LEONARD MALTIN'S

151

BEST MOVIES

YOU'VE NEVER SEEN

ALSO BY LEONARD MALTIN

LEONARD MALTIN'S

151

BEST MOVIES
YOU'VE NEVER SEEN

LEONARD MALTIN

harperstudio

An Imprint of HarperCollins*Publishers*

HarperCollins books may be purchased for educational, business, or sales promotional use. For information please write: Special Markets Department, HarperCollins Publishers, 10 East 53rd Street, New York, NY 10022.

For more information about this book or other books from HarperStudio, visit www.theharperstudio.com.

FIRST EDITION

Designed by Renato Stanisic

Library of Congress Cataloging-in-Publication Data

Maltin, Leonard.
    Leonard Maltin's 151 best movies you've never seen / by Leonard Maltin. — 1st ed.
        p. cm.
    ISBN 978-0-06-173234-8 (pbk.)
    1. Motion pictures — Catalogs. I. Title. II. Title: Leonard Maltin's one hundred fifty-one best movies you've never seen. III. Title: One hundred fifty-one best movies you've never seen.
    PN1998.M275 2010
    791.43'75—dc22
                                                                        2009043098

10 11 12 13 14   OV/RRD   10 9 8 7 6 5 4 3 2 1

CONTENTS

PREFACE

As our media culture continues to evolve, with seismic changes affecting the journalistic landscape, a number of film critics have lost their jobs. Some people have questioned their relevance. After all, it's easy to find opinions about anything, including movies, on the Internet.

But wait—as they say on those TV infomercials. Check out a movie ad, be it on the Internet, on television, or in a newspaper. What do you see? Review quotes. If critics are irrelevant, why do studios and distributors rely on them to promote their movies?

The answer is simple: people want recommendations, preferably from someone they know and trust. Let's call that the human factor. Years ago, Blockbuster Video spent a lot of money developing a computer kiosk to help customers find their ideal video selections, only to discover that most people wanted a human being to help them, not a machine. Millions of renters approached the anonymous guy or gal behind the counter to ask, "Is this movie any good?"

A certain segment of the population prefers an informed opinion to that of the man on the street. And people who do put stock in critics tend to seek out someone they agree with most of the time. (If you don't agree with my opinions, why would you even peruse a book with my name on it?)

I don't present myself as a sage or an oracle. I love movies, and I've spent a great many years watching, writing, and thinking about them. Like any critic, I see more bad films than good, but the best part of my job is leading people to worthwhile movies they might otherwise overlook. That's what inspired this book.

My goal is simple: to introduce you to unfamiliar films and whet your appetite to see them. I define "unfamiliar" as any movie that failed to find a large audience. While that includes some major studio releases, most of the selections in this volume are independent or foreign films, including documentaries. Many of them are offbeat; even if they had multimillion-dollar advertising campaigns behind them, chances are they wouldn't appeal to a mass audience. If you have a taste for this kind of entertainment, you may already know some of these titles. Other selections *should* have developed a following, in my opinion, but didn't. I hope to offer a sense of discovery even to experienced cinephiles.

Because I want to reach as broad an audience as possible, I have resisted the temptation to stock the pond with movies from Hollywood's golden age. I love films from the silent era, and the 1930s and '40s, but that is a very particular pursuit, for another book.

Instead, I've concentrated on films from the last twenty years and offered just a smattering of oldies. If you're not accustomed to viewing movies of the 1930s, you might experiment with *Lady for a Day*. If you think Westerns are a collection of clichés, you might try *Seven Men From Now*. If you think issues involving politics and media are strictly a product of our time, you might be surprised by *State of the Union,* which came out in the presidential election year of 1948.

Otherwise, I've restricted most of my proselytizing to films of recent vintage. I like to think of myself as having eclectic taste, and a curiosity about all kinds of films. I don't think there is a common thread that runs through this list of titles, except perhaps for originality. It probably isn't coincidental that so many of them are the work of writer-directors who are passionate about telling their stories—as opposed to journeymen who are simply carrying out an assignment— or that a number come from first-time filmmakers whose enthusiasm permeates their work. My synopses are brief because I don't want to outline the entire plot—just enough to intrigue you. I am not a fan of so-called spoilers.

I've also avoided movies that are hard to find, although every rule has its exceptions. I couldn't compile a list of unsung films and leave out such longtime favorites as *Resurrection* (1980), *Queen of Hearts* (1989), and *King of the Hill* (1993). I live in hope that their owners will see the light and release them on DVD, or at least make them available for downloading. In the meantime, I encourage you to search the Web, check out eBay, fire up that dormant VHS machine, and/ or purchase an all-region DVD player that can accommodate foreign-issue discs, which are easy to purchase online.

As you peruse this book you will find references to the Telluride Film Festival, which has offered me unique moviegoing experiences for the past thirty years, and my weekly class at the University of Southern California, where I have the opportunity to interview filmmakers and see how their movies play to a young demographic. If I lean on these two sources, it's because they consistently inform my life as a critic and an observer of the current movie scene.

A note about cast and credit information: I have strived to be consistent with my annual reference book, *Leonard Maltin's Movie Guide*. For instance, I cite the year of a film's theatrical release in its home country, as opposed to some online sources that go by a film festival debut. My cast lists are selective, but I've tried to include any actor of note.

I am grateful to all of my colleagues at DirecTV, where I introduce movies, and ReelzChannel, where I single out hidden gems every week on my show *Secret's Out*. Writing scripts for those outlets has helped me to clarify my thoughts about many of the films I cite in this book.

My thanks go to Darwyn Carson for fact-checking the manuscript and serving as a sounding board for this material. She is thorough and intelligent, but just as important, she loves movies.

I am indebted to Richard Curtis for introducing me to Bob Miller at HarperStudio, who responded so enthusiastically to my idea for this venture. Bob's a movie buff, too, which has made the experience especially rewarding.

My wife, Alice, and daughter, Jessie, provide endless, continual, and immeasurable love and support. Nothing I do would matter without them.

With that, I offer a wide-ranging menu of movies for your edification and amusement. I don't present these as forsaken masterpieces: they're just good movies that I'm glad I saw. If you take my recommendations to heart, I hope you will feel the same way.

Leonard Maltin
July 2009

1. AMERICAN DREAMZ

(2006)

Directed by Paul Weitz

Screenplay by Paul Weitz

Actors:

HUGH GRANT

DENNIS QUAID

MANDY MOORE

WILLEM DAFOE

CHRIS KLEIN

JENNIFER COOLIDGE

SAM GOLZARI

MARCIA GAY HARDEN

SETH MEYERS

JOHN CHO

JUDY GREER

SHOHREH AGHDASHLOO

TONY YALDA

MARLEY SHELTON

There is nothing new about amateur contests. Frank Sinatra made his first step toward stardom when he and the

Hoboken Four appeared on *Major Bowes Amateur Hour,* a radio sensation in the 1930s and '40s. (I grew up watching the major's successor, Ted Mack, who hosted the long-running show on television.) Ella Fitzgerald enjoyed her first taste of success on the stage of the Apollo Theater in Harlem during one of its legendary amateur nights. But *American Idol* has taken this time-worn concept to a new level of popularity and slickness of production; in the process it has become a pop-culture phenomenon.

Anything this popular deserves scrutiny and invites satire. That's what struck writer-director Paul Weitz and inspired *American Dreamz,* which not only takes on the wildly successful talent show but, in the same breath, post-9/11 feelings toward Middle Eastern immigrants and even the president of the United States. This George W. Bush–like figure (played as a sincere dimwit by Dennis Quaid) faces a crisis of confidence that may or may not be cured by an appearance on the *American Dreamz* television program.

Hugh Grant would seem to be an ideal choice to play a character inspired by *Idol'*s caustic producer-host Simon Cowell. But Weitz, who codirected Grant in *About a Boy,* wasn't merely looking for a personable Brit. He realized that the actor was capable of playing the variation on Cowell he had in mind, a man who has every trapping of success but still isn't happy. Not every actor could portray a self-loathing individual and still retain our interest in him. Grant manages that feat.

The character meets his match in the unlikely guise of Mandy Moore, a sweet-faced girl from the Midwest who's chosen as a contestant on the show. Her all-American looks are deceiving, as the people around her are doomed to learn for themselves: she's about as warm as an Eskimo Pie.

I have a feeling that these cold-blooded characters kept *American Dreamz* from becoming the box-office hit it deserved to be. What's more, it dares to make fun of a show people genuinely love. But that's exactly what I like about this movie: it's a satire that spares no one. Weitz holds a mirror up to American society and uses humor to help us see ourselves at our best, and at our worst.

2. THE ANIMAL FACTORY

(2000)

Directed by Steve Buscemi

Screenplay by Edward Bunker and John Steppling

Based on the novel *The Animal Factory* by Edward Bunker

Actors:

WILLEM DAFOE

EDWARD FURLONG

MICKEY ROURKE

TOM ARNOLD

STEVE BUSCEMI

JOHN HEARD

DANNY TREJO

SEYMOUR CASSEL

We've all seen plenty of prison dramas, from such emblematic Hollywood yarns as *The Big House* (1930) to starker, modern-day variations like *In the Name of the Father* (1993). Camp followers are fond of the women-in-prison subgenre that was launched, unintentionally, with *Caged* (1950) and became exploitation fodder in the decades to follow.

With all of these movies in our collective consciousness, a prison picture has to offer something fresh or it's headed toward cliché city. *The Animal Factory* avoids the obvious at every turn.

Unlike other stories set behind bars, its strength comes not from melodrama but matter-of-factness. The setting is a state institution where the formidable Willem Dafoe— looking particularly menacing with his head shaved—plays a quiet, cunning prison veteran who believes, not without justification, that he runs the joint. He even has a wicked sense of humor. Edward Furlong is an unworldly twenty-one-year-old newcomer, locked up for marijuana dealing, who becomes Dafoe's latest protégé. At first he's reluctant to form any alliances, wanting to fight his own fights, but he gradually comes to understand that he needs a mentor. The film contends that it's impossible to avoid playing "the game" in order to survive.

Yet Dafoe isn't a traditional heavy, and his feelings toward Furlong aren't blatantly sexual; in fact, he feels almost fatherly toward the young man. The nuances of their relationship help make the film as compelling as it is.

Every member of the ensemble is well cast, from Seymour Cassel as an old-time prison guard to Mickey Rourke as a transvestite who's overjoyed to have a young stud like Furlong as his new cell mate. Tom Arnold is also quite good as a prisoner who's on the prowl for the new kid and makes no bones about it.

Actor Steve Buscemi's debut film behind the camera, *Trees Lounge,* showed talent and style; his sophomore project reveals maturity. (Since that time he's piloted episodes of *The Sopranos* and *Nurse Jackie* and two excellent indie features, *Lonesome Jim* and *Interview*.) And if the setting and the performances owe a debt to him, the film owes its credibility to screenwriter Edward Bunker, who served time in San Quentin and adapted this script from his same-named novel. (An earlier book of his became the Dustin Hoffman vehicle *Straight Time*.) Bunker also appears briefly onscreen as a character named Buzzard.

3. AURORA BOREALIS

(2006)

Directed by James Burke

Screenplay by Brent Boyd

Actors:

JOSHUA JACKSON

DONALD SUTHERLAND

JULIETTE LEWIS

LOUISE FLETCHER

ZACK WARD

JOHN KAPELOS

STEVEN PASQUALE

TYLER LABINE

It must be frustrating for actors to do outstanding work in a film hardly anyone sees. I'm sure they take satisfaction in a job well done, but we all need approbation. The performances in a little movie called *Aurora Borealis* are deeply felt, and it shows. When I screened this film for my class, most of my students still thought of Joshua Jackson as the guy they'd grown up watching on the popular TV series *Dawson's Creek*. They were (pleasantly) surprised to see him inhabit an entirely different character, and enjoyed watching him relate so convincingly to his costars.

Duncan (Jackson) is twenty-five years old and his life in Minneapolis is going nowhere. He's living out an extended adolescence, hanging out with the same friends he's had for years. He can't hold down a job, and has no sense of direction or self-worth. (He even allows his hardworking brother, played by Steven Pasquale, to use his apartment to cheat on his wife.) We learn that Duncan's promising hockey career came to an end with the death of his father ten years ago, apparently from a cocaine overdose. He's never gotten over—or past—this life-changing experience.

His brother nags him about visiting their grandparents (Donald Sutherland and Louise Fletcher), and when he finally does, Duncan establishes a bond with the old man, who's suffering from Parkinson's and the early stages of dementia but still has a roguish spark. The young man even takes a job as a handyman in his grandparents' apartment building—a major step, for him—and enjoys spending time with them, all the more so when he meets his grandfather's visiting nurse, Kate (Juliette Lewis).

Kate genuinely likes Duncan but perceives that he's unable, or unwilling, to move out of his carefully proscribed comfort zone with his pals in Minneapolis. Is there a future to their relationship? And is Duncan's grandfather serious when he talks about ending his own life?

What could play out as soap opera becomes convincing drama because the performances are so sincere. Jackson has a way of underplaying that makes what he does look easy. Lewis is lively and likable as a good-hearted person with a sound head on her shoulders.

Then there is Donald Sutherland, who has the ability to play colorful, slightly-larger-than-life characters without slipping into caricature. He is completely endearing as an old man with an independent streak and a sly sense of humor. Neither screenwriter Brent Boyd nor director James Burke wanted him to be cute—as so many older people are personified in Hollywood movies—and he dodges that quite neatly. In fact, Sutherland spent time researching people with Parkinson's disease before filming began.

During a discussion about the film with my class at USC, an interesting point arose. There is a scene in which Louise Fletcher and Juliette Lewis try to help wheelchair user Sutherland to the bathroom in time to meet his urgent needs. They don't quite make it, but instead of despairing they all begin to laugh, at Sutherland's cue. Some people in the class found this forced—a cheap laugh—but two other students raised their hands: one spoke of how it reminded her of a grandparent who'd reacted in exactly the same way, and another called on her experience in health care to confirm that many older people develop a sense of humor about their problems as a means of coping.

It's this kind of sensitivity that makes *Aurora Borealis* worthwhile. A great movie? No, but definitely a good one. If you see it, agree with me, and happen to run into one of its actors someday, be sure to tell them.

4. BAADASSSSS!

(2004)

Directed by Mario Van Peebles

Screenplay by Mario Van Peebles

Actors:

MARIO VAN PEEBLES

JOY BRYANT

TERRY CREWS

OSSIE DAVIS

DAVID ALAN GRIER

NIA LONG

RAINN WILSON

T. K. CARTER

SAUL RUBINEK

PAUL RODRIGUEZ

VINCENT SCHIAVELLI

KHLEO THOMAS

LEN LESSER

SALLY STRUTHERS

ADAM WEST

GLENN PLUMMER

JOHN SINGLETON

TROY GARITY

There are many movies about moviemaking, but even within that category *Baadasssss!* is unique. It is at once a period piece, a cultural document, a family diary, and an unblinking look at guerrilla filmmaking. Its title, although entirely appropriate, apparently put people off. (I wonder how it would have fared had it been released with its working title, *How to Get the Man's Foot Outta Your Ass?*)

In the early 1970s there was no independent film movement,

as we know it today, and there were no avenues for black film-makers to tell their stories. Melvin Van Peebles had enjoyed his first success in Hollywood with a sardonic comedy called *Watermelon Man,* but he didn't want to make another studio movie. He was fired up to create something original and relevant, and he did just that, by any means necessary. This is Mario Van Peebles's dramatic account of how his father made the landmark 1971 movie *Sweet Sweetback's Baadasssss Song.*

Mario portrays his iconoclastic father, who's got the drive and enthusiasm to make a street-smart movie for black audiences, and a makeshift crew of people who are willing to help him out. But Melvin is also his own worst enemy, repeatedly alienating the very people who can help him realize his goals and often putting them at risk. He also casts his young son Mario (played by Khleo Thomas) in the movie, enacting scenes that even some of his colleagues consider inappropriate.

Baadasssss! is a portrait of a contrary but unique artist and a vivid, often hilarious look at underground moviemaking long before digital video cameras made the medium accessible to just about anyone. The cast is extremely well chosen, offering solid opportunities to such talented people as Joy Bryant, Terry Crews, David Alan Grier, Nia Long, Rainn Wilson, T. K. Carter, Saul Rubinek, and Paul Rodriguez. The legendary Ossie Davis appears as Melvin's father, and director John Singleton (who made his mark a generation after Melvin with *Boyz N the Hood*) has a cameo role as a disc jockey. But it's the younger Van Peebles's bold performance as his father that stands out most.

Mario Van Peebles has written, directed, and starred in a number of films over the years but this is his most personal piece of work—and I think his best.

5. THE BALLAD OF LITTLE JO

(1993)

Directed by Maggie Greenwald

Screenplay by Maggie Greenwald

Actors:

SUZY AMIS

BO HOPKINS

IAN MCKELLEN

ANTHONY HEALD

DAVID CHUNG

HEATHER GRAHAM

RENE AUBERJONOIS

CARRIE SNODGRESS

MELISSA LEO

SAM ROBARDS

RUTH MALECZECH

When I saw this film, prior to its release in 1993, I thought it would rise to the top on a wave of critical acclaim. I was wrong. It was ignored by pretty much everyone, yet it remains one of my favorite unsung movies of the 1990s. It also holds a special place in the heart of its leading actress, Suzy Amis, who appreciated what a rare opportunity it afforded her.

The Ballad of Little Jo was the brainchild of underappreciated writer-director Maggie Greenwald. Her inspiration was the obituary of a man who lived in the Old West; when it came time to lay him to rest, it was discovered that he was in fact a she.

Greenwald did further research, but once she understood the context of that obituary, the screen story unfolded in her mind: Amis plays a naive young woman who is seduced by a photographer in Boston. When she bears his child, she is ostracized by polite society and flees to the West where no one will know her. She quickly learns that there is no place for a single woman there unless she is a prostitute, so she decides to masquerade as a man. In time, she ingratiates herself within the community . . . and the plot thickens.

The excellent supporting cast includes Ian McKellen, Bo Hopkins, Heather Graham, Rene Auberjonois, Carrie Snodgress, Anthony Heald, David Chung, and Melissa Leo. Amis's real-life husband at the time, Sam Robards, plays the seducer who sets the story in motion.

A former fashion model, Amis had a decade-long career in films, and while she never became a household name, she appeared in a number of interesting movies including *Rocket Gibraltar, The Usual Suspects,* and *Cadillac Ranch.* Then James Cameron cast her in *Titanic,* as the granddaughter of "Old Rose" (Gloria Stuart) in the film's modern-day sequences. A short time later she married Cameron and retired to raise a large family. She was ideally suited for the role of Jo Monaghan because she grew up on a ranch in Oklahoma and already knew how to handle a gun. She worked with a coach to develop the proper body language for her male character and brought real conviction to her performance. She was nominated for an Independent Spirit Award, as was David Chung, who plays her unexpected love interest, but the film made little impact on critics or audiences. It deserves to be much better known.

6. BETTER THAN SEX

(2000)

Directed by Jonathan Teplitzky

Screenplay by Jonathan Teplitzky

Actors:

DAVID WENHAM

SUSIE PORTER

CATHERINE MCCLEMENTS

KRIS MCQUADE

SIMON BOSSELL

IMELDA CORCORAN

We Americans are rather cocky about our place in the world—although we've taken a lot of lumps in recent years—but there is one area in which we remain utterly provincial, if not downright prudish: sex. All it takes is a brief survey of European films to see how childlike and backward we are in our attitude toward one of the most natural aspects of life.

If I were to describe the film at hand as a sex comedy, most Americans would expect sniggering jokes, most likely from a male point of view. What makes *Better Than Sex* so refreshing is that it isn't that at all. It's about two adults and their mutual attraction. It probably wouldn't hold much interest for hormonal teenagers, even though there's plenty of nudity on display, because it isn't about the quest for sex. In fact, as the movie opens we discover that the leading man and leading woman have already spent an active night in bed together. Writer-director Jonathan Teplitzky is interested in what happens to those two people *after* that proverbial one-night stand.

We all put on a face for the world, especially when we meet someone to whom we're attracted. Getting to know that person is one of the most challenging rituals any man or woman faces in life. Part of this cheerful movie's appeal is the direct contact we have with its players as they go through this awkward stage. Cin (Susie Porter) and Josh (David Wenham) talk directly to us in the film's opening scene; at other times we hear their thoughts and observe how they contrast with what they're actually saying to each other, even during sex.

It seems that they met the night before and shared a taxi ride following a party. Cin invited Josh up to her apartment and they haven't left yet, even though she's keenly aware that he is based in London and is headed back there in three days. The question is, will he want to leave?

Both Porter and Wenham (who are well known in Australia, much less so here) are attractive, appealing actors who seem completely comfortable being naked in front of the camera, which helps us get accustomed to the idea, too. Can you picture any American actors doing the same for almost the entire duration of a film? The frankness of their inner conversations is equally rare in Hollywood movies—and thus, disarming. We may hatch many of the same thoughts, but we've been taught to suppress them, or to confide only in our closest friends.

But *Better Than Sex* isn't an instructional film: it's a piece of light entertainment that's thoroughly engaging.

7. THE BIG HIT

(1998)

Directed by Che-Kirk (Kirk) Wong

Screenplay by Ben Ramsey

Actors:

MARK WAHLBERG

LOU DIAMOND PHILLIPS

CHRISTINA APPLEGATE

CHINA CHOW

AVERY BROOKS

BOKEEM WOODBINE

ANTONIO SABATO JR.

LAINIE KAZAN

ELLIOTT GOULD

SAB SHIMONO

LELA ROCHON

ROBIN DUNNE

Like other critics I'm often asked to make lists, and the toughest kind for me to do is a selection of Guilty Pleasures. If I don't feel guilty about liking Jerry Lewis, the Three Stooges, or *Bela Lugosi Meets a Brooklyn Gorilla,* what's left? But I will say I am slightly sheepish about my fondness for *The Big Hit.* In some ways it's indefensible, but this unabashed mélange of politically incorrect comedy and in-your-face action is great fun to watch. It expands its ideas to such a ludicrous extreme that you can't take it seriously . . . and that's just what I like about it.

Mark Wahlberg plays Melvin Smiley, a hit man who works for crime boss Avery Brooks and tries his best to hide his sordid activities from his fiancée, Christina Applegate.

Melvin hangs out with a none-too-bright posse—played by Lou Diamond Phillips, Bokeem Woodbine, and Antonio Sabato Jr.—and one day they decide to pull a fast one on their boss by kidnapping the daughter of a Japanese businessman. Little do they dream that the Asian mogul has just gone broke—and the girl is Brooks's goddaughter.

Things go from bad to worse with every move they make. And to add to the chaos, Applegate's Jewish parents show up for a visit. They're played with gusto by Elliott Gould and Lainie Kazan.

A simple outline can't do justice to this frenetic farce, which turns racial and ethnic stereotypes upside down and wears its outlandishness on its sleeve, to coin a phrase. You might even call this a recruiting film for bad behavior.

Most critics despised *The Big Hit,* and audiences didn't flock to see it, perhaps confused as to whether it was a comedy or an action movie—especially with John Woo's name as executive producer—and never dreaming it was a hybrid of the two. Hong Kong veteran Kirk Wong hasn't directed a movie since, and screenwriter Ben Ramsey didn't earn another big-screen credit for a decade afterward.

That said, you might want to approach the film with caution, but I've met a number of people who cheerfully confess that they like it. I can't defend my opinion; I can only tell you that it made me laugh, and I do that with my gut, not my intellect.

8. BLOOD AND WINE

(1997)

Directed by Bob Rafelson
Screenplay by Nick Villiers and Alison Cross
Story by Nick Villiers and Bob Rafelson

Actors:

JACK NICHOLSON

MICHAEL CAINE

JUDY DAVIS

STEPHEN DORFF

JENNIFER LOPEZ

HAROLD PERRINEAU JR.

MIKE STARR

Jack Nicholson's name on a movie should be enough to place it firmly in the spotlight, but the dark qualities of *Blood and Wine* seem to have soured its distributor on the film's potential, and that sentiment was passed along to potential viewers. They weren't wrong about the tone of the picture: it's tough and violent, an ultra-hard-boiled caper picture set in Florida. The cast includes Judy Davis, Stephen Dorff, Harold Perrineau, and a young Jennifer Lopez, but the main reason to see it is to savor the moments when Nicholson and Michael Caine share the screen.

This 1997 release marks the fifth time Nicholson was directed by Bob Rafelson, who helped forge the actor's reputation with *Five Easy Pieces* in 1970. While none of their subsequent efforts (*The King of Marvin Gardens* in 1972, *The Postman Always Rings Twice* in 1981, and *Man Trouble* in 1982) enjoyed the same degree of critical and commercial success, their friendship endured. They met each other while working on *The Monkees* television series in the late 1960s, which gave Rafelson his first directing experience and Nicholson a chance to contribute to the freewheeling scripts. They subsequently collaborated on the underrated Monkees feature film *Head* (1968).

If you listen to the commentary track and interviews on the well-produced DVD release of *Blood and Wine,* you'll learn a great deal about the unusual push-pull relationship between the director and his star. They are obviously more than coworkers, and they can read each other well. (Rafelson talks a great deal more than Nicholson, but you still get both perspectives.)

One might think *Blood and Wine* was based on a novel, like so many well-plotted film noirs peopled with colorful characters, but the story was concocted by Rafelson and Nick Villiers, who then wrote the final screenplay with Alison Cross.

Nicholson plays a high-end wine dealer who's been a neglectful parent to his stepson (Dorff) and a poor excuse for a husband to Davis, whose money he has wantonly squandered. He wants to be free of her, especially since he's taken up with a sexy Cuban nanny (Lopez). His solution to all of his problems is to steal a valuable necklace from one of his well-heeled customers—Lopez's employer, in fact. To pull this off he calls on a professional jewel thief named Victor, played with great panache by Caine. Victor has a consumptive cough and a fatalistic worldview, but he's ready for action. There is nothing redeeming about Nicholson's character, or Caine's, for that matter, but you can't take your eyes off them: that's the mark of a great script and two consummate actors.

Because this is a film noir, we already know that things are going to go askew; the only question is when and how. The story is solid, but it's the detail of the characterizations, the sudden bursts of violence, and the fully committed performances that make *Blood and Wine* so good, and so memorable.

9. BRICK

(2006)

Directed by Rian Johnson

Screenplay by Rian Johnson

Actors:

JOSEPH GORDON-LEVITT

LUKAS HAAS

NORA ZEHETNER

NOAH FLEISS

MATT O'LEARY

NOAH SEGAN

MEAGAN GOOD

EMILIE DE RAVIN

BRIAN WHITE

RICHARD ROUNDTREE

rick was made in about a month's time for less than half a million dollars, but if it weren't any good those statistics would be meaningless. The fact that it *is* so good is a tribute to an inspired idea, a clever screenplay, a talented acting ensemble, and a filmmaker who had the passion and determination to get this movie made. It also proves that money is irrelevant to a film's success: it all starts with a good idea.

In this instance the idea was to transpose the hard-boiled world of film noir to a Southern California high school. The talented (and underappreciated) Joseph Gordon-Levitt stars as Brendan, a student who's pretty much a loner until he discovers the dead body of his former girlfriend at the edge of a sewage tunnel. He then takes it upon himself to discover who is responsible for the murder, which means infiltrating various social strata in and around his school—and ultimately getting in to see the local "Mr. Big" drug dealer.

Brick is not without a sense of humor; there's a wonderful irony in setting a dark story like this in sunny California. But the reason the movie works is that it isn't a spoof or a parody: what's at stake here is deadly serious. The characters speak in a stylized argot that writer-director Rian Johnson patterned after the dialogue of Dashiell Hammett; it takes a little getting used to, but it's worth the effort. Another ingredient that recalls bona fide film noirs of the '40s—but is conspicuously missing from contemporary movies about teens—is a series of fistfights. Again, this isn't playacting: you can feel that those punches really hurt.

The tone is everything in a movie like this, and *Brick* never missteps. Its visual style, its performances, and most of all its screenplay coalesce remarkably well. If I have any criticism it's that it goes on longer than it needs to, but that's a small price to pay for such an exhilarating piece of entertainment.

Brick marks Rian Johnson's feature-film debut. He wrote the script shortly after graduating from USC, and spent the next nine years visualizing it (along with fellow grad Steve Yedlin, who shot the film). Perhaps that's why it's as polished as it is: a lot of thought went into the project before the cameras ever rolled.

When my daughter and I saw *Brick* at the Sundance Film Festival in 2005, we learned that distributors were reluctant to acquire it because they thought it was "too smart" for average teenage audiences. Given the typical run of teen movie fare, they may have been right . . . but that doesn't take away from the film's unique qualities or its singular achievement.

10. BROTHERS

(2004)

Directed by Susanne Bier

Screenplay by Anders Thomas Jensen

Story by Anders Thomas Jensen and Susanne Bier

Actors:

CONNIE NIELSEN

ULRICH THOMSEN

NIKOLAJ LIE KAAS

BENT MEJDING

SOLBØRG HØJFELDT

PAW HENRIKSEN

In 2004 I traveled to the Sundance Film Festival with my teenage daughter in tow. We arrived the day after the event began and canvassed a handful of people in the press office for recommendations of what to see, based on early buzz. Hearing good things about a Danish film called *Brothers* that was screening that night, we latched on to a pair of tickets. We knew nothing about the film or its director (Susanne Bier, whose *Open Hearts* had played at the festival several years earlier), but we were game. As *Brothers* unspooled we sat transfixed, and although that screening took place in January 2004, I didn't see a better film the rest of the year.

The story revolves around a middle-class Danish family, in which one brother has always lived up to his reputation as the black sheep. He has just been released from prison and his future is up in the air. The "good brother" is happily married and the father of two adorable daughters whom he must leave to fulfill his military service in Afghanistan. His sibling promises to look after the wife and kids while he's gone.

It would be unthinkable to reveal what happens next, but suffice it to say that each brother must deal with choices that defy expectations, not to mention their prescribed roles within the family. The drama is almost unbearably tense at times, both in the war zone and on the home front—and all of it seems palpably real.

Bier was schooled in the Dogme doctrine of bare-bones filmmaking—in fact, *Open Hearts* was also known as Dogme number 28—and while *Brothers* doesn't follow all of its rigid rules, it does strip away any vestige of Hollywood-style storytelling. The "sets" are all practical locations where the handheld camera roams freely and often frames actors in tight close-ups that demand absolute truthfulness in their work. (It doesn't hurt that leading lady Connie Nielsen is a natural beauty as well as a talented actress.)

Unlike most films at Sundance, *Brothers* already had distribution in place, a partnership between Universal's Focus Features and IFC. But *Brothers* never made a dent in the public consciousness despite its excellence and the presence of a recognizable actress in the leading role.

Bier and her screenwriting partner Anders Thomas Jensen followed this brilliant film with another drama nearly as good called *After the Wedding,* which was nominated for a Best Foreign Language Film Academy Award. The director then made a creditable American debut with *Things We Lost in the Fire* starring Halle Berry and Benicio Del Toro.

I'm sure she is still in the early stages of a long and fruitful career . . . but I don't think I will ever forget my first screening of *Brothers* and the impact it had on me.

11. BUBBA HO-TEP

(2003)

Directed by Don Coscarelli

Screenplay by Don Coscarelli

Based on the story by Joe R. Lansdale

Actors:

BRUCE CAMPBELL

OSSIE DAVIS

ELLA JOYCE

BOB IVY

HEIDI MARNHOUT

DANIEL ROEBUCK

Most films can be pigeonholed, by genre or by comparing them to other recent pictures. It isn't commonplace to find a movie that's truly original, but that is the only way to describe Don Coscarelli's *Bubba Ho-Tep*. I'm tempted to call it a hybrid of horror film and comedy but even that's off the mark.

The title offers a clue to the film's cheeky tone. Fans of classic horror films know that the mummy character played by Boris Karloff in 1932 was called Im-Ho-Tep. Bubba is a nickname popular in the South. But what do these names mean *together*?

The setting for this fanciful tale (inspired by Joe R.

Lansdale's short story) is a nursing home in East Texas. Here we find none other than Elvis Presley—not a fake Elvis, as you might think, but a man who says he switched places with an Elvis impersonator years ago. Bruce Campbell offers a persuasive performance as the fabled entertainer who must now endure the double indignity of bedpans and a community of people (both nurses and patients) who think he's crazy.

But wait—he may not be the craziest man in the home. Jack's room is filled with memorabilia relating to President John F. Kennedy, because that's who he is. How did he survive the assassination attempt? And how did a famous white man turn black? Jack has answers—and because he's played by the imposing Ossie Davis, those answers have weight.

Jack tells Elvis that the spirit of an Egyptian mummy is invading their rest home at night and stealing souls. There do appear to be some strange goings-on, and in Jack's mind only the two of them can stand up to this eerie presence and defeat it.

Bubba Ho-Tep is fun to watch because it has the courage of its convictions. What could be utter silliness in lesser hands is made tangible by the ingenuity of writer-director Coscarelli (best known for such genre pictures as *Beastmaster* and *Phantasm*), who creates a genuinely creepy atmosphere for his nocturnal horror moments, and the rich performances of his stars. Campbell, who has built a one-man industry out of his cult stardom in the *Evil Dead* movies, does a terrific job as the Vegas-style Elvis, and the always imposing Davis plays his whacked-out role with gusto and gravitas.

Whether or not you get caught up in the story, you'll have to admit that *Bubba Ho-Tep* is one of a kind.

12. CAREER GIRLS

(1997)

Directed by Mike Leigh

Screenplay by Mike Leigh

Actors:

KATRIN CARTLIDGE

LYNDA STEADMAN

KATE BYERS

MARK BENTON

JOE TUCKER

ANDY SERKIS

MARGO STANLEY

MICHAEL HEALY

Mike Leigh makes films like no one else in the world, and he goes about it in a most unusual way: when he's starting a project, he gathers a group of actors he likes who are willing to make a major commitment of time (usually six months). They then participate in workshops where Leigh suggests ideas and the actors develop their characters (and histories). This sparks improvisation, and Leigh gently pushes them in one direction or another, not knowing himself which characters will take center stage in the finished film. When they have reached a certain point, he goes off and creates a screenplay based on the initially improvised material.

This is the main reason Leigh's films don't resemble one another, and why even his staunchest admirers (like me) don't know what to expect. I haven't loved all of his work, but for me there are definitely more hits than misses, and his best films (*High Hopes*, *Life Is Sweet*, *Secrets & Lies*, *Topsy-Turvy*, *Happy-Go-Lucky*) have garnered widespread acclaim.

Secrets & Lies was perhaps his greatest success, earning five Oscar nominations, including Best Picture, and it played to a wider audience than he'd ever reached before. Newcomers to the fold were surprised, then, when his follow-up effort was so different in its ambitions, and in its tone. Yet taken on its own terms, *Career Girls* is quite wonderful.

Leigh explores working-class Brits the way John Osborne and the creators of the famous "kitchen sink" school did in their plays and films of the 1950s and early '60s. In this case, his heroines are two former roommates who are reunited after six years' time. As Annie (Lynda Steadman) visits Hannah (Katrin Cartlidge) in her London flat and the two begin to reminisce, flashbacks fill us in on their college lives, and the rather dramatic transformations their personalities have undergone since they were young, when Hannah was a mass of tics and Annie was, in her friend's words, "a walking open wound."

Both their shared memories and current experiences revolve around men and their misadventures with the opposite sex. At one point they run into a man they both dated once upon a time, who caused their friendship considerable stress—yet he doesn't remember either one of them.

If you're still wondering about the story line, you apparently don't know Mike Leigh's movies. *Career Girls* doesn't really have a story, per se; it's a character portrait of two young women who have matured since their giddy youth but still haven't figured out where they belong in the scheme of things. All we know is that they're trying to get along, and in the process, they come to realize how much their friendship has meant.

If you become attuned to the leisurely rhythm of Leigh's

work, and immerse yourself in the workaday world of his characters, *Career Girls* is exceedingly satisfying entertainment. It also features two terrific performances, by Lynda Steadman and Katrin Cartlidge (who later appeared in Leigh's *Topsy-Turvy*). It's sad to note that this gifted actress, whose career was on the rise—and who received particular acclaim for her work in *Career Girls*—died in 2002.

Two other footnotes: the music for this film was composed by Tony Remy and Marianne Jean-Baptiste, who was nominated for an Oscar for her breakthrough role in Leigh's *Secrets & Lies*—and who then became a fixture on TV's long-running series *Without a Trace*.

And the showy role of a weed-smoking, self-styled ladies' man who propositions Cartlidge is played by Andy Serkis, who later gained screen immortality as Gollum in *The Lord of the Rings*.

13. CASANOVA

(2005)

Directed by Lasse Hallström

Screenplay by Jeffrey Hatcher and Kimberly Simi

Story by Kimberly Simi and Michael Christofer

Actors:

HEATH LEDGER

SIENNA MILLER

JEREMY IRONS

OLIVER PLATT

LENA OLIN

OMID DJALILI

STEPHEN GREIF

KEN STOTT

HELEN MCCRORY

CHARLIE COX

NATALIE DORMER

TIM MCINNERNY

LEIGH LAWSON

LAUREN COHAN

Whenever a talented actor is cut down in the prime of life, it's left to fans and pundits to speculate about what might have been. But in the case of Heath Ledger, one of his best (and most endearing) performances was roundly ignored at the peak of his youthful career. Released right after *Brokeback Mountain,* which netted Ledger an Oscar nomination, *Casanova* was given a desultory theatrical release at the busiest time of the movie year, Christmas 2005, and never made more than a blip on most people's radar.

They missed out on one of the most delightful adult comedies in recent memory.

Casanova is a romp, in the manner of *Tom Jones,* but reinvented for the post-feminist era. Ledger plays the fleet-footed serial womanizer of eighteenth-century Venice, stealing into bedrooms and out of windows one step ahead of angry husbands and protective matrons. He finally meets his match in the person of Francesca Bruni (Sienna Miller), a spirited young woman who not only can handle a sword with the best of men but has the gumption to write a series of feminist tracts that she distributes throughout the city (taking the precaution to sign a man's name to those unpopular diatribes). She is the first woman who hasn't heaved a sigh at the mere sight of Casanova and that presents the great lover with a unique challenge.

Miller is as charismatic as Ledger here, and that's one of the reasons *Casanova* is so appealing.

The political wrangling and sexual high jinks veer into the world of farce through the presence of Oliver Platt, as a bloated merchant who's been promised to Miller in marriage, and Jeremy Irons (possibly channeling Boris Karloff) as a self-important bishop who has been dispatched to Venice to put a lid on the citizens' errant behavior. These two fine actors go to town with their pompous characterizations that invite comic deflation from the moment they appear on screen.

With deft support from Lena Olin as Miller's mother, Omid Djalili as Ledger's quick-witted servant, and Charlie Cox as Miller's lovesick brother, Lasse Hallström's handsome production never allows the opulent settings to overwhelm the action in the foreground. Although the authentic Venetian backgrounds are a treat for the eye, this is still a comedy in which character and incident take precedence and the director never loses sight of that. Kimberly Simi and Michael Cristofer wrote the story, which was turned into a screenplay by Simi and Jeffrey Hatcher.

The result is a modern-day rarity: a smart, sexy comedy for grown-ups. It's also a major credential for Heath Ledger, whose performance as a lighthearted romantic hero couldn't be more different from the repressed gay rancher he played so well in *Brokeback Mountain*.

14. CHOP SHOP

(2008)

Directed by Ramin Bahrani
Screenplay by Ramin Bahrani and Bahareh Azimi

Actors:

ALEJANDRO POLANCO

ISAMAR GONZALES

CARLOS ZAPATA

AHMAD RAZVI

ROB SOWULSKI

Having captured the attention of film festival audiences and critics with his brilliant feature *Man Push Cart,* Ramin Bahrani followed it with another movie just as potent, and just as good. Once again, he began by exploring a little-known area of New York City and getting to know it well before he even attempted to fashion a story with his writing partner, Bahareh Azimi.

He later explained the origins of *Chop Shop* in this official statement:

Willet's Point, Queens, is twenty blocks of junkyards, dumping grounds, and row upon row of auto-body repair shops. Over seventy-five years ago, F. Scott Fitzgerald described it as "The Valley of the Ashes" in The Great Gatsby. More recently the current mayor of New York has named it, "The bleakest point of New York." Across the street from the junkyards and repair shops looms Shea Stadium, whose giant billboard reads, "Make Dreams Happen." I was curious to know what dreams can happen in this place, and who these dreamers are, so I set out to make Chop Shop.

During the year I spent in the location, I became increasingly drawn to the lives of the young Latino kids who work and live in the auto-body shops. My story is about one of them, a twelve-year-old Latino who has an immense yet flawed love for his sixteen-year-old sister. In their world there is no room for sentimentality and even less for judgment.

As in his previous film, Bahrani found his stars through a lengthy audition process—this time, at city schools—and then spent months rehearsing with them, to get to a point where they would feel at ease in front of the camera and their scenes would seem genuine, not scripted.

Alejandro Polonco plays the young boy known as Ale, an orphan who has learned to fend for himself—selling candy on subway trains, bootleg DVDs wherever he can, snatching the occasional handbag, and learning a trade under the benevolent eye of Rob, who owns an auto-body shop in the Queens neighborhood known as the Iron Triangle. Rob also lets Ale sleep in a tiny upstairs room. Ale seems to have his life in order, but he isn't content: he fears that his older sister is falling under the influence of the wrong friends and wants to take her under his protective wing. His dream is to save enough money for them to buy a lunch wagon that they will run together. He also persuades her to move in with him so she will be safe.

Chop Shop is a slice of life with vivid, indelible characters. Young, precocious Ale is a force of nature, blessed with street smarts yet still a child—in ways he can't fully understand.

In describing *Chop Shop,* most critics invoked the names of landmark Italian neorealist films like *Open City, Paisa,* and *Bicycle Thieves,* with good reason. Like those films, Bahrani ennobles his disenfranchised characters, shooting day and night in real locations (with his usual cinematographer, Michael Simmonds), and using nonprofessional actors, including the actual owner of the auto-body shop and the leading player from his previous film, Ahmad Razvi. But as he immersed himself in the Iron Triangle, the director wasn't thinking of the Italians who made such moving stories about the under-classes. He recalls saying to himself, "If Luis Buñuel's *Los Olvidados* were to be made today and in America, it would be made here." If you've ever seen that unforgettable film about juvenile delinquents, you know this much about the gifted Ramin Bahrani: he has excellent role models.

15. CITIZEN RUTH

(1996)

Directed by Alexander Payne

Screenplay by Alexander Payne and Jim Taylor

Actors:

LAURA DERN

MARY KAY PLACE

KURTWOOD SMITH

SWOOSIE KURTZ

KELLY PRESTON

M. C. GAINEY

KENNETH MARS

DAVID GRAF

ALICIA WITT

BURT REYNOLDS

TIPPI HEDREN

Satire, Broadway playwright George S. Kaufman once famously observed, is what closes on Saturday night. That sentiment is as true today as it was when he made his caustic remark, because audiences haven't changed much since the 1920s. They generally want to be entertained, and when they go to see a comedy (or something purporting to be a comedy) they want to laugh. They don't want to have their foibles pointed out to them, nor do they particularly want to think. For these and other reasons, satire is a rare commodity on stage and screen.

All the more reason to celebrate the work of filmmaker Alexander Payne and his longtime writing partner Jim Taylor. *Citizen Ruth* marked their feature-film debut, and the promise in this endeavor has been realized in their subsequent work, which includes *Election, About Schmidt,* and *Sideways.* They specialize in social satire and observations about the American psyche. They have been criticized from time to time for being mean-spirited, but I prefer to think that they're expressing their point of view about characters who just possibly deserve to be made fun of.

The gifted Laura Dern plays the title character in *Citizen Ruth,* set in Payne's hometown of Omaha, Nebraska. Ruth Stoops is a mess, a woman who lives on the streets and subsists by inhaling paint fumes from a brown paper bag. When she is arrested—not for the first time—and it's discovered that she is pregnant, a judge orders her to have an abortion or face jail time. At this point, a pro-life activist couple (played to perfection by Mary Kay Place and Kurtwood

Smith) come to Ruth's "rescue," taking her into their home where they try to indoctrinate her to their way of thinking. This sets off a battle of wills between the pro-lifers and an equally vocal abortion-rights group.

Payne and Taylor don't take sides; they allow both groups to express their feelings about this hot-button issue. Instead, they make fun of extremists and their behavior—and the hypocrisy of their campaign to "save" a woman whose only concern is getting high.

Citizen Ruth is a modest film but it scores a bull's-eye, without an ounce of preachiness or pretention. The casting is flawless, with supporting parts filled by Swoosie Kurtz, Kelly Preston, M. C. Gainey, Kenneth Mars, David Graf, Alicia Witt, Burt Reynolds, and Tippi Hedren, among others. But it's Laura Dern's unself-conscious, go-for-broke performance as Ruth—the unlikely poster girl for *any* issue—that seals the deal.

16. CONNIE AND CARLA

(2004)

Directed by Michael Lembeck

Screenplay by Nia Vardalos

Actors:

NIA VARDALOS

TONI COLLETTE

DAVID DUCHOVNY

STEPHEN SPINELLA

DASH MIHOK

ALEC MAPA

DEBBIE REYNOLDS

Every year or two a movie defies the odds and becomes a hit through the most timeworn form of advertising known to mankind: word of mouth. Every independent filmmaker dreams of a success to compare with *My Big Fat Greek Wedding,* but not many have that movie's wide-ranging appeal—or a distributor who's willing to nurture it on a city-by-city, week-by-week basis. (It cost $5 million to make, and earned $200 million in its U.S. theatrical run, returning greater dividends to its investors than *Spider-Man* or any of 2002's expensive blockbusters.)

So what do you do for an encore?

The writer and star of *Greek Wedding,* Nia Vardalos, wisely offered her next screenplay to Tom Hanks, whose company had produced the first hit, and he and his wife, Rita Wilson, readily served as coexecutive producers of *Connie and Carla.* But this film was released by Universal, not a hungry independent firm, and the studio threw it into theaters to sink or swim. If it had enjoyed the tender loving care accorded *Greek Wedding,* I think it would have found a large and appreciative audience.

Connie (Vardalos) and Carla (Toni Collette) are struggling lounge singers who work at a Chicago airport motel, belting out classic show tunes to a tiny, pathetic audience. When they accidentally witness a mob "hit," they take it on the lam—just like Tony Curtis and Jack Lemmon in *Some Like It Hot.* In Los Angeles they stumble on to success through another, happier, accident—by pretending to be drag queens. Here they find their most devoted audience: gay men who love Broadway musicals. Their private life grows complicated when Connie falls in love with David Duchovny—who doesn't know she's really a woman.

Connie and Carla was savaged by many reviewers, although even Stephen Holden in the *New York Times* acknowledged, "She brings to the [movie] the same warmhearted ebullience and sense of people as one big, happy (if eccentric) family that lent *My Big Fat Greek Wedding* such mass appeal."

This is clearly not a critic's film, but it is a lot of fun to watch; if you love show tunes, you'll certainly be happy. Vardalos and Collette throw themselves into their roles, holding nothing back. Director Michael Lembeck is a veteran of television comedy and films (and teaches a workshop founded by his father Harvey). The actresses couldn't have placed themselves in better hands for a good-time farce that also has heart.

17. C.R.A.Z.Y.

(2005)

Directed by Jean-Marc Vallée

Screenplay by François Boulay and Jean-Marc Vallée

Actors:

MICHEL CÔTÉ

MARC-ANDRÉ GRONDIN

DANIELLE PROULX

ÉMILE VALLÉE

PIERRE-LUC BRILLANT

MAXIME TREMBLAY

ALEX GRAVEL

JOHANNE LEBRUN

French-language films from Canada get little if any recognition here in the States, which seems to me a crime. A good film is a rare and precious thing and ought to be cherished—especially if it comes from a neighboring country.

C.R.A.Z.Y. is the saga of a dysfunctional family over twenty years' time. It opens on a whimsically amusing note but grows more serious as the story progresses. Veteran French-Canadian actor Michel Côté stars as the blustery patriarch of a Catholic family that grows to have five sons . . . but when the fourth, Zac, is born on Christmas Day 1960, his wife is convinced that it's a sign. Her eccentric ideas set Zac onto the road of life in oddball fashion, but it's only later in life, when the boy realizes that he isn't attracted to girls, that he begins to understand what "different" can mean in a tight-knit family with a macho father. (Zac is played as a young boy by the director's son Émile Vallée, and later by Marc-André Grondin.)

Director Jean-Marc Vallée (who wrote the expansive and emotionally charged screenplay with François Boulay) makes canny use of popular music—from David Bowie to the Rolling Stones—to signify the passage of time and the societal shifts of the late 1960s and '70s. He also establishes early on that the father is inordinately fond of Patsy Cline and Charles Aznavour, and insists on singing along with Aznavour records at almost every official family gathering. This seemingly tangential piece of business turns out to have surprising resonance in the film's later passages.

Although the setting is Montreal, the language is French, and the family is Catholic, the family dynamic in *C.R.A.Z.Y.* is so well developed that the story is universally relatable. That, and the touchstones of social change that audiences of a certain age will remember, give the film broad appeal.

Indeed, while *C.R.A.Z.Y.* swept the Canadian GENIE Awards and won Best Canadian Feature Film at the Toronto Film Festival, it is significant to note that it also won the Audience Award at the AFI Fest—in Los Angeles.

18. CRIMINAL

(2004)

Directed by Gregory Jacobs

Screenplay by Gregory Jacobs

and Steven Soderbergh (as Sam Lowry)

Based on a screenplay by Fabián Bielinsky

Actors:

JOHN C. REILLY

DIEGO LUNA

MAGGIE GYLLENHAAL

PETER MULLAN

JONATHAN TUCKER

ENRICO COLANTONI

ZITTO KAZANN

MICHAEL SHANNON

MALIK YOBA

ELLEN GEER

JACK CONLEY

Hollywood has a spotty record when it comes to remaking successful films from other countries for American consumption. There are, of course, standouts: *Three Men and a Baby* comes to mind, and on a smaller scale, *Tortilla Soup,* a likable Latino paraphrase of *Eat Drink Man Woman.* My daughter would argue for *The Birdcage,* which I don't dislike, but my memory of screenwriter Francis Veber's original *La Cage aux Folles,* is just too strong to surrender to the American copy.

In a similar vein, film buffs who saw the Argentine import *Nine Queens* have no use for its modest remake, *Criminal.* I missed Fabián Bielinsky's 2000 release the first time around, so I was both charmed and fooled by Gregory Jacobs's interpretation, which resets the story in Los Angeles. (Jacobs wrote the screenplay with his longtime colleague Steven Soderbergh, who chose to use the pseudonym Sam Lowry.)

I also happen to like the actors Jacobs cast in the leading roles, John C. Reilly and Diego Luna. Reilly, the everyman with a perennial hangdog expression, strolls into a low-rent casino and spots Luna, a likable young hustler, pulling a scam, insisting he hasn't received proper change from a waitress. He intercedes, posing as a plainclothes cop, and "arrests" Luna, escorting him outside to the parking lot. There he chastises the younger man for his obviousness, reveals his own duplicity, and offers him a job as an apprentice for a series of cons he's about to pull. Luna, who needs money badly, readily agrees, and Reilly takes on the role of teacher and mentor.

Then a big score presents itself. Reilly is called by his sister (Maggie Gyllenhaal), a concierge at a major Los Angeles hotel. A notorious counterfeiter has taken ill at the hotel just as he's about to put over a deal with an Irish collector of rare currency (Peter Mullan), who's scheduled to return home within twenty-four hours. There is bad blood between Gyllenhaal and her brother, but she needs him to get the forger off her hands, and there's a lot of money at stake.

This is big, much bigger than the day-to-day scams that make up Reilly's life, and he needs Luna to help him pull it off. Time is of the essence, and every piece of the puzzle must fit exactly. Needless to say, there are many twists and turns, and nothing is as it seems. Unless you've seen *Nine Queens* I don't think you could figure out where the story is headed . . . and that's the fun of watching *Criminal*.

Los Angeles is probably the most photographed city in the world, but Jacobs offers a fresh perspective here, utilizing little-seen locations and making excellent use of the downtown area, including the historic Biltmore Hotel. As with so many films, it's the characters who make or break a film, and Reilly and Luna make a terrific team, while L.A. provides a perfect backdrop for their shady dealings.

19. CRUSH

(2002)

Directed by John McKay
Screenplay by John McKay

Actors:

ANDIE MACDOWELL

IMELDA STAUNTON

ANNA CHANCELLOR

KENNY DOUGHTY

BILL PATERSON

CAROLINE HOLDAWAY

Does a movie have to be 100 percent believable to work? It all depends. I can think of many instances where I've allowed myself to go along with a story and put credibility aside for the sake of entertainment. If I'm having a good time, and I like the characters enough, that doesn't seem so much to ask.

I can't pretend that *Crush* doesn't demand a certain leap of faith, but I think this British comedy-drama (by first-time writer-director John McKay) has what it takes to win over an audience that's looking for a bit of escape. Predictably enough, the film divided critics, some of whom surrendered to it while others found it absurd. (Some couldn't—or wouldn't—even accept Andie MacDowell in the leading role, even though it's explained that she's an American living in England.)

MacDowell has one of her all-time best roles in this story of three forty-ish women who enjoy a weekly tell-all session. Kate (MacDowell) is the headmistress at an exclusive prep school, Janine (Imelda Staunton) is a local police detective, and Molly (Anna Chancellor) is a much-married doctor. Their jobs require all three women to carry themselves with a certain authority, so their get-togethers, where they let their hair down and talk openly over drinks and cigarettes, are a tonic.

Then Kate falls into a passionate affair with a former student—now all of twenty-five years old. What seems like a fling at first turns serious, and instead of cheering her on, her friends actively disapprove. Moreover, they take it upon themselves to bring Kate to her senses—whatever the cost.

One reason some viewers don't like this movie is that the tone changes completely, from lighthearted, barb-tongued comedy to dark, intense drama—but I think it works, largely because of the empathetic performances. We're meant to root for MacDowell, and we do.

Please note that this movie bears no relation to the 1992 film of the same name with Marcia Gay Harden or the 1993 movie *The Crush,* which stars Cary Elwes and Alicia Silverstone.

20. DARK DAYS

(2000)

Directed by Marc Singer

The story behind some films is more interesting than the films themselves, but in the case of *Dark Days* it's a tie as to which is more compelling. It's also difficult to separate the two because Marc Singer's journey is inextricably tied up with the film he made.

Dark Days is a documentary about people who live in abandoned railroad tunnels under the streets of Manhattan. The first question one must ask is, "How would anyone know of such a community?"

Having recently left England to live with a friend in Manhattan, Singer took an interest in the homeless people he saw every day on the street . . . but unlike most of us, he began to engage them in conversation. With no career path of his own, he spent more and more time with homeless men. Eventually, one of them showed him the secret entrance to their underground shelter.

Here he discovered an amazing environment, populated by people who had fallen through the cracks of society. Some left loved ones behind; others admit that they ruined their own lives through drugs. They seemed content underground, by and large, having fashioned their own defined spaces using materials they scavenged off the street. They quickly educated Singer about the rules of survival, aboveground and below: where to find the best discarded food, how to trap rats, how to protect your possessions, etc. Some of them were downright ingenious in making something out of nothing.

Singer had never made a movie before—hadn't even thought about it—but once he entered this world he felt driven to document it. However, he understood that in order to do so he would have to earn his subjects' complete trust. So he moved underground and lived with them. (How many people would, or could, do that?) Then one day he went to a camera supply store to rent a 16 millimeter camera and asked how to load and operate the device! His next move was truly inspired: he "hired" the residents of the tunnel to be his crew.

One must understand that not only did Singer live underground for the better part of two years, without any income, he also had no idea how his film would turn out. Would there be clearly defined characters and a story to tell, or would he wind up with a sociological study of limited interest to a general audience?

As it happens, certain characters did command the screen, and in the course of time, a climactic event did present itself. The resulting film, edited by Melissa Niedich, is mesmerizing and unique.

Dark Days won three awards at the Sundance Film Festival and gathered more acclaim in the months that followed, including Best Documentary prizes from the Independent Spirit Awards and the Los Angeles Film Critics Association.

It was at one of those ceremonies that I met Marc Singer and invited him to my class at USC. He readily accepted and provided one of the most memorable evenings the class has ever experienced. My students were moved by the film, but it was Singer himself who knocked us out. He spoke with a total lack of guile or pretention, and revealed that when a New York City Housing Authority representative told him about the possibility of apartment vouchers being made available to the subjects of his film, he put his camera down and spent the next six months helping his friends acclimate to a new life aboveground. He may not be a professional filmmaker, but he is quite possibly some sort of saint.

One wonderful postscript: I asked him what it was like to be the object of so much attention at Sundance. He told me that as a result of the clamor there he was contacted by several agents who wanted to know if he'd be interested in directing Hollywood movies. They even offered him scripts to consider. Clearly, they hadn't seen the film, or paid attention to it, only to the response throughout Park City.

P.S. Singer hasn't made another film since *Dark Days*.

21. THE DEAD GIRL

(2006)

Directed by Karen Moncrieff

Screenplay by Karen Moncrieff

Actors:

TONI COLLETTE

PIPER LAURIE

ROSE BYRNE

MARY BETH HURT

MARCIA GAY HARDEN

BRITTANY MURPHY

KERRY WASHINGTON

GIOVANNI RIBISI

JAMES FRANCO

MARY STEENBURGEN

BRUCE DAVISON

NICK SEARCY

JOSH BROLIN

he Dead Girl is a dark, daring picture with juicy roles for
some of the most talented actresses around: Toni Collette,
Marcia Gay Harden, Rose Byrne, Kerry Washington, Mary
Beth Hurt, Piper Laurie, Mary Steenburgen, and Brittany
Murphy. In spite of that cast, the somber tone of the movie
(and its title) kept people away. They missed out on a provocative film and a couple of powerhouse performances.

The Dead Girl was written and directed by Karen
Moncrieff, a former actress who had long runs on several
daytime soap operas before deciding that she wanted to
write—and just possibly, write material that was better than
what she was being handed to perform. She made her filmmaking debut with *Blue Car,* which was very well received.
Her second film presents us with five vignettes about women
who have little in common except troubling and unresolved
issues in their lives.

Toni Collette stars in the first segment, about a woman
who lives under the thumb of her demanding mother
(Piper Laurie), until she discovers the body of a dead girl
near her house. In a strange way this becomes a liberating
experience for her, and indirectly leads to her meeting
a young man (Giovanni Ribisi) who may free her from
servitude.

We then meet a forensics student (Rose Byrne, now familiar to viewers of the TV series *Damages*), who works
in the local morgue, and may have a personal link to the

deceased . . . a haggard housewife (Mary Beth Hurt) who makes a shocking discovery involving her husband . . . a distraught mother (Marcia Gay Harden) who's trying to find her runaway daughter, and a brain-fried hooker (Kerry Washington) who may have some clues. Finally we meet the dead girl when she was alive—played by Brittany Murphy.

Karen Moncrieff told me that her inspiration for this mosaic of stories was a gnawing anger she felt about violence against women and how it's regarded in our society. Her script was so good that it attracted a high caliber of actors, none of whom had to make an enormous time commitment in order to participate: The movie was filmed in twenty-five days as if it were five separate short films. There are no weak links, but I want to single out Marcia Gay Harden and Kerry Washington, who are both great in the penultimate segment of the film, a highly emotional confrontation between two women who would never meet under any other circumstances. (Ironically, Washington was rejected more than once for the part because she was considered too pretty.)

Moncrieff says, "I like movies that shake me up. I go to the theater to see something reflected back to me that looks like life. My idea of a chick flick is anything by Kieslowski. *Red, White,* and *Blue,* those are some good chick flicks." That kind of passion for challenging drama shouldn't go unrewarded: *The Dead Girl* is downbeat, to be sure, but never dull.

22. THE DEVIL'S BACKBONE

(2001)

Directed by Guillermo del Toro

Screenplay by Guillermo del Toro, Antonio Trashorras, and David Muñoz

Actors:

EDUARDO NORIEGA

MARISA PAREDES

FREDERICO LUPPI

IÑIGO GARCÉS

FERNANDO TIELVE

IRENE VISEDO

BERTA OJEA

Some film buffs and critics became aware of Mexican filmmaker Guillermo del Toro when his first, ambitious science-fiction feature *Cronos* first played in the United States in 1994. Others caught on when he brought his personal touch to such mainstream movies as *Mimic* and *Blade II,* and his following grew with the release of a film borne of his love for comic books, *Hellboy.* By the time the dark fairy tale *Pan's Labyrinth* arrived on the scene in 2006, del Toro was being hailed as a master by critics and fans alike.

Yet somehow, even people who admired *Pan's Labyrinth* seem to be unaware of his previous endeavor in this arena, *The Devil's Backbone.* Like the later, better-known feature, this one is also set against the backdrop of the Spanish Civil War and tells its tale from a child's point of view. A highly stylized blend of suspense and the supernatural, it takes place in an orphanage on the outskirts of a town seemingly cut off from the world. In the courtyard of the ancient compound lies an unexploded bomb embedded in the ground—a visual metaphor not easily dismissed.

Our hero is ten-year-old Carlos, who's been dropped at this institution to fend for himself. The people in charge are nice enough, but he is tormented by a bully and spooked by a caretaker who doesn't like the boys snooping around.

Then there's the ghost of a boy named Santi, who used to live at the orphanage. He chooses to communicate with Carlos and will not let him rest, warning him of impending death. Del Toro takes these basic story elements and augments them with character quirks and visual details it would be pointless to describe.

The filmmaker has been writing and drawing in a series of notebooks since he was a boy. When it comes time to prepare a screenplay, he goes back to inspirations that struck him weeks, months, even years earlier. Each of his films has been gestating in his overactive imagination for some length of time. That's why his most personal films, *The Devil's Backbone* and *Pan's Labyrinth,* are so richly layered.

Del Toro has known real terror in his own life; his father was once kidnapped and held for ransom. That's one reason he is able to blend reality and fantasy in such a beguiling way. He sees the bizarre and surreal even in everyday settings, and has a gift for realizing that vision on-screen.

A great ghost story with an all-too-believable setting, *The Devil's Backbone* is unrelentingly eerie—a thinking person's Halloween movie.

23. DIAMOND MEN

(2001)

Directed by Daniel M. Cohen

Screenplay by Daniel M. Cohen

Actors:

ROBERT FORSTER

DONNIE WAHLBERG

JASMINE GUY

BESS ARMSTRONG

GEORGE COE

KRISTEN MINTER

One of the most arresting films I saw when I was a teenager was Haskell Wexler's *Medium Cool,* a vivid, highly charged drama about a TV reporter covering the 1968 Democratic National Convention in Chicago when rioting breaks out. I've never forgotten the impact it had on me, or how good its leading actor was. Somehow, Robert Forster never got the breaks he should have in the years that followed that triumphant role. He starred in a short-lived TV series, *Nokia,* and eventually took whatever jobs came along, even in low-end direct-to-video fare. I met him during this period and was struck by the fact that he didn't express any bitterness about his career. On the contrary, he signed up with a speaker's bureau to talk (gratis) at various clubs and civic groups about the power of positive thinking.

Finally, in 1997, Quentin Tarantino wrote a leading role in *Jackie Brown* with Forster in mind, and refused to hear of anyone else playing the part of the world-weary bail bondsman. His pitch-perfect performance earned Forster an Oscar nomination as Best Supporting Actor, and he hasn't stopped working since. He plays a lot of cops and a fair number of fathers, but there is one common thread: he's always believable.

There aren't many leading roles for an older actor, but at least one stands out, in a modest but irresistibly likable film called *Diamond Men*. Forster is right on the money as Eddie Miller, a veteran diamond salesman who supplies local jewelry stores throughout Pennsylvania. After he recovers from a heart attack, he is told that he can no longer be insured to carry his supply of diamonds. This is a crippling blow, much worse than the heart attack: selling gems is all he's ever done. But before he's put out to pasture, he reluctantly agrees to break in a new guy on his route, a neophyte named Bobby (Donnie Wahlberg).

As the two men drive around the state, visiting old and trusted clients, Eddie tries to impart some wisdom, and tricks of the trade, to his would-be replacement. Gradually, Bobby begins to appreciate that Eddie knows his stuff and isn't a bad guy, even if he is "old." In fact, the younger man tries to help his widowed mentor open himself up to female companionship, for the first time since his wife passed away some years ago.

Diamond Men is built on a formula, but it's well done, and first-time writer-director Daniel Cohen draws on his own experience as a diamond salesman to give the movie a foundation of credibility. Those telling details of salesmanship, along with keen observations of life on the road, add up. Cohen's screenplay takes off in unexpected directions, leading to a denouement that you may or may not be willing to swallow, but Wahlberg's amiability, and Forster's unshowy, rock-solid performance, make the movie impossible to dislike.

24. DICK

(1999)

Directed by Andrew Fleming

Screenplay by Andrew Fleming and Sheryl Longin

Actors:

KIRSTEN DUNST

MICHELLE WILLIAMS

DAN HEDAYA

SAUL RUBINEK

WILL FERRELL

BRUCE MCCULLOCH

DAVE FOLEY

JIM BREUER

TERI GARR

ANA GASTEYER

HARRY SHEARER

RYAN REYNOLDS

G. D. SPRADLIN

Not many comedies can be clever and silly at the same time, but *Dick* can make that claim. Director and cowriter Andrew Fleming (who made *The Craft* and more recently *Hamlet 2*) bemoans the fact that almost everyone in the movie became famous *after* its release. But perhaps its two appealing stars and supporting cast of able comedic performers who gained fame on *Kids in the Hall, Saturday Night Live,* and elsewhere will attract people to this little-known film. *Dick* remains a bright, original comedy with an ingenious premise.

Kirsten Dunst and Michelle Williams play teenage best friends, one of whom happens to live at the Watergate complex in Washington, D.C., in the early 1970s. When they sneak downstairs one night to mail a letter to the Bobby Sherman fan club, they put tape over the lock on a security door so they can climb back upstairs—but forget to remove the tape. That's what catches the attention of a security guard and leads to his discovery of burglars inside the Democratic Party National Headquarters.

In other words, our two young heroines set in motion the Watergate scandal. Not that they notice. In fact, the girls remain blissfully unaware of everything going on around them throughout the story: that's the central joke. While Woody Allen's Zelig and Tom Hanks's Forrest Gump reveled in being in the right place at the right time, these airheads don't realize they've been accidental eyewitnesses to history.

Dan Hedaya is well cast as President Nixon, who eventually hires the teenagers to walk his dog, Checkers. Saul Rubinek is Secretary of State Henry Kissinger, who reveals more than he should within earshot of the girls. Will Ferrell and Bruce McCulloch are *Washington Post* reporters Bob Woodward and Carl Bernstein, Dave Foley is Bob Haldeman, Jim Breuer is John Dean, Ana Gasteyer is Nixon's secretary Rose Mary Woods, and Harry Shearer is Watergate mastermind G. Gordon Liddy.

If you're old enough to have lived through the Watergate years and these names are receding in your memory, you may enjoy reliving that difficult period through a welcome prism of comedy. If you haven't a clue as to who these people were, or the nature of the events that led to President Nixon's resignation in 1974, you'll get a sugar-coated history lesson. Either way, *Dick* is good fun.

25. THE DINNER GAME

(1998)

Directed by Francis Veber
Screenplay by Francis Veber
Based on the stage play *Le dîner de cons*
by Francis Veber

Actors:

JACQUES VILLERET

THIERRY LHERMITTE

FRANCIS HUSTER

ALEXANDRA VANDERNOOT

DANIEL PRÉVOST

CATHERINE FROT

EDGAR GIVRY

CHRISTIAN PEREIRA

PÉTRONILLE MOSS

When people ask me to name the funniest movie I've ever seen, I usually rattle off the names of classic comedies of the silent and early talkie era (from Chaplin to the Marx Brothers) . . . and as I do, I see their eyes glaze over. "No, no, no," they're thinking, "I don't mean something ancient."

All right then. How about a picture from 1998? I can't remember any film that's made me laugh out loud as much as Francis Veber's *The Dinner Game*. The audience I saw it with was practically in tears—even my daughter, then just nine years old, loved it—yet it's another foreign film that received only scant release in the United States.

The premise is simple but ingenious: a successful book editor (played by popular French leading man Thierry Lhermitte) chances to meet a man on a train trip who strikes him as a perfect candidate to bring to his weekly dining group. The object of this dinner game, played by a gathering of successful, self-confident men, is to bring along the stupidest guest they can find . . . and this latest patsy (Jacques Villeret), a tax accountant whose wife ran off with another man, is very stupid indeed.

In the best tradition of French farce, this idea grows and grows, like a snowball gaining momentum as it rolls downhill. Before long the well-meaning interloper plays havoc with the publisher's well-ordered life, upsetting his relationship with his ex-wife, his mistress, his son, and various others. Yet this cherub-faced fellow remains clueless about the chaos he is creating, while the victim becomes increasingly frantic.

The story plays out with effortless precision, because it was honed to perfection onstage in Paris by its creator, Francis Veber.

Veber is hardly unknown on these shores: he is the man who wrote and directed *La Cage aux Folles* back in 1978, which was later transformed into a popular stage musical and a successful American movie called *The Birdcage,* with Robin Williams and Nathan Lane. He has continued to write and often direct extremely popular farces for stage and screen in France, and many of his movies have been acquired by Hollywood studios with English-language remakes in mind.

I was lucky enough to attend a screening of his subsequent film, *Tais-Tois* (or *Ruby et Quentin*) in Los Angeles, which is almost as funny as *The Dinner Game,* and also involves a character who is blissfully stupid, played in that case by the great Gérard Depardieu. That evening, at the annual City of Lights–City of Angels Festival, Veber discussed his philosophy of filmmaking—and comedy.

First and foremost, he believes in simplicity. He explained that he lives in fear of boring an audience, so in recent years he has streamlined his plots to revolve around one main character and has jettisoned any subplots that might seem extraneous.

He also believes the old axiom that brevity is the soul of wit. *The Dinner Game* runs a mere eighty minutes, while *Tais-Tois* is eighty-five, and *The Valet* is also just under an hour and a half. I doubt that anyone leaves the theater feeling shortchanged. (Veber said his script supervisor estimates that these films will run longer, but he tells his actors to hurry!) Universal Pictures thought enough of the film to acquire U.S. distribution rights, but gave it only a halfhearted release. The remake rights were purchased by a Hollywood studio and numerous scripts were generated over a decade's time as various contributors insisted on "opening it up!" It finally went into production as *Dinner for Shmucks,* with Steve Carell and Paul Rudd in the leading roles, in 2009.

The Dinner Game (*Le Dîner de cons* in its original language) was nominated for six César Awards, France's equivalent of the Oscar, and won three, for Best Actor (Jacques Villeret), Best Supporting Actor (Daniel Prévost), and Best Writing (Veber).

To get the most out of this film I would urge you to watch it with friends, to create the feeling of an audience; the trigger effect of laughter will be your reward.

26. DINNER RUSH

(2001)

Directed by Bob Giraldi

Screenplay by Rick Shaughnessy and Brian S. Kalata

Actors:

DANNY AIELLO

EDOARDO BALLERINI

VIVIAN WU

MIKE MCGLONE

KIRK ACEVEDO

JOHN CORBETT

SANDRA BERNHARD

SUMMER PHOENIX

POLLY DRAPER

MARK MARGOLIS

AJAY NAIDU

JAMIE HARRIS

Television offers a full menu of restaurant reality shows, but I prefer watching movies like *Dinner Rush* that combine a love of food, a peek behind the scenes of a busy restaurant, and a healthy dose of New York flavor. It shouldn't come as a great surprise that the man who made it also owns an Italian restaurant in Manhattan.

The movie unfolds during one exceptionally eventful night at the eatery run by that quintessential Italian-American New Yorker, Danny Aiello. The restaurant is his pride and joy. Sure, he runs numbers on the side, but that's just business. He hopes to turn the neighborhood bistro over to his son, who (to his father's dismay) has no use for traditional Italian dishes. That's one headache; another is caused by two tough-looking guys who show up and insist on muscling into co-ownership of the place.

Aiello isn't the only one who's having a busy night. There's drama to spare in the kitchen, where the sous-chef is in hot water with his bookie. Out front, the servers have their hands full with a rude, imperious customer (and would-be trendsetter), played by Mark Margolis, and a venomous food critic (who's also been sleeping with the chef) played by Sandra Bernhard.

There are enough plot threads to fill a miniseries. Some are more believable than others, just as some of the film's images are overly self-conscious, but the diverse ingredients ultimately mesh as the evening progresses. The atmosphere rings true, inside the kitchen and out front, and that's crucial to the picture's success, while Aiello brings warmth and honesty to his character.

This film was a labor of love for director Bob Giraldi, who's made a reported 2,500 television commercials and such memorable music videos as Michael Jackson's "Beat It." He's also a New York City restaurateur. He willed this movie into existence and shot it in three weeks. *Dinner Rush* barely got a theatrical release, but everyone I know who's seen it has enjoyed it. Why not cook up some pasta, rent the DVD, and make a night of it?

27. THE DISH

(2000)

Directed by Rob Sitch

Screenplay by Santo Cilauro, Tom Gleinser,

Jane Kennedy, and Rob Sitch

Actors:

SAM NEILL

KEVIN HARRINGTON

TOM LONG

PATRICK WARBURTON

GENEVIEVE MOOY

TAYLOR KANE

BILLIE BROWN

ROY BILLING

JOHN MCMARTIN

People often ask me for recommendations of films to rent, and one of my perennial suggestions is the Australian comedy *The Dish*. It's the living definition of a feel-good movie, but not the simplistic, button-pushing formula kind. It has a personality all its own and I daresay it's irresistible.

Like so many great comedies, this one is rooted in the observation of human nature. It has a great premise that's well developed (by screenwriters Santo Cilauro, Tom Gleinser, Jane Kennedy, and director Rob Sitch) but it's the quirkily amusing array of characters that really brings it to life.

The Dish is based on a real-life incident. In 1969, as the United States was about to send a man to the moon, NASA realized that it needed a backup satellite to ensure that there would be no cutoff of communication when its space capsule reached the Southern Hemisphere. The likely candidate turned out to be located in the village of Parkes in New South Wales, situated in the middle of a sheep pasture.

The honor of being selected to participate in this historical event sends the residents of Parkes into a tizzy, and even occasions an official visit from the U.S. ambassador and the Australian prime minister.

It also places considerable pressure on the hardworking team of scientists who operate "the dish" on a daily basis, led by studious, unflappable, pipe-smoking Sam Neill. NASA has sent one of its own men (Patrick Warburton) to supervise the Aussie crew but the locals want to prove their mettle, especially when a couple of minicrises erupt.

Director Sitch weaves news footage from 1969 into his narrative and manages to build suspense into every stage of the story (even though we know the outcome of the moon mission already). Although the film opens in the year 2000 as an elderly Neill visits the scene of his former triumph, the movie unfolds in the present tense and has an ingratiating immediacy about it.

Sitch and his writing colleagues collaborated three years earlier on another highly entertaining film, *The Castle* (1997), and have since worked together on such television shows Down Under as *Thank God You're Here* and *The Hollowmen*. But I suspect it's *The Dish* that will have the longest life here in the States.

28. DISNEY'S TEACHER'S PET

(2004)

Directed by Timothy Björklund

Screenplay by Bill Steinkellner and Cheri Steinkellner

Source material by Gary Baseman

Actors:

NATHAN LANE

KELSEY GRAMMER

SHAUN FLEMING

DEBRA JO RUPP

DAVID OGDEN STIERS

JERRY STILLER

PAUL REUBENS

MEGAN MULLALLY

ROB PAULSEN

WALLACE SHAWN

ESTELLE HARRIS

JAY THOMAS

This may be the craziest animated movie ever to bear the Disney name. I know that's a tall statement but I stand by it. In 2000, the studio's TV animation division commissioned a Saturday-morning show from comedy writers Bill and Cheri Steinkellner and contemporary artist Gary Baseman, and hired a bright animator-turned-director named Timothy Björklund (who made his reputation on the hip series *Rocko's Modern Life*) to direct. *Teacher's Pet* never became a solid hit, but having waited a bit too long to commission a theatrical-feature version of its previous TV success *Doug,* the company gave a green light to the team to make this movie. I'm so glad they did.

So were other critics, who (like me, I must confess) had never seen the series. The theatrical arm of the Disney company had little faith in this feature and opened it without fanfare in January 2004—whereupon it won a bushelful of great reviews! Its lackluster promotion and marketing—and the fact that it's so darned weird—kept it from becoming a mainstream hit, but I love it.

Here's the premise; pay close attention. Mrs. Mary Lou Helperman is a schoolteacher, and as it happens, one of her students is her own son Leonard. Another pupil named Scott is in reality the family dog Spot (voiced with great comic brio by Nathan Lane). When Mrs. Helperman wins a special citation, she decides to take a road trip to Florida to collect the award . . . but that means leaving Spot at home, which he simply cannot bear. So Spot—I mean, Scott— convinces Mrs. Helperman to take him along on the trip, so Scott—I mean, Spot—can avail himself of a mad scientist named Ivan Krank who claims he can turn animals into human beings!

Teacher's Pet doesn't look, sound, or feel like a Disney movie. The look was created by Baseman, an award-winning artist and designer whose work resembles a post-modern version of children's drawings. The sound track includes hilariously over-the-top voice work by a sterling cast including Lane, Kelsey Grammer (as Ivan Krank), David Ogden Stiers, Paul Reubens, Jerry Stiller, Megan Mullally, Wallace Shawn, Jay Thomas, Rob Paulsen, Shaun Fleming (as Leonard), and Debra Jo Rupp, who's wonderfully ditsy and endearing as Mrs. Helperman. What's more, many of these players get to sing, as *Teacher's Pet* is a full-scale musical, filled with silly and clever songs—including a memorable paean to the United States sung as the Helperman trailer makes its way across the country.

As for the feel of the film, it's hip, funny, strange, and totally disarming. There are a handful of Disney in-jokes that kids will enjoy spotting, but I suspect this film may be of greater interest to adults with childlike minds (like me) than actual children.

29. THE DOOR IN THE FLOOR

(2004)

Directed by Tod Williams

Screenplay by Tod Williams

Based on *A Widow for One Year*

by John Irving

Actors:

JEFF BRIDGES

KIM BASINGER

JON FOSTER

ELLE FANNING

BIJOU PHILLIPS

MIMI ROGERS

ROBERT LUPONE

DONNA MURPHY

LOUIS ARCELLA

In the annual media circus that Oscar season has become, would-be pundits attempt to ascribe all sorts of motivations and agendas to the academy voters. Many of them express outrage over Oscar history. How, they wonder, could the Academy of Motion Picture Arts and Sciences have failed to give Alfred Hitchcock (or Cary Grant) an Academy Award?

With a little thought, the answer becomes clear: in the years they did great work, academy voters thought someone else did even better. No one has the benefit of hindsight when it's time to fill out a ballot: if voters had thought it might be their best (or last) opportunity to honor one of the industry giants, they surely would have done so.

I don't do a lot of second-guessing about Oscars past, but I do feel strongly about at least one overlooked performance. Jeff Bridges should have been nominated for his incredible work in *The Door in the Floor*. The film is good, but he is unforgettable.

Bridges plays an unsuccessful novelist who has settled for a lesser form of literary success as the author and illustrator of children's books. One summer he hires a naive sixteen-year-old prep-school boy, who aspires to become a writer himself, to work as his assistant. But the boy (Jon Foster) has no idea what lies in store for him when he arrives at Bridges's beautiful home in fashionable East Hampton, New York.

Bridges and his wife, well played by Kim Basinger, are waging a kind of war against each other, brought on by their inability to grieve together for the tragic loss of their twin teenage sons. She has become one of the walking dead, and even her seduction of the "new boy" is accomplished without real passion. Bridges, on the other hand, is acting out in the worst way, recklessly womanizing and causing no little embarrassment in their community. Caught in the middle is their loving four-year-old daughter (Elle Fanning), who doesn't understand what's going on but clings to the secondhand memories of her brothers, as told to her in storybook fashion when she gazes at their framed photos on the wall.

The Door in the Floor is taken from the first section of John Irving's sprawling novel *A Widow for One Year*. His characters have multiple layers, and in filmmaker Tod Williams's adaptation the actors manage to convey the many facets of their splintered personalities. Basinger almost wordlessly expresses the heartbreak that has rendered her lifeless.

But it's Bridges, in a perfectly considered performance as a swaggering character, who commands the screen, and the lion's share of our attention. He could have been portrayed as a monster, but the actor doesn't make him a complete boor. In fact, the film derives its lighter moments from his rambunctious, often outrageous, behavior (as with his latest conquest, artsy neighbor Mimi Rogers).

If someone ever decides to award consolation Oscars, I hope they'll put Jeff Bridges high on the list.

30. DRIVING LESSONS

(2006)

Directed by Jeremy Brock

Screenplay by Jeremy Brock

Actors:

JULIE WALTERS

RUPERT GRINT

LAURA LINNEY

NICHOLAS FARRELL

MICHELLE DUNCAN

JIM NORTON

TAMSIN EGERTON

OLIVER MILBURN

JIM NORTON

By and large, Americans don't like foreign-made films, even those in the English language. Some of that resistance may be melting away in the age of Harry Potter, since those extraordinarily successful movies feature many of the UK's finest actors. *Driving Lessons* stars two faces familiar to Potter fans: Rupert Grint, who plays Ron Weasley, and the wonderful Julie Walters, who plays Ron's mother in the Potter movies.

Walters made her mark on American moviegoers in a star-making part opposite Michael Caine in *Educating Rita* (1983) and has maintained a high-profile career on both sides of the Atlantic ever since, including an Oscar-nominated turn as the dancing teacher in *Billy Elliot* and a costarring role in the pop musical *Mamma Mia!* as one of Meryl Streep's singing pals.

In *Driving Lessons,* Walters plays a lonely, aging actress named Eve Walton who hires a teenage boy to be her helper and companion. Grint plays Ben Marshall, a sixteen-year-old trying desperately to break free from his iron-willed mother and an enervating home life. He needs the job, but has no idea what he's in for. Laura Linney affects a British accent to play Grint's mother, who's a religious zealot and a hypocrite, which drives her husband, a mild-mannered minister, to distraction.

Eve takes a theatrical approach to almost everything in life, and introduces the sheltered teenager to a world in which his poetic nature can blossom. Despite their age difference, these two characters create a strong bond of friendship—and need.

Driving Lessons is a real charmer, but it's never cute or precious. It has the ability to take us from comedy to drama and back again without ever sounding a false note—all the more impressive because it marks the directing debut of screenwriter Jeremy Brock. His past work includes *Mrs. Brown* with Judi Dench, *Charlotte Gray,* and *The Last King of Scotland,* for which he shares credit with Peter Morgan. When I heard him speak after a showing of this film, he was self-effacing about what he'd accomplished, admitted that a great deal of the story was based on his own life (including the key characteristics of his parents and the aging actress), and gave the bulk of the credit for the movie's success to his actors. I wouldn't entirely disagree, but like so many good movies, this one is built on a strong foundation: truth. Brock's real-life experiences gave him the best possible material to work with.

31. DUCK SEASON

(2004)

Directed by Fernando Eimbcke

Screenplay by Fernando Eimbcke and Paula Markovitch

Actors:

ENRIQUE ARREOLA

DIEGO CATAÑO

DANIEL MIRANDA

DANNY PEREA

CAROLINA POLITI

A low-key comedy without stars in it would normally face an uphill climb in American theaters. *Duck Season* is Mexican, so it never stood a chance. It swept virtually every award there was to give in its native country (even from MTV Mexico) and played at film festivals around the world. It even won the Grand Jury Prize at the AFI Fest in Los Angeles, but it never made the impression it should have here in the United States.

This modest black-and-white film probably wouldn't appeal to hardcore fans of Adam Sandler or Will Ferrell movies even if it were in English. It plays like a cross between *Napoleon Dynamite* and a Jacques Tati vehicle. It's unpretentious and takes time building its comic ingredients. It's also incredibly engaging and funny.

Our heroes are fourteen-year-old pals Flama and Moko, who've been left alone for a Sunday afternoon in their well-appointed high-rise apartment. They plan to spend their time playing a video game, pausing now and then to peruse their secret stash of forbidden magazines. Then things begin to happen: an "older" teenage girl who lives down the hall asks if she can borrow the use of their oven to bake brownies. A pizza delivery boy shows up just past the thirty-minute mark—at least, according to Flama and Moko—and refuses to leave without his money. And so on . . .

If it were merely a series of unrelated incidents, *Duck Season* might be just an amusing trifle, but first-time feature-film director Fernando Eimbcke and his cowriter Paula Markovitch manage to give us a rich portrait using very few brushstrokes. We can draw our own conclusions about the boys' relationship to their parents, their loneliness and escape into the world of television and video games, the isolation of life in an apartment complex that offers luxury but no feeling of a neighborhood, and more.

Duck Season filters this perceptive look at modern-day adolescence through a layer of whimsy, with felicitous results. It's well worth a look.

32. EAST IS EAST

(1999)

Directed by Damien O'Donnell

Screenplay by Ayub Khan-Din

Based on the play by Ayub Khan-Din

Actors:

OM PURI

LINDA BASSETT

JORDAN ROUTLEDGE

ARCHIE PANJABI

EMIL MARWA

CHRIS BISSON

JIMI MISTRY

RAJI JAMES

IAN ASPINALL

LESLEY NICOL

GARY DAMER

EMMA RYDAL

RUTH JONES

JOHN BARDON

Some storytelling themes are as universal as they are timeless. The idea of children wanting to live their own lives, causing their parents some degree of anguish in the process, can be found in everything from *Romeo and Juliet* to *Fiddler on the Roof.* It's surefire dramatic fodder because it's based on a real-life situation we all recognize.

In the British comedy-drama *East is East,* the leading character is a Pakistani immigrant now living in England who talks a good show but sends mixed signals to his children. He's played by the wonderful Indian actor Om Puri, who's one of the busiest, best-loved performers in his native country and a recognized actor of distinction around the world.

The year is 1971 and George Khan (Puri) expects his seven children to abide by his old-world Muslim customs and traditions, even though he left a wife behind in Pakistan twenty-five years ago to marry their mother, who helps him run a very British fish-and-chips shop. What's more, they've all grown up in England and don't feel the same bond that he does to the old country . . . to put it mildly.

The family is put to its ultimate test when the bombastic father sets up arranged marriages for two of his sons. He has no idea that one of the boys is in love with the blond girl next door, whose father has no use for immigrants of any kind.

George Khan is a blustery fellow and Puri paints him with broad strokes, but he always seems real, not a cardboard comic character. Even more important, we respect his relationship with his wife and believe their love for each another.

You'd never guess that this lively, entertaining film was based on a play; its movement through the neighborhood, in and out of various locations, seems absolutely natural. Ayub Khan-Din adapted his stage work for the screen without missing a beat, and Damien O'Donnell's direction guarantees that there's never a dull moment.

I don't think you have to know anything about England in the '70s to understand or appreciate this story. You could substitute almost any setting, any time period, and any ethnicity and it would still play. That the characters and incidents in *East is East* all seem so authentic makes it an especially fruitful variation on a time-tested idea.

33. EVERYTHING PUT TOGETHER

(2001)

Directed by Marc Forster

Screenplay by Catherine Lloyd Burns,

Adam Forgash, and Marc Forster

Actors:

RADHA MITCHELL

MEGAN MULLALLY

JUSTIN LOUIS

CATHERINE LLOYD BURNS

ALAN RUCK

MICHELE HICKS

MATT MALLOY

VINCE VIELUF

MARK BOONE JUNIOR

Every time I kick off a new semester at the University of Southern California, I tell my students—a large and varied group—that who they are as individuals, where they come from, what they've experienced and not yet experienced will color their opinions of the films we're going to screen.

Because my wife suffered three miscarriages before giving birth to our daughter, and we both went through

the emotional wringer each time, I'm sure I'm more sensitive to the content of *Everything Put Together* than someone
else might be (even though the mother in this film suffers
an even worse fate than Alice did). But I can't imagine not
finding this film to be provocative and interesting under any
circumstances.

Everything Put Together is an unusual chamber piece set
in American suburbia that treats an intimate human drama
as if it were gothic horror. For its main character, a happily
married woman played by the talented (and underappreciated) Australian actress Radha Mitchell, it *is* a horror film
come to life.

Mitchell and her two best friends are sharing the joy
of pregnancy together, a felicitous example of good timing
that enables them to shop, decorate, attend classes, and prepare themselves for the great adventure that lies ahead. But
Mitchell is prone to anxiety, and in a cruel twist, her worst
fears are realized when one day after giving birth her baby
dies of sudden infant death syndrome.

The rest of the film deals with both a reality and an
unreality. In the real world, Mitchell is shocked when her
friends seem to shun her, as if her terrible misfortune will
rub off on them. In her mind, she undergoes a much worse
ordeal, torturing herself with grief and obsessing about her
baby. As others withdraw from interaction with her—or
counsel her to get on with her life—she becomes increasingly isolated, which only fuels her sense of going through
a living nightmare.

This early effort by Swiss-born director Marc Forster
(who has gone on to make such films as *Monster's Ball,
Finding Neverland,* and *Stranger Than Fiction*) reveals both

his ambitions and his nascent skills, showing us this story from the young mother's point of view and making sure we feel every chilling moment, both real and imagined, as she slides toward madness.

Fortunately, there is a light at the end of the tunnel, and it is this that distinguishes *Everything Put Together,* with its realistic trappings and sharp observations about middle-class rituals, from a sadistic horror movie. Because Mitchell's character undergoes a catharsis, we do, too.

Forster coscripted the film with Catherine Lloyd Burns (who plays Judith, one of the pregnant women) and Adam Forgash. He found his collaboration with cinematographer Roberto Schaefer (who also shot his first feature back in 1995) and editor Matt Chesse so fruitful that he has made them part of his permanent team. It's amusing to think that the same people responsible for this micromovie also made the James Bond extravaganza *Quantum of Solace.*

34. FAST, CHEAP & OUT OF CONTROL

(1997)

Directed by Errol Morris

Actors:

DAVE HOOVER

GEORGE MENDONÇA

RAY MENDEZ

RODNEY BROOKS

Errol Morris has carved out a unique career in the field of documentaries, or as some people prefer to call it, nonfiction filmmaking. He made news in the world of cinema when the celebrated director Werner Herzog "dared" him to make a movie. When Morris's first documentary feature, *Gates of Heaven*, was not only finished but well received, Herzog paid off on his bet in Les Blank's self-explanatory film *Werner Herzog Eats His Shoe.*

Since that time Morris has made a wide variety of films that have stirred controversy (*The Thin Blue Line*), tackled unthinkable subjects (*Mr. Death*), and earned him widespread acclaim, including an Academy Award for *The Fog of War,* his hard-hitting interview feature about former U.S. secretary of defense Robert A. McNamara.

But I have a special place in my heart for one of Morris's most unusual and endearing films, *Fast, Cheap & Out of Control.* It's almost impossible to capture in words. Morris profiles four disparate individuals: a topiary artist who creates beautiful and whimsical garden sculptures, a wild animal trainer, an obsessive robot scientist who is living in future tense, and a scientist whose specialty is the study of mole rats.

Any one of these people might merit a documentary study, at least in short-subject form. What do they have in common that warrants juxtaposing (and intercutting) their stories as a feature-length movie? That is the elusive quality that makes this film so intriguing. (I feel certain that Morris was inspired by the robot scientist's quote, "If you analyze it too much, life becomes almost meaningless.") As it progresses, the pace of intercutting between the subjects accelerates and we begin to see the film as a kind of cinematic fugue—a comparison only enhanced by the driving, melancholy (and quite beautiful) music score by Caleb Sampson.

Some movies can't, and shouldn't, be described: they should be experienced. *Fast, Cheap & Out of Control* is a quintessential example.

For the record, it won Best Documentary award from the New York Film Critics Circle and the National Society of Film Critics, and was given the Truer Than Fiction prize at the Independent Spirit Awards.

35. 15 MINUTES

(2001)

Directed by John Herzfeld
Screenplay by John Herzfeld

Actors:

ROBERT DE NIRO

EDWARD BURNS

KELSEY GRAMMER

AVERY BROOKS

MELINA KANAKAREDES

KAREL RODEN

OLEG TAKTAROV

VERA FARMIGA

JOHN DIRESTA

CHARLIZE THERON

KIM CATTRALL

DARIUS MCCRARY

DAVID ALAN GRIER

JAMES HANDY

One of the challenges of being a critic is that sometimes you find yourself swimming against the tide, cheering for a movie that no one else seems to like. That's what tests your mettle. I really like *15 Minutes*; I find it exciting, original, highly charged entertainment with a sharp point of view and a terrific cast. But I'm almost alone in my opinion.

What didn't other critics like about it? They said it's far-fetched: *I don't think it's trying to be realistic.* They said it's heavy-handed: *I think the filmmaker is responding to the out-landishness of his chosen targets.* They said it takes itself too seriously: *I think they missed the point.*

The overall subject is the media, and everyone's desire to have their fabled fifteen minutes of fame. In this case, the people who shoot for that goal are amoral, violent criminals who learn how to work the system to their advantage—even the legal system in a country where they've just arrived.

Robert De Niro plays a New York City detective who has a habit of making headlines, and frankly, he likes it. In fact, he often gives tips to Kelsey Grammer, the host of a scandalous TV show called *Top Story*—and Grammer is a little too hungry for the kind of eyebrow-raising fodder that makes his show a hit.

Then along come two foreigners—Karel Roden as Emil and Oleg Taktarov as Oleg—from Eastern Europe, who plan to rob, murder, pillage, and document themselves doing it on video, then sell the evidence to *Top Story*. They're greedy for notoriety and they have no shame about it because they realize that in America, celebrity is its own reward and the legal system can be manipulated.

There are other story threads involving fire inspector Edward Burns and TV reporter Melina Kanakaredes, who's in love with De Niro. The screenplay covers a lot of ground but gives each of its characters a fair shake. Charlize Theron turns up in a tiny role as a favor to the director, who gave her her first break in his debut picture, *2 Days in the Valley*.

John Herzfeld wrote and directed this (literally) explosive film, which seldom stops to take a breath and features incredible action set pieces filmed all around the city. *15 Minutes* is in your face from the word go and it's clear that Herzfeld is swinging for the fences. Does it bear scrutiny after the fact? Not according to its critics. But it takes you on a hell of a ride.

36. FIND ME GUILTY

(2006)

Directed by Sidney Lumet

Screenplay by T. J. Mancini,

Robert J. McCrea, Sidney Lumet

Actors:

VIN DIESEL

PETER DINKLAGE

LINUS ROACHE

RON SILVER

ALEX ROCCO

ANNABELLA SCIORRA

RAÚL ESPARZA

JERRY ADLER

RICHARD PORTNOW

JOSH PAIS

To those well-meaning folks who believe that movie reviewers have the same kind of power as a prominent New York theater critic, I submit the sad case of *Find Me Guilty*.

Many of the most prominent critics in the United States encouraged their readers and TV audiences to see this entertaining film from director Sidney Lumet. No one listened.

I know the reason why, because I saw it in the faces of the people I proselytized: they could not, *would* not, believe that Vin Diesel could possibly be starring in a movie worth seeing.

We all fall into the trap of pigeonholing actors, but this was an unfortunate case. Diesel, who has solid theater training but rose to fame as an action-movie star, altered his appearance and worked tirelessly with Lumet to bring a fascinating character to life on-screen.

Actually, Jackie DiNorscio is *larger* than life—but his story is real. Lumet and cowriters T. J. Mancini and Robert J. McCrea use verbatim dialogue from trial transcripts to tell the amazing tale of a low-level New Jersey hood who decides to act as his own attorney in a massive Federal case against the Lucchese crime family. He sees himself as a stand-up comic, but the trial judge (well played by Ron Silver) tries to control his cut-up tendencies for the sake of courtroom decorum. Jackie Dee is a loud, big-hearted lug but he's not stupid, and part of the fun in watching the movie is seeing how so-called smarter people underestimate him, and the power of his disarming candor.

Lumet shows us both sides of the case in and out of court, and populates the film with superior actors right down the line: Linus Roache as the government prosecutor, Peter Dinklage as the mob's defense attorney, Alex Rocco as one of the mob elders, and Annabella Sciorra as Jackie's estranged wife.

But the movie's success hinges on Diesel, and he delivers. If you don't believe me, it's your loss.

37. FIRELIGHT

(1998)

Directed by William Nicholson

Screenplay by William Nicholson

Actors:

SOPHIE MARCEAU

STEPHEN DILLANE

DOMINIQUE BELCOURT

KEVIN ANDERSON

LIA WILLIAMS

JOSS ACKLAND

SALLY DEXTER

Movies used to be about storytelling, but nowadays they are more often about sensations; there's a good reason many Hollywood hits are compared to thrill rides. But I don't think there's an audience in the world, regardless of age, that doesn't respond to a good story.

From the silent-film era through the 1960s there were certain warhorses that were remade time and again, like *Madame X,* a story of mother love and sacrifice. Among its many imitators were *Stella Dallas* (filmed three times . . . so far) and a 1931 film called *The Sin of Madelon Claudet* that won Helen Hayes an Academy Award.

One doesn't find that theme very often in modern cinema, but *Firelight* proves that it hasn't lost its potency, if handled well. It probably helps that the story is set in 1838.

The beautiful Sophie Marceau (a French star best known to American audiences as *Braveheart*'s melancholy queen) is ideally cast as a troubled, and impoverished, Swiss woman who becomes the nineteenth-century equivalent of a surrogate mother. British sheep farmer Stephen Dillane's wife lies in a coma and can't provide him with an heir. Marceau agrees to accept payment for her services and then disappear, but after giving birth, cannot separate herself emotionally from her child. Seven years later she applies for—and wins—the job as the girl's governess, unbeknownst to the master of the house.

Call it soap opera if you like, but this is a beautifully rendered story of passions, both repressed and unleashed. It was written by William Nicholson, best known as the playwright of the wonderful biographical drama about C. S. Lewis, *Shadowlands,* which he later adapted for the screen, earning an Oscar nomination in the process. (He later shared a nomination for the screenplay of *Gladiator.*) This marks his only directorial effort to date, which is surprising given the skill with which he brought this story to life. The film has a masterful look and feel. Nicholson provides a realistic setting for a story where emotions ebb and flow—like the color palette itself, from a gray, icy island playhouse where the young girl finds escape, to the warm glow of the firelight where inner feelings are stirred.

Firelight offers the same kind of satisfaction one derives from reading a good novel where you get lost in the story and don't want it to end.

38. FOLLOWING

(1999)

Directed by Christopher Nolan

Screenplay by Christopher Nolan

Actors:

JEREMY THEOBALD

ALEX HAW

LUCY RUSSELL

JOHN NOLAN

In the year 2001 an audacious independent film called *Memento* became a sensation, inspiring rave reviews and tremendous word of mouth. It launched the career of director Christopher Nolan, who adapted the screenplay from a story by his brother Jonathan. They have gone on to make box-office history with their reinvention of the Batman saga in *Batman Begins* and *The Dark Knight*.

I saw *Memento* several months before its release (and attendant hoopla) at a press screening and utterly dismissed it, finding it pretentious and unappealing. No one was more surprised by its success than I.

Then I saw Nolan's first feature film, made two years earlier, and wondered why it hadn't earned the full-fledged American release, and acclaim, it warranted.

Following shows how a talented filmmaker with a great idea can realize his ambitions without a multimillion-dollar budget. Nolan spent six months working with his cast, and another year's worth of Saturdays shooting the black-and-white feature. (He served as his own cinematographer.) It runs a scant seventy minutes and offers more satisfaction than most bloated two-hour Hollywood movies.

The premise is immediately intriguing: a man named Bill (played by Jeremy Theobald) gets his kicks by following strangers on the street. This amusing, seemingly harmless pastime turns dangerous when one of his victims, named Cobb (Alex Haw), confronts him. It turns out that Cobb has his own idea of fun, stealing people's identities, and persuades Bill to become a partner in crime.

The story would be strong enough to support a film, but *Following* messes with our minds by injecting flashbacks and flash forwards, without warning or explanation. As Nolan explained at the time, "I decided to structure my story in such a way as to emphasize the audience's incomplete understanding of each new scene as it is first presented."

Indeed. This is what takes *Following* to a higher level, beyond film noir homage.

Best of all, it never betrays its microbudget origins. You couldn't ask for more appropriate settings or moody camerawork, and you wouldn't want to see anyone else playing these parts. *Following* is a genuine sleeper, and though I'm apparently alone on this one, I like it better than *Memento*.

39. GILLES' WIFE

(2004)

Directed by Frédéric Fonteyne

Screenplay by Philippe Blasband, Marion Hänsel

and Frédéric Fonteyne

Based on the novel by Madeleine Bourdouxhe

Actors:

EMMANUELLE DEVOS

CLOVIS CORNILLAC

LAURA SMET

COLETTE EMMANUELLE

GIL LAGAY

M any big Hollywood movies these days make almost continual use of tight close-ups. Three recent examples come to mind (*Star Trek, Terminator Salvation,* and *Watchmen*) in which we become eerily familiar with every nook, cranny, and blemish on the leading actors' faces. That may eventually pay off when people watch those movies on their iPhones, but it can be disconcerting when you're sitting in a theater and the faces are twenty feet high. D. W. Griffith and his cameraman Billy Bitzer, who developed the idea of the close-up, meant it to be used for emphasis, or punctuation, in a scene. In the decades that followed, smart directors adhered to that idea. Think of the frequently excerpted scene from George Stevens's *A Place in the Sun* where Montgomery Clift and Elizabeth Taylor get lost in each other's faces. ("Tell Mama . . . tell Mama all.") The impact of that moment would be diminished—or lost altogether—if the rest of the film had been shot the same way.

Silent films had more occasion to rely on close-ups because the actors' faces had to tell the story. Surely it is not coincidental that the exquisite French film *Gilles' Wife,* which relies so much on its leading lady's expressive face, also uses a minimum of dialogue.

Gilles' Wife takes place in a rural French village in the 1930s and beautifully evokes that time and place. The pace is leisurely and the camera lingers over the simple qualities that made up daily life at a time before television, video games, and the Internet became ubiquitous. When was the last time you saw a movie that paid attention to the sun streaming through the slats of a barn? The sound track is similarly serene, uncomplicated by the roar of jet engines overhead or music playing when a character walks inside a village store.

But this is more than simply a mood piece: it is a powerful story of relationships. Emmanuelle Devos plays Elisa, the loving wife of a factory worker, whose day is filled with household chores and the raising of their twin daughters. She and Gilles make love at night. Their life is uncomplicated and they are content. Elisa's sister Victorine comes to visit on a regular basis and enjoys spending time with her nieces. Gilles has always liked her but at some point his interest becomes more than casual. Elisa is unaware of the change at first.

When the reality of the situation becomes clear to her, Elisa is distraught. She feels betrayed twice over, but she decides not to let her emotions control her response. She addresses Gilles with calmness and understanding, and says, "I'll wait till you're over it." He responds, "I'll never be over it." What is Elisa to do?

Gilles' Wife is a richly textured movie that almost feels as if it were made in the period it depicts. That is to the credit of director Frédéric Fonteyne, who adapted Madeleine Bourdouxhe's period novel with Philippe Blasband and Marion Hänsel. He takes his time and makes every scene count. Words cannot express the beauty of Virginie Saint-Martin's cinematography, which is almost painterly. But the main attraction here is Emmanuelle Devos's face, which registers so many emotions over the course of the film. We watch her think, gaze, contemplate, and suffer—and we fill in the gaps of dialogue in our mind.

I only wish more filmmakers understood the power of silence, and the way an audience responds to someone *thinking* on screen.

40. GLOOMY SUNDAY

(1999)

Directed by Rolf Schübel

Screenplay by Rolf Schübel and Ruth Toma

Based on the novel by Nick Barkow

Actors:

ERIKA MAROZSÁN

JOACHIM KRÓL

BEN BECKER

STEFANO DIONISI

ANDRÁS BÁLINT

GÉZA BOROS

ROLF BECKER

ILSE ZIELSTORFF

ULRIKE GROTE

G *loomy Sunday* is a foreign film that's had an unusual history here in the United States. Several years after its release in Europe, it opened in a neighborhood theater in Wilmette, Illinois, and local word of mouth kept it going for more than a year. Another theater in Beverly Hills then gave it a try with the same results. Its leading lady, Erika Marozsán, even made personal appearances there on weekends. How could a film without recognizable stars or a major ad campaign attract this kind of following? The answer lies in the film itself, which has an emotional pull for an older audience, and a European sensibility that speaks to a substantial segment of our population.

Gloomy Sunday is a well-made, old-fashioned romantic drama—the type Hollywood rarely even attempts anymore. It opens in Budapest in the 1990s. An elderly man visits an old haunt for the first time in fifty years. As he dines, he gazes at a framed photograph of a woman who inspired the title song. We then flash back in time.

The story revolves around the gregarious owner of this same restaurant during the late 1930s. Laszlo Szabo (Joachim Król) is in love with his beautiful waitress, Ilona (Marozsán). When he hires a starving pianist named Andras (Stefano Dionisi) to play in his café, he doesn't anticipate that Ilona will fall in love with him. Or that one of their best customers, a German salesman (Ben Becker) will also fall under her spell. Yet they all manage to remain friends. Then World War II erupts and changes their lives.

A major subplot involves Andras's haunting composition, which becomes his (and the café's) signature tune. Although customers insist that he play it nightly, it gains unexpected notoriety throughout Europe as "the suicide song" because it is found playing on gramophones as scores of people do themselves in. (In real life, it didn't have the same effect here in America, where it was made popular by Billie Holiday.)

The melancholy song becomes a perfect accompaniment for a bittersweet story of love and fate that unfolds against the tumultuous backdrop of Europe during the 1930s and '40s.

I don't think anyone would make a case for this being a great movie, but there is something about its old-world milieu, its unabashed romanticism, and its appealing cast that makes it hard to resist. At a time when most movies are cool and ironic, this one dares to be warm and direct. Perhaps that's why people who were raised on old Hollywood movies (like me) find this one so agreeable.

41. GO TIGERS!

(2001)

Directed by Kenneth A. Carlson

I'm not a sports fan, so I didn't expect to find a film about high school football terribly interesting. But *Go Tigers!* turns out to be something more: a revealing look at small-town America.

The setting is working-class Massillon, Ohio, where for 106 years the town has cheered, coddled, and generally gone crazy for its championship high school football team. The residents eat, sleep, and breathe football. In fact, in the movie's opening moments, we bear witness to a unique ritual: when a baby is born, a representative from the chamber of commerce comes to the hospital and presents the newborn with a tiny football!

The 1999 team feels particular pressure, for several reasons. Their last season was an embarrassment and they're in need of a comeback. Even more important, the school district itself is on the rocks, subject to severe budget cuts. The city wants to impose a tax levy and citizens will be loath to vote for that in the upcoming referendum unless the Massillon Tigers deliver the goods. Without a winning season, the team may have to go into hibernation.

Filmmaker Carlson becomes a fly on the wall as we get

to know key members of the team, some of whom have academic challenges to meet, and at least one of whom has been in trouble with the law.

Go Tigers! is a fascinating look at traditional small-town values, as embodied by a cast of real-life characters that would do any novelist proud. Carlson grew up in Massillon, so he paints an empathetic—but not whitewashed— picture of star athletes, coaches, teachers, parents, boosters, and even naysayers in town.

This is less a film about sports than it is about pride, tradition, values, and the American way. That's why I like it.

42. GOING IN STYLE

(1979)

Directed by Martin Brest

Screenplay by Martin Brest

Based on the story by Edward Cannon

Actors:

GEORGE BURNS

ART CARNEY

LEE STRASBERG

CHARLES HALLAHAN

PAMELA PAYTON-WRIGHT

MARK MARGOLIS

I'd like to think that filmmaker Martin Brest won't go down in the history books as the man who made the notorious high-profile flop *Gigli,* or the bloated remake of *Death Takes a Holiday* called *Meet Joe Black.* I remember with fondness his antic, award-winning student film *Hot Dogs for Gaugin* and his early Hollywood efforts like *Beverly Hills Cop, Midnight Run,* and the lesser-known film from 1979 called *Going in Style,* which he wrote and directed, from a story by Edward Cannon.

It takes a certain sensibility for a young man (then twenty-eight years old) to make a movie about old people and show empathy and respect as well as a sense of humor. *Going in Style* is a comedy, but not, as its wacky poster (and DVD) artwork would imply, a parade of belly laughs. It's the story of three senior citizens who live together in Astoria in Queens, New York. They barely get by on social security and pass the time feeding pigeons in the park. Then Joe (George Burns), who's bored with their sedentary lives, hatches a scheme that will spice things up and give them some spending money at the same time: they're going to rob a bank.

This seemingly outlandish premise succeeds because the movie isn't played as farce; in fact, aside from the robbery itself, it's quite realistic, especially in its depiction of the old men's dead-end existence. These characters don't ask for pity, but the situation speaks for itself. Brest's thoughtful screenplay is filled with nuance, and his staging pays great attention to detail.

But the icing on the cake is the performances of his stars: George Burns, Art Carney, and Lee Strasberg. Burns earned an Oscar for his performance in the Neil Simon comedy *The Sunshine Boys,* and this film, made four years later, reaffirms what a skillful actor he was. (And why not? After all, he spent his entire life in show business.) His Joe is not cute or coy; he's a pragmatist and the driving force behind the scheme that changes the three friends' lives.

Art Carney also won an Oscar late in life, for his touching performance in *Harry and Tonto* in 1974. Although he was beloved for his work in comedy, creating the iconic role of Ed Norton opposite Jackie Gleason in *The Honeymooners,* he, too, was a fine actor who could find many colors in a well-written character.

Least known to the general public was Lee Strasberg, the legendary acting teacher and Actors Studio guru. He made a strong impression in a rare screen appearance as Hyman Roth in *The Godfather, Part II* and was persuaded to act again in a handful of projects in the late 1970s, including this one. His character is the most serious of the senior-citizen trio, which works to the movie's benefit: we aren't watching colorful old codgers, but three lonely men who find purpose in life in an unconventional way. The bank heist is just a springboard for a thoughtful story about old age.

43. THE GREAT BUCK HOWARD

(2009)

Directed by Sean McGinly

Screenplay by Sean McGinly

Actors:

JOHN MALKOVICH

COLIN HANKS

EMILY BLUNT

RICKY JAY

TOM HANKS

STEVE ZAHN

DEBRA MONK

GRIFFIN DUNNE

WALLACE LANGHAM

MATTHEW GRAY GUBLER

ADAM SCOTT

GEORGE TAKEI

I'm a sucker for show-business stories, especially when they originate somewhere off the beaten path. Writer-director Sean McGinly based *The Great Buck Howard* on his own experiences—and it shows. I don't think anyone would set out to invent such a main character or story line. Some critics dismissed the film as "slight," but I think it offers rich rewards, even on a small scale.

The title character is a mentalist, reminiscent of the Amazing Kreskin, an old-school performer whose heyday has come and gone; he still mourns the demise of *The Tonight Show with Johnny Carson*. John Malkovich wouldn't have been the first name that popped into my head when casting this role, but he is both charming and convincing as a man who has deluded himself into believing that a major comeback is just around the corner.

Colin Hanks plays an aimless law school dropout who stumbles into the job of Malkovich's assistant and roadie, a thankless task given his new boss's mercurial nature and many eccentricities. (The actor's real-life father, Tom, was one of the film's producers, and appears briefly as the young man's disapproving dad.)

The Great Buck Howard is essentially a character portrait, from the new roadie's point of view as he travels the hinterlands with his demanding employer. Along the way he develops a grudging admiration for his employer's work ethic, his showmanship, and the fact that even after all these years, he still draws an admiring audience.

Filmmaker McGinly, who inhabited this world, re-creates it with affection, bemusement, and care, offering plum supporting roles to such good actors as Emily Blunt, Steve Zahn, Debra Monk, Ricky Jay, and Griffin Dunne, who make the most of them. There are cameo appearances by a variety of television hosts, some old-time entertainers, and, in a curious plot twist, *Star Trek*'s George Takei. All of this is certain to amuse show-biz buffs and observers.

They do not constitute the great American moviegoing public, however, and *The Great Buck Howard* sat on the shelf for more than a year before receiving a desultory theatrical release in 2009. It doesn't deserve such obscurity, any more than Buck Howard himself does.

44. THE GREATEST GAME EVER PLAYED

(2005)

Directed by Bill Paxton

Screenplay by Mark Frost

Based on the book *The Greatest Game Ever Played:*
Harry Vardon, Francis Ouimet, and the Birth
***of Modern Golf* by Mark Frost**

Actors:

SHIA LABEOUF

STEPHEN DILLANE

JOSH FLITTER

PEYTON LIST

MARNIE MCPHAIL

ELIAS KOTEAS

STEPHEN MARCUS

LEN CARIOU

LUKE ASKEW

PETER FIRTH

JOE JACKSON

DAWN UPSHAW

JAMES PAXTON

There are countless movies about baseball, and a healthy supply of films about such other pastimes as football and basketball. Golf has never struck Hollywood as an especially compelling sport, but when writer-producer Mark Frost (whose television credits include *Hill Street Blues* and *Twin Peaks*) came upon the story of the 1913 U.S. Open Tournament, he knew he'd struck gold. The true story offered so much great raw material that he researched and wrote a book called *The Greatest Game Ever Played,* and then sold the screen rights to the Disney company.

Shia LaBeouf was on his way toward stardom when he landed the leading role in this period picture as Francis Ouimet, a golf-crazy kid from the wrong side of the tracks who repeatedly defied the odds and wound up playing opposite the British champion Harry Vardon (well played by Stephen Dillane) in the U.S. Open.

It turns out that Ouimet and Vardon have something unexpected in common: they both overcame poverty, yet they'll never be accepted by the self-styled aristocrats who populate the golf clubs of the world. *The Greatest Game Ever Played* turns out to be more than just a good sports yarn: it's also a highly relatable story about class conflict.

Actor Bill Paxton had already directed two feature films when he heard about this property. When he met with the Disney executives to pitch himself for this project, he came prepared: he had consulted with a conceptual artist who gave him sketches to show how he planned to "goose" the golfing sequences and make them riveting to a generation of moviegoers raised on video games. That sealed the deal.

Those eye-popping moments—following a golf ball in mid-air (with a ladybug sitting calmly on its surface) or adopting the golfer's point of view as everything vanishes from sight except the hole, hundreds of yards away—give the film a flashiness that takes some getting used to. But in the end, it works.

Those cutting-edge visuals stand out in sharp relief from the rest of the film, which captures the look and feel of its period so well. No detail seems to have escaped the attention of production designer François Séguin, from the hand-lettered chalk scoreboard to the contents of the haberdashery where LaBeouf works after school. Cinematographer Shane Hurlbut bathes the film in a warm, nostalgic glow.

Paxton even decided to go against the modern trend of saving credits for the end of the film and build an elaborate opening-title sequence, using photographs and illustrations, to set the stage for his audience and draw us back in time.

Unfortunately, being a PG-rated Disney film put off adults from seeing the film, while kids apparently found no allure in a story about golf. A negative review in *Sports Illustrated* didn't help. If it had been released after *Disturbia* or *Transformers,* Shia LaBeouf would have saved the day, but he wasn't yet a household name. (He later credited Paxton with helping him to grow as an actor, and indeed, his performance in this film is sincere and strong.)

Because I liked it so much, I put this film to the ultimate test, showing it to my USC class of twenty-somethings, as tough a crowd as any filmmaker ever had to face. At first they felt superior to it because it was a Disney movie, but it soon won them over and they wound up loving it. I think you will, too.

45. THE HARD WORD

(2002)

Directed by Scott Roberts

Screenplay by Scott Roberts

Actors:

GUY PEARCE

RACHEL GRIFFITHS

ROBERT TAYLOR

JOEL EDGERTON

DAMIEN RICHARDSON

RHONDDA FINDLETON

KATE ATKINSON

VINCE COLOSIMO

DORIAN NKONO

Heist movies are usually fun to watch if the filmmaker can continually engage and surprise us—like a vaudevillian who's got to keep six or eight plates spinning at the same time. *The Hard Word* pulls this off with élan, carrying out a story that's hard-edged and contemporary without falling into pseudo-Tarantino posturing or Guy Ritchie–like self-consciousness. Like its criminal heroes, it's simply out to get the job done so everyone can enjoy the payoff.

This particular yarn comes from Australian writer-director Scott Roberts, who had the good fortune to land two major stars, Guy Pearce and Rachel Griffiths, for the leading roles.

Pearce plays Dale Twentyman, who's made a career out of armed robbery, along with his brothers Mal and Shane—and in cahoots with their slick criminal lawyer Frank Malone (Robert Taylor), who knows all the angles. To their minds, serving a stretch in prison is a small price to pay for the rewards awaiting them upon release. But while his clients are behind bars, Malone gets cocky and starts fooling around with Dale's wife (Griffiths), little dreaming that the sexy blonde is just as smart—and devious—as he is.

The film hinges on the brothers being sprung from prison long enough to pull—you guessed it—one last job, and it's here that everyone's plans begin to unravel.

Guy Pearce is a versatile actor who tends to disappear into whatever part he's playing. The role of Dale offers him the chance to summon up a gritty bravado we don't often get to see. Griffiths, too, can be mousy or malevolent, depending on the role; here she's a self-assured sexpot who always seems to know the score.

The Hard Word received a mixed response from critics, but I think it can hold its own alongside any caper movie of recent vintage. Its characters are colorful and well drawn, its action scenes are exciting, and its story twists are unfailingly clever. The Australian cast and setting make it particularly fresh for American viewers.

46. THE HARMONISTS

(1997)

Directed by Joseph Vilsmaier

Screenplay by Klaus Richter

Based on the story by Jürgen Büscher

Actors:

BEN BECKER

HEINO FERCH

ULRICH NOETHEN

HEINRICH SCHAFMEISTER

MAX TIDOF

KAI WIESINGER

MERET BECKER

KATJA RIEMANN

DANA VÁVROVÁ

OTTO SANDER

In the first years of the twenty-first-century, a number of German and Austrian filmmakers have attempted to deal with the emotionally volatile subjects of World War II, Nazism, and the Holocaust. From *Blind Spot,* a stark documentary interview of Hitler's secretary; to *Downfall,* the saga of the führer's final days; to the Academy Award–winning *The Counterfeiters,* about a Nazi-controlled counterfeiting ring that operated inside a concentration camp, these (and other) compelling films evoke the turbulent feelings of a modern generation that wants to understand how their parents and grandparents responded to the events of the 1930s and '40s, and why.

But there is at least one film that predates this recent cycle. It never received the same degree of attention in the United States, although it was a great success in Germany, and in the grand scheme of things it doesn't tackle as weighty a subject . . . but *The Harmonists* (known overseas as *The Comedian Harmonists*) paints a vivid picture of how the Nazis affected, and subverted, every aspect of German life—even its light entertainment.

The Comedian Harmonists were a hugely popular, much loved six-man vocal group that formed in 1927 when Berlin was one of the world's cultural capitals. As we see in this well-told chronicle, a singer named Harry Frommermann (Ulrich Noethen) is inspired by a popular American vocal group called the Revelers, who sold millions of records (and even appeared on-screen in some Vitaphone short subjects). He sets out to create a German equivalent of this close-harmony group, and aspires to the highest musical standards. One by one he recruits the five men who will become his partners—men who are willing to endure hours of relentless rehearsal in order to achieve perfection.

Naturally there are setbacks on the road to success, including personal matters that intrude on the Harmonists' professional lives. (Harry and his first partner in the enterprise, Robert Biberti, played by Ben Becker, are in love with the same woman.) But through perseverance, and fidelity to the musical goals they all share, the Comedian Harmonists succeed.

Three of the singers are Jewish, and three are not, but by the early 1930s they are all affected by the demands of the National Socialist Party. Here the film effectively dramatizes the way many Germans responded to anti-Semitic outbursts and capricious orders, dismissing them as little more than a nuisance, at first, and refusing to believe that their country could succumb to such a fringe movement.

When I first saw this film I was so intrigued that I sought out the Comedian Harmonists' music (which is quite wonderful, and available on various CD collections) and went out of my way to see Eberhard Fechner's long, exhaustive documentary about the group, filmed in the mid-1970s when most of the original members were still alive to tell their story. (One of them, Roman Cycowski, became a cantor in San Francisco and lived to be ninety-eight.)

But even if you've never heard, or heard of, the group, their story is undeniably interesting. The unkindest word most critics had for it was "conventional," noting its resemblance to a vintage Hollywood biographical drama. That it may be, but it is also evocative of its era, and solidly entertaining.

47. HEDWIG AND THE ANGRY INCH

(2001)

Directed by John Cameron Mitchell

Screenplay by John Cameron Mitchell

Adapted from the stage musical by

John Cameron Mitchell and Stephen Trask

Actors:

JOHN CAMERON MITCHELL

MIRIAM SHOR

STEPHEN TRASK

THEODORE LISCINSKI

ROB CAMPBELL

MICHAEL ARONOV

ANDREA MARTIN

MICHAEL PITT

ALBERTA WATSON

While traditional movie musicals have made a welcome comeback in recent years, with everything from *Hairspray* to *High School Musical* finding favor with audiences, other less conventional films have expanded the genre's boundaries. The offbeat content and themes of *Hedwig and the Angry Inch* virtually ensured that it wouldn't find the same level of acceptance as, say, *Mamma Mia!* But if people would just give it a try they would discover a funny, bracingly original piece of work with a terrific song score.

Like many contemporary movie musicals this one originated onstage, where its star, John Cameron Mitchell, and his cocreator Stephen Trask, created a flamboyant performance piece about Hedwig, an "internationally ignored" German-born rock star. A self-styled diva, she has survived a botched sex-change operation (hence the "angry inch" reference) but hasn't gotten over being dumped by the boy-toy rock idol she helped nurture on his way to success. He's even stolen Hedwig's highly personal repertoire of songs. This has left Hedwig (née Hansel) dazed and embittered, as we see during her current tour of low-rent restaurants called Bilgewater's, where she has the misfortune of tracing the same route as her much more popular protégé.

Even if transsexuality isn't normally your cup of tea, you may find yourself drawn into this buoyant film. First off, Mitchell's performance as the glamorous, self-deluded Hedwig is astonishing. She's an ego-driven oddball, to be sure, but she's not a freak, and her expressive songs help to flesh out a memorable, curiously touching character. The songs are clever and funny, and their staging is so inventive it's hard to believe that this material was originally designed for theater instead of film. In many ways, first-time director Mitchell's greatest achievement is turning that stage piece into a fresh movie concoction that never belies its origins. Clever animation by Emily Hubley adds to the cinematic quality of the piece. (There's even a sing-along with the bouncing ball.)

Most of all, *Hedwig and the Angry Inch* is fun to watch: audacious and entertaining, a musical that doesn't seem tied to any familiar traditions but knows how to make perfect use of the medium.

48. HIDALGO

(2004)

Directed by Joe Johnston

Screenplay by John Fusco

Actors:

VIGGO MORTENSEN

OMAR SHARIF

LOUISE LOMBARD

SAÏD TAGHMAOUI

PETER MENSAH

J. K. SIMMONS

ZULEIKHA ROBINSON

SILAS CARSON

JOSHUA WOLF COLEMAN

ADAM ALEXI-MALLE

FLOYD RED CROW WESTERMAN

C. THOMAS HOWELL

MALCOLM MCDOWELL

When I interviewed director Joe Johnston after seeing *Hidalgo,* I couldn't wait to ask him what films had influenced him most. I expected him to cite *Lawrence of Arabia,* not only because his movie involves a grueling horse race across the Arabian desert, but because he cast *Lawrence*'s Omar Sharif in a key supporting role. But when Johnston said *Gunga Din,* I broke into a big smile. I had a feeling he was trying to invoke that kind of entertainment and I was happy to learn I was right.

Hidalgo marks a rare return to a genre Hollywood used to own: high adventure. The term is probably meaningless to younger moviegoers. Some might say *Raiders of the Lost Ark* and its sequels would qualify, but Indiana Jones is a fantastic character with only one foot in reality and that's not quite the idea. Exaggeration is acceptable in a high-adventure yarn but there *is* a limit.

For *Hidalgo,* screenwriter John Fusco turned to the little-known story of Frank T. Hopkins (Viggo Mortensen), a celebrated horseback rider who is working for Buffalo Bill's Wild West Show in 1890—and haunted by the memories of what he witnessed at Wounded Knee when he was working for the U.S. Army. A sheik invites Hopkins and his remarkable horse Hidalgo to participate in the Ocean of Fire, a three-thousand-mile race that few can endure, let alone hope to win. What's more, Hidalgo is a mustang and will be pitted against the finest of purebred Arabian horses. Hopkins accepts the challenge but doesn't know quite the extent of the adventure that awaits him.

Hopkins is a somewhat controversial character in real life, but Fusco and director Johnston are not out to teach us a history lesson. Their goal was to create a larger-than-life action-adventure yarn that could be called a Western—if it didn't happen to take place halfway around the world. The screenplay is cleverly laced with subplots and colorful characters (including Hopkins's rivals in the race and the independent-minded daughter of the sheik).

But the emphasis is on big-screen action and *Hidalgo* definitely delivers the goods. Johnston and his company traveled the world to make this movie. The director also realized that if he relied too much on CGI to "paint" the images, his film would have the same unrealistic look as an outer-space fantasy, so he built as many full-scale sets as possible and used as many stuntmen and extras as he could afford to give each scene visual credibility.

Viggo Mortensen, fresh from his triumphant work in *The Lord of the Rings* trilogy, is a perfect choice to play Hopkins. A horseman in real life, the actor conveys both the physicality and the emotional fragility of his character.

Hidalgo is the kind of movie that makes me feel like a twelve-year-old again. In fact, I know at least one father who took his adolescent son to see this movie as part of a birthday-party group, and the kids loved it. They also acknowledged that they'd never seen any other film quite like it. I only wish people could discover *Hidalgo* on a big screen, where it was meant to be seen . . . but in the best home theaters I'm sure it will come to life.

49. A HOME AT THE END OF THE WORLD

(2004)

Directed by Michael Mayer
Screenplay by Michael Cunningham
Based on the novel by Michael Cunningham

Actors:

COLIN FARRELL

ROBIN WRIGHT PENN

DALLAS ROBERTS

SISSY SPACEK

MATT FREWER

ERIK SMITH

HARRIS ALLAN

ANDREW CHALMERS

RYAN DONOWHO

WENDY CREWSON

JOSHUA CLOSE

Some movies defy pigeonholing, and more often than not, they suffer for it. Audiences respond to pithy descriptions ("*The Terminator* meets *When Harry Met Sally*") or punchy ad lines; the more complicated a film sounds, the warier people tend to be.

A Home at the End of the World can't be boiled down to a simple sentence. As it is, Michael Cunningham had to condense his 352-page novel to transform it into a workable screenplay. But the very quality that makes the movie difficult to summarize is also what makes it so good.

This is a saga that spans several decades. We first meet Bobby as a boy in the late 1960s, in thrall to his older brother, then as an adolescent in the mid-1970s, when he forms a friendship with Jonathan. After the latest in a series of traumatic experiences, he moves in with Jonathan's family, welcomed by his understanding mother (Sissy Spacek) and father (Matt Frewer). They provide a safe haven for the sensitive teenager, who just wants a simple, happy life.

Jonathan is gay, and while he fools around with Bobby early on, Bobby isn't so certain about his sexual identity. In the early 1980s Jonathan (now played by Dallas Roberts) leaves his hometown of Cleveland for New York City. Bobby (Colin Farrell) stays behind, but when his surrogate parents retire to Arizona, he comes to Greenwich Village and catches up with Jonathan, who has moved in with a hippieish "older woman," nicely played by Robin Wright Penn.

Together they form a family unit, and while there are complications in this triangle relationship, and crises to be dealt with, the characters come to realize they have a bond that can't be shaken.

Cunningham's characters reflect their times, and changing attitudes around them; the result is a delicate and moving story about redefining the traditional notion of family. Acclaimed theater director Michael Mayer never directed a film before this, but clearly understood all the nuances of the screenplay. The acting is exceptionally good, with standout work from Colin Farrell, atypically cast as a gentle soul, screen newcomer Dallas Roberts as his lifelong friend, Robin Wright Penn as a woman who's been around and is still searching for answers, and Sissy Spacek as an open-hearted mom.

A Home at the End of the World is superior adult drama that unfolds like a good novel.

50. THE HOUSE OF SAND

(2005)

Directed by Andrucha Waddington
Screenplay by Elena Soárez
Story by Luiz Carlos Barreto, Elena Soárez,
and Andrucha Waddington

Actors:

FERNANDA MONTENEGRO

FERNANDA TORRES

RUY GUERRA

SEU JORGE

LUIZ MELODIA

ENRIQUE DÍAZ

STÊNIO GARCIA

EMILIANO QUEIROZ

I love movies that take me to another time and place, and that's one of the qualities that makes a Brazilian film called *The House of Sand* worth seeing. From the very first scene—set in 1910—we're swept away to a desolate spot at the edge of the desert called Maranhão, in the northern part of Brazil, where a madman brings his wife and her mother, intending to make a home there. He is caught up in a crazy scheme and they are his unfortunate victims. The wife is played by Fernanda Torres, and the mother is played by the grande dame of Brazilian cinema, Fernanda Montenegro. If you saw *Central Station* in 1998, I'm certain you'll remember her; she was nominated for an Academy Award for that performance, and she does exceptional work again in this unusual story.

At first, the young wife will do anything to get away from this place, but fate, and the elements, are against her. In time she begins to make her peace with the environment and meets a fisherman (Seu Jorge) who is able to help her and her daughter, as they are now forced to fend for themselves. There are other occasional (and intriguing) encounters with visitors to their remote spot on the map, but this remains their home as one generation melts into another. The story elapses over sixty years' time altogether, and in an audacious but fascinating pas de deux, the two actresses switch the roles of mother and daughter to reflect the passage of the years. (I can't think of another film where this has been done.)

The House of Sand is a mood piece that casts an almost-hypnotic spell with haunting images (photographed in wide screen by Ricardo Della Rossa), sounds, and performances. I was completely caught up in that spell, but I'm going to let you in on something I didn't know while I was watching the film: the two female stars are mother and daughter in real life. That wouldn't be a secret in Brazil, where both of them are well known, but it was news to me, and it adds resonance to the remarkable performances both women give here.

Even after quite some time, I still have pictures in my mind from this movie. Any film with that kind of staying power is worth seeing, it seems to me.

51. HOW TO LOSE FRIENDS & ALIENATE PEOPLE

(2008)

Directed by Robert Weide

Screenplay by Peter Straughan

Based on the book by Toby Young

Actors:

SIMON PEGG

KIRSTEN DUNST

JEFF BRIDGES

DANNY HUSTON

GILLIAN ANDERSON

MEGAN FOX

MIRIAM MARGOLYES

BILL PATERSON

MAX MINGHELLA

DIANA KENT

THANDIE NEWTON

MARGO STILLEY

I think Simon Pegg is going to have a long and prosperous career; he's a modern-day everyman with a gift for comedy. So far he's made a smooth transition from cult figure on British TV (in such series as *Spaced*) to star and writer of cult movies (*Shaun of the Dead, Hot Fuzz*) to leading man (*Run, Fat Boy, Run*), with a high-profile detour as Scotty in the latest *Star Trek* movie. But when *How to Lose Friends & Alienate People* came out in 2008, the fact that he wasn't a household name, combined with the distributor's obvious indifference to the movie, dealt it a death blow.

Critics were unkind, as well, but this is another instance

where it seemed to me that they reviewed what the film wasn't, or what they thought it should be, rather than what it was. In England, where Pegg is a star and the book on which the film was based was a bestseller, reviews were positive and the box office was strong.

Again, I can't explain why other people didn't like this comedy: I can only tell you that I did.

Toby Young's cheeky memoir dealt with his experiences while working for *Vanity Fair* magazine. Peter Straughan's screenplay uses the book as a starting point for a series of largely—though not wholly—fictional comedic and romantic misadventures that also take us inside the world of celebrity culture. (Having worked at *Entertainment Tonight,* I can tell you that much of this rang true to me.) The charm of the film derives from the fact that it's rooted in reality but isn't afraid to incorporate slapstick and silliness into the proceedings.

Simon Pegg plays Sidney Young, a gate-crashing British journalist whose audacity gets him a job working for eccentric editor Jeff Bridges at *Sharp's* magazine in New York. The younger man reminds Bridges of himself when he was starting out, but Sidney is now in the big leagues and his bull-in-a-china-shop approach doesn't go over well in the office, or at parties where the staff tries to chat up young stars and their publicists.

He gets off on the wrong foot with fellow worker Kirsten Dunst but, eventually, they form a kinship. The relationship is strained when Sidney goes overboard for a sexy starlet played by Megan Fox. But Sidney comes to learn that hobnobbing with the stars comes with a high price tag—if you value your integrity.

The cast is well chosen, top to bottom. Jeff Bridges is

great fun to watch as the Graydon Carter prototype; he's even made up to resemble the real-life *Vanity Fair* editor. Kirsten Dunst is quite likable in the best part she's had in years. Danny Huston is excellent as a *Sharp's* editor and celebrity sycophant, and Gillian Anderson is perfect as a publicist who wields her power like a royal scepter. There are also fine contributions from such expert character actors as Miriam Margolyes and Bill Paterson.

Director Robert Weide steers everyone on the right path in his feature-film debut, after an Emmy-winning career crafting documentaries on comedy icons from W. C. Fields to Lenny Bruce, and piloting Larry David's *Curb Your Enthusiasm* from its inception through its first five seasons. (Full disclosure: Bob is an old friend of mine. I really hoped I would like this movie and I'm happy to say I did.)

Any movie that makes repeated reference to *La Dolce Vita* is setting its sights above the rabble. But *How to Lose Friends & Alienate People* has something for everyone—enough lowbrow humor and sexy women to please the crowd and plenty of smarts to satisfy discerning moviegoers as well.

52. I SERVED THE KING OF ENGLAND

(2006)

Directed by Jiri Menzel

Screenplay by Jiri Menzel

Based on the novel by Bohumil Hrabal

Actors:

IVAN BARNEV

OLDRICH KAISER

JULIA JENTSCH

MARTIN HUBA

MARIÁN LABUDA

MILAN LASICA

JOSEF ABRHÁM

ISTVÁN SZABÓ

In the late 1960s, film critics and discerning moviegoers took note of some striking imports that came to represent the Czech New Wave. One such import, called *Closely Watched Trains,* won the Academy Award as Best Foreign Language Film for 1968. Forty years later, that same filmmaker, Jirí Menzel, sent another movie to our shores from a novel by the same author who wrote that Oscar winner. It's a story that manages to be whimsical and wise, serious and sexy.

The film opens in the 1930s. Ivan Barnev plays Jan, a slight but ambitious young man whose goal is simple: he wants to be a millionaire. He notices, early on, that money has extraordinary power—so much so that even wealthy men will get down on all fours to pick up change on the floor. Jan works his way up the ladder as a waiter in a series of increasingly plush restaurants, cafés, and hotels, learning about human nature in the process, witnessing the indulgences of the wealthy, and loving a series of beautiful women.

The last woman he meets is the one he marries, and here he makes a fateful mistake. He's never had any interest in politics, so it means nothing to him that his bride is German, but when the Nazis invade Czechoslovakia he has to choose which side he's on . . . and his decision will affect the rest of his life.

The story is told as a series of flashbacks, after Jan, now an old man, has been released from prison. It's a wistful story of how even a seeming innocent can be swept up by the winds of political change.

It's been a long time since I've seen a film that embraced so many emotions, or was so open in its treatment of sexuality. *I Served the King of England* is based on a novel by one of Czechoslovakia's leading writers, Bohumil Hrabal, who knew of what he spoke: his book was banned by the Communist government that seized control of the country in 1968.

Menzel manages to combine elements of whimsy—perfectly realized by his innocent-looking leading man—and visual flights of fancy with a serious story. With a flair for illustrating life's incongruities, this charming, disarming, highly sexual film is like a breath of fresh air that comes to us from the hands of an old master.

53. IDIOCRACY

(2006)

Directed by Mike Judge

Screenplay by Mike Judge and Etan Cohen

Story by Mike Judge

Actors:

LUKE WILSON

MAYA RUDOLPH

DAX SHEPARD

TERRY ALAN CREWS

DAVID HERMAN

ANDREW WILSON

BRAD "SCARFACE" JORDAN

JUSTIN LONG

THOMAS HADEN CHURCH

SARA RUE

STEPHEN ROOT

NARRATED BY EARL MANN

I'm sure I'm not the only one who's concerned about the dumbing down of America, but you wouldn't automatically think that this issue would be important to the man who brought us Beavis and Butthead. In truth, Mike Judge is a very bright guy who also created *King of the Hill* (and provided the voice of its hero, Hank Hill). He also wrote and directed the enduring cult-favorite feature *Office Space.* He certainly can't be accused of cultural elitism; that makes him the perfect candidate to take on the issue of rampant stupidity.

In *Idiocracy* he states his case right up front: stupid people procreate at a much higher rate than smart people. Hilarious "interviews" with prospective—and actual—parents prove his point. (And remember—this movie was written long before the Octomom came along.) Just think what that means about our future as a society!

Luke Wilson plays a soft-headed army file clerk who's chosen to participate in a time-travel hibernation experiment, along with a hooker, played by Maya Rudolph. Naturally, things don't go as planned and the two are propelled five hundred years into the future, when the world has devolved into a planet of morons. There's ample evidence everywhere they turn, from tumbling skyscrapers to mountains of garbage. (In fact, this is one of the funniest-*looking* films I've ever seen, the result of a fruitful collaboration between Judge and production designer Darren Gilford.) The utter haplessness of society is illustrated in everything from vending machines to fast-food restaurants. In this arena, Wilson is regarded as the smartest man alive.

Unfortunately, Judge's setup is much better than his payoff. The film wanders, repeats itself, and loses momentum. Normally, I wouldn't recommend a movie this uneven, but there are so many hilarious ideas and gags during the film's first half hour, I can't resist calling it to your attention. I don't see many films that make me laugh out loud, repeatedly; this one did, so I'm willing to forgive its inconsistency.

Incidentally, if you're wondering why you haven't heard of this film before, it was unceremoniously dumped into theaters with virtually no advertising or publicity. Mike Judge thought the studio was deliberately sabotaging his movie because he dared to make fun of the establishment. Maybe they just don't have a sense of humor.

54. IN THE SHADOW OF THE MOON

(2007)

Directed by David Sington

With:

BUZZ ALDRIN

ALAN BEAN

EUGENE CERNAN

MICHAEL COLLINS

CHARLES DUKE

JAMES LOVELL

EDGAR MITCHELL

HARRISON SCHMITT
DAVID SCOTT
JOHN YOUNG

When I heard seemingly unanimous praise for *In the Shadow of the Moon* at the 2007 Sundance Film Festival, I wasn't surprised. After all, it's a documentary about the United States's *Apollo* space program, with NASA footage that hasn't been seen since it was shot in the late 1960s and early '70s, and interviews with ten surviving *Apollo* astronauts. How could it be bad? But until I saw it I couldn't have appreciated what a moving experience it would be. It turned out to be one of my favorite films of the year.

Some astronauts, like Buzz Aldrin, have remained in the public eye, but others who flew to the moon never sought the limelight, and it's their presence that helps make this film so special. Ten of the fifteen survivors agreed to appear on camera. As the film reminds us, these hand-picked space soldiers were the best and the brightest of their generation, groomed to be heroes. They remain also highly intelligent and articulate men today. Mike Collins comes off especially well.

Some of them spent their careers in the air force, while others moved on to other pursuits. Most of them are in their late seventies now and have a real sense of perspective about their experiences in space. They think about their place in the universe in a way no one else on earth possibly could.

They also speak with great feeling about their colleagues who died in the horrifying fire on a launchpad in Houston.

The one man who doesn't appear in the film is Neil Armstrong, who first set foot on the moon in 1969 . . . yet his absence also says something about the character of the man, who doesn't feel like a hero and shuns the limelight.

British director David Sington deserves our gratitude for persuading so many astronauts to sit for extensive, candid interviews. If the film relied solely on these conversations it would be worthwhile, but Sington discovered that while NASA shot miles of color movie footage documenting every aspect of the space program, only a fraction of it was ever seen by the public. (Generally speaking, the agency would prepare a half-hour film about each mission, and that's what news organizations and documentarians have drawn upon ever since.) He dug into the NASA vaults and came up with pure gold—incredible images in remarkable condition.

As the filmmaker told me, "It was one of those projects where everything miraculously seemed to come together."

I may be prejudiced, having lived through this era, but I'd like to think that even young people who don't know much about the U.S. space program would be impressed with these men, their missions, and what it all meant to Americans who'd been rocked by the Vietnam War and the social revolution of the time. Here was something we could all be proud of. Ron Howard captured those feelings beautifully in *Apollo 13,* as did the subsequent TV miniseries *From the Earth to the Moon.* But there is no substitute for the firsthand recollections of these amazing men.

In the Shadow of the Moon is an extraordinary—and hugely entertaining—film about an exceptional human endeavor.

55. INDIGÈNES (DAYS OF GLORY)

(2006)

Directed by Rachid Bouchareb

Screenplay by Rachid Bouchareb and Olivier Lorelle

Actors:

JAMEL DEBBOUZE

SAMY NECÉRI

ROSCHDY ZEM

SAMI BOUAJILA

BERNARD BLANCAN

MATHIEU SIMONET

BENOIT GIROS

MÉLANIE LAURENT

ANTOINE CHAPPEY

Will filmmakers ever run out of stories to tell from World War II? It doesn't seem likely. *Indigènes* (given the blander title *Days of Glory* for its U.S. release) casts light on an unfamiliar facet of the war: the recruitment of the "indigenous" people of North Africa to fight for France, even though Frenchmen still looked down on them as second-class citizens. This riveting drama was nominated for Best Foreign Language Film at the Academy Awards but failed to capture a sizable American audience.

The film was greeted as a call to arms in France and caused then-president Jacques Chirac to reexamine the country's treatment of nonnative veterans. It was nominated for a raft of César Awards, winning Best Screenplay, and received a special prize at the Cannes Film Festival for its director and another for its leading cast members who collectively took home the Best Actor prize.

Those same actors admitted that they never knew about the discrimination that their countrymen faced until they read Rachid Bouchareb and Olivier Lorelle's script.

The reason that screenplay works so well is that it doesn't attempt to capture a sweep of history: instead it tells a big story in a personal way, focusing on specific characters. We follow young North African and "Black African" men as they prepare for the adventure of going to war, despite hasty and ineffectual training. Saïd (played by Jamel Debbouze, a familiar face from his usually comedic roles in films like *Amélie*) is so thrilled to be part of the army that he's unwilling to complain, even in the worst circumstances. Corporal Abdelkader (Sami Bouajila) believes in the cause he's fighting for, and also naively believes that his dedication and bravery will force the French commanders to recognize the North Africans' contribution. The most complex character is Sergeant Martinez (Bernard Blancan), a martinet who recognizes his troops' bravery but won't fight for their rights. That's because he is conflicted about his own identity.

Some critics thought *Indigènes* fell short of greatness because it applied its specific story to a familiar template of war movies, alternating vignettes of the soldiers in quiet moments with bursts of action in battle. That may be, but if it is a flaw, it's a minor one given the potency (and relevancy) of the drama and its ability to grapple with issues of prejudice and injustice in the midst of war. *Indigènes* packs a wallop.

56. INNOCENT BLOOD

(1992)

Directed by John Landis

Screenplay by Michael Wolk

Actors:

ANNE PARILLAUD

CHAZZ PALMINTERI

DAVID PROVAL

ANTHONY LAPAGLIA

ROBERT LOGGIA

ANGELA BASSETT

DON RICKLES

LUIS GUZMÁN

ROCCO SISTO

TONY SIRICO

TONY LIP

KIM COATES

MARSHALL BELL

I grew up watching classic Hollywood horror movies on television—*Frankenstein, Dracula, The Mummy,* et al—and I must confess I've never developed a stomach for modern-day horror, which substitutes graphic gore and torture for atmosphere. When pressed to name a relatively recent movie that might be suitable for Halloween viewing, I always cite John Landis's *Innocent Blood,* a sexy, funny, extremely bloody vampire yarn that ought to be better known.

One selling point that didn't help the movie in 1992 is its cast, which includes Anthony LaPaglia, the terrific actor who's now well known as the lead in the long-running TV series *Without a Trace;* Angela Bassett, who was just on the verge of stardom; and several familiar faces who became regulars on *The Sopranos.* Throw in Don Rickles—in a serious role—and Luis Guzmán and you've got a highly watchable cast. Oddly enough, the top-billed actors (Anne Parillaud, David Proval, the always good Robert Loggia, Chazz Palminteri) don't mean as much today.

French actress Parillaud, who caused a sensation in *La Femme Nikita,* is perfectly cast as a sexy vampire who walks the streets of Pittsburgh at night in search of sustenance. It turns out she has a predilection for "bad boys," and once she sinks her teeth into ruthless mob boss Loggia, she wants more of the same. Undercover cop LaPaglia forms an unholy alliance with her and tries to stop the rabid Loggia from infecting the entire city.

As usual, Landis takes the concept of in-jokes to extremes by fleshing out his cast (ahem) with the likes of B-movie babe Linnea Quigley, horror-makeup master Tom Savini, *Famous Monsters of Filmland* guru Forrest J. Ackerman, pop culture publisher Russ Cochran, Muppet master and filmmaker Frank Oz (a Landis regular), and a handful of fellow directors: Michael Ritchie and horror maestros Sam Raimi and Dario Argento.

Most people who don't care for this film—and that includes many of the critics who wrote it up in 1992—found its tone wildly uneven. They're not wrong—it can be gruesome at one moment, funny the next—but I find that a heady brew. And if the result isn't quite as cohesive as John Landis's earlier gem *An American Werewolf in London,* I still enjoy the roller-coaster ride.

I don't often use the term "guilty pleasure" to describe movies I like, but this is a notable exception.

57. INTERMISSION

(2003)

Directed by John Crowley

Screenplay by Mark O'Rowe

Actors:

COLIN FARRELL

SHIRLEY HENDERSON

KELLY MACDONALD

COLM MEANEY

CILLIAN MURPHY

GER RYAN

BRIAN F. O'BYRNE

BARBARA BERGIN

MICHAEL MCELHATTON

DEIRDRE O'KANE

DAVID WILMOT

TOM O'SULLIVAN

OWEN ROE

TAYLOR MOLLOY

JEFF O'TOOLE

LAURENCE KINLAN

Colin Farrell had just had a run of films that cemented his stardom in the United States (*Minority Report, Phone Booth, The Recruit, S.W.A.T.,* and especially *Daredevil*) when he turned up as part of an ensemble in *Intermission.* I thought his star wattage would draw attention to this terrific film, but it didn't. In the wake of Guy Ritchie's success stateside with *Lock, Stock, and Two Smoking Barrels* and *Snatch,* this boisterous Irish blend of crime, romance, and comedy should have attracted the same audience . . . but it's never too late.

Intermission lets us know what we're in for in the opening scene, in which a friendly conversation is punctuated with an unexpected burst of violence. In a prime example of post-Tarantino storytelling, writer Mark O'Rowe and director John Crowley keep us on our toes, fearlessly and flawlessly veering from comedy to drama, from romance to action, as they weave a daunting number of ingredients together. (*Variety*'s Derek Elley counted eleven story lines and at least fifty-four speaking parts.)

All you really have to know is that *Intermission* profiles people from various walks of life, from a married woman who's just been dumped to a cop who thinks he belongs on a reality TV show. They're all searching or striving for something in their lives: respect, tenderness, sex, cash, a chance to break free, a chance to fit in.

As it turns out, all of these lives are intertwined, in ways we can't possibly predict. While it's highly entertaining to see how the threads eventually connect, what really matters is that each character is so fully realized.

Best of all, each part is perfectly cast. *Intermission* features an all-star cast of Irish and British actors whose names may not be of the household variety, although their faces are. In the years since *Intermission* was made, such sterling actors as Colm Meaney, Kelly Macdonald, Shirley Henderson, Cillian Murphy, Brian F. O'Byrne, and David Wilmot have continued to thrive on stage, screen, and television in the UK and the United States. (A little girl named Emma Bolger who appears in the opening scene made an even stronger impression when *In America* opened in the States later in 2003. She plays one of Paddy Considine's daughters in that lovely film.)

In the immediate wake of *Pulp Fiction* I suffered through a seemingly endless number of Tarantino-wannabe movies before Guy Ritchie rescued the hip crime movie from oblivion. If you're a fan of the genre you really ought to know *Intermission,* which tells its story on an even bigger canvas, to great effect.

58. ISLAND IN THE SKY

(1953)

Directed by William A. Wellman

Screenplay by Ernest K. Gann

Based on the novel by Ernest K. Gann

Actors:

JOHN WAYNE

LLOYD NOLAN

WALTER ABEL

JAMES ARNESS

ANDY DEVINE

ALLYN JOSLYN

JIMMY LYDON

HARRY CAREY JR.

HAL BAYLOR

SEAN MCCLORY

WALLY CASSELL

REGIS TOOMEY

LOUIS JEAN HEYDT

BOB STEELE

DARRYL HICKMAN

TOUCH (MIKE) CONNORS

GORDON JONES

FRANK FENTON

PAUL FIX

CARL (ALFALFA) SWITZER

FESS PARKER

ANN DORAN

GEORGE CHANDLER

H ow could a movie starring John Wayne possibly be considered obscure? Be patient; I'll explain.

In the 1950s, Wayne, like many other top stars, began producing his own films, first with Robert Fellows as Wayne-Fellows Productions and then under the name Batjac (named for the shipping firm in his 1948 movie *Wake of the Red Witch*). Although Warner Bros. and United Artists distributed the films, the rights and negatives reverted to Batjac after a certain period of time. Thus, Batjac wound up owning such films as *Hondo, The High and the Mighty, McLintock!,* and *Island in the Sky* outright. They were all sold to television at one time or another, but were withdrawn in the 1970s and with rare exceptions went into limbo for more than thirty years.

In the early 1980s, the home-video market boomed and demand for those titles was high but Wayne's son Michael held out. Ironically, it was only after his untimely demise in 2003 that his widow, Gretchen, began to investigate the possibility of restoring and reissuing those films.

All during that limbo period the one picture people asked to see most often was *The High and the Mighty*. This wasn't hard to understand. It had been an enormous hit in 1954—in fact, the sixth-highest-grossing movie of the year—and it was considered the forerunner of *Airport* and other such multicharacter sagas. Shot in color and the new Cinema-Scope process, it was directed by William A. Wellman and written by Ernest K. Gann, based on his best-selling book.

Just one year earlier, the same powerful team worked with Wayne on another aviation saga. *Island in the Sky* was filmed in black and white, didn't boast an all-star cast as *The High and the Mighty* did, and told a very different kind of story, with bittersweet drama and only a qualified happy ending. Perhaps for these reasons it was not a resounding hit, and to this day it stands in the shadow of its more popular successor.

But in my opinion it's a better film—and director Wellman thought so, too.

Island in the Sky was inspired by a real-life story about a cargo plane that was forced to crash-land in snowy Newfoundland, where its small crew fought the elements (and a broken radio) in a desperate struggle to survive until they could be located—and rescued. In those days before sophisticated radar and tracking devices, their plight galvanized virtually every pilot who was familiar with their route.

In this fictionalized version of the tale, it is up to the captain (Wayne) to maintain morale as one day melts into another. He cannot give in to despair, lest his crew lose the will to live. Meanwhile, back at base camp every available pilot takes to the air in search of the downed plane and its men.

Wellman plays all of this for its humanity and never allows the film to descend into melodrama. There are highly dramatic moments, to be sure, and one scene in which Wayne uncharacteristically has to portray genuine fear (not, perhaps, his strongest suit as an actor). But it's the character vignettes and flashbacks that give this film its color, and the authenticity of the crew's valiant struggle, furiously turning the handle of a hand-cranked radio, that gives it bite.

The cast couldn't be better, filled with veterans both young and old. The crew members are played by Hal Baylor, Sean McClory, Wally Cassell, and Jimmy Lydon (who considers it the best adult role of his career—and he's right). Some people who saw this film in their youth have never forgotten McClory's haunting final scene (which I won't spoil).

Other roles are filled by Lloyd Nolan, Walter Abel, Wayne's protégé James Arness, Allyn Joslyn, a young Mike Connors, an equally young Fess Parker, and such longtime Wayne "regulars" as Andy Devine, Harry Carey Jr., Paul Fix, and Bob Steele. Old-movie buffs will also recognize Gordon Jones, Frank Fenton, Darryl Hickman, Louis Jean Heydt, Ann Doran, and two of director Wellman's favorites, character actor George Chandler and *Our Gang* veteran Carl "Alfalfa" Switzer.

Island in the Sky benefits from William H. Clothier's aerial photography and an effective music score credited to Emil Newman and Hugh Friedhofer (though mostly written by the latter). It's an extremely well-crafted film that deserves a bigger reputation than it has—especially since it's now so readily available on DVD.

59. JULIA

(2008)

Directed by Erick Zonca

Screenplay by Aude Py and Erick Zonca

Actors:

TILDA SWINTON

AIDAN GOULD

SAUL RUBINEK

KATE DEL CASTILLO

JUDE CICCOLELLA

BRUNO BICHIR

KEVIN KILNER

EUGENE BYRD

Tilda Swinton is one of those actresses whose mere presence in a film is a seal of approval, whether it's a mainstream movie like *The Chronicles of Narnia: The Lion, the Witch and the Wardrobe,* where she played the White Witch; *The Curious Case of Benjamin Button*; *Michael Clayton*; or a small indie effort like *Thumbsucker, Stephanie Daley,* or *Julia.* We've seen this versatile actress in many kinds of roles, but I don't think anyone would picture her playing a party girl in a slinky dress who's had too much to drink. Yet that's exactly how we meet her in the opening scene of Julia, a smart move on the part of director Erick Zonca. I almost felt like saying to the screen, "Okay, you've got my attention!"

Julia is a thoroughly messed-up woman who's burned almost every bridge in her life, yet refuses to straighten herself out and stop drinking. It's only because she isn't thinking straight that she allows herself to get involved in a crazy scheme. A desperate Latina neighbor offers her money to help her kidnap her young son, who's living with his grand-father. Naturally, everything goes awry.

Before long, Julia is on the run with the boy, an innocent who doesn't understand what's going on. The two cross the California border into Mexico, where things get hairier and downright dangerous. Julia is playing with dynamite, but she's both foolish and fearless.

It's because I respond to Swinton so positively that I was willing to be taken for the wild ride this movie turns out to be. I don't want to tell too much of the story because I think it's best to see the film as I did, knowing as little as possible. All you really need to know is that it is anchored by Swinton, and she's never off camera.

Although filmmaker Zonca is French (best remembered for *The Dreamlife of Angels*), this project was filmed in the United States and Mexico and has the feel of a hybrid: an American movie with European sensibilities. *Julia* is long, involved, and (though I rarely use this word to describe a movie) crazy . . . but I thoroughly enjoyed it.

60. KEEPING MUM

(2005)

Directed by Niall Johnson

Screenplay by Richard Russo and Niall Johnson

Based on a story by Richard Russo

Actors:

ROWAN ATKINSON

KRISTIN SCOTT THOMAS

MAGGIE SMITH

PATRICK SWAYZE

TAMSIN EGERTON
TOBY PARKES
LIZ SMITH
EMILIA FOX

There is no such thing as a typically British comedy; after all, the Mother Country has given us both Noël Coward and Benny Hill. Yet a little film like *Keeping Mum* would seem out of place if it took place anywhere but England, since it incorporates both Hitchcockian gallows humor and sex farce. Given that, one couldn't find a better lineup of stars to inhabit this black comedy than Maggie Smith, Rowan Atkinson, and Kristin Scott Thomas.

The setting is a tiny village called Little Wallop. Atkinson plays the local vicar, who's a bit absentminded. Among other things, he's forgotten to maintain good sexual relations with his wife, Scott Thomas, which has led her to have a fling with her golf pro, an American stud (played by Patrick Swayze in the broadest possible manner). The couple's children—a sexually active daughter and a boy who's always being bullied—face challenges of their own until housekeeper Smith arrives on the scene. This efficient newcomer to their lives has a knack for solving problems . . . by eliminating the people who cause them. (She doesn't limit herself to humans: an annoyingly noisy dog belonging to a neighbor is quietly dispatched, offscreen of course.)

We learn the truth about the housekeeper in a flashback prologue, but naturally it takes her new employers considerably longer to catch on to what's happening right under their noses.

Keeping Mum doesn't aspire to be a comedy for the ages,

but it achieves its modest goals with expertise—a word I can't apply to an overwhelming number of contemporary comedies—and that's what makes it entertaining.

The thought of Dame Maggie as a cheerful ax murderer may startle some, but she's played all kinds of characters in her long and varied career. Young viewers who only know her from the *Harry Potter* films might do well to see her in a different light here.

What a pleasure it is to watch these actors at work. Atkinson and Smith are past masters at comedy, but we rarely get to see Scott Thomas cut loose this way and she's wonderful.

Oddly enough, this quintessentially British comedy was cowritten by director Niall Johnson and American Richard Russo, the novelist who gave us *Empire Falls* and such screenplays as *Nobody's Fool*. So much for clichés.

61. KILL ME LATER

(2001)

Directed by Dana Lustig

Screenplay by Annette Goliti Gutierrez

Story by Dana Lustig and Annette Goliti Gutierrez

Based on a short film by María Ripoll

Actors:

SELMA BLAIR

MAX BEESLEY

O'NEAL COMPTON

LOCHLYN MUNRO

D. W. MOFFETT

BRENDAN FEHR

TOM HEATON

Utilizing suicide as a plot point provides a challenge to any filmmaker, no matter how experienced. If the script is a black comedy, audiences can accept the idea, played out in absurdist terms. If the tone is more serious, viewers may feel uncomfortable or downright squeamish. Yet Dana Lustig, a director with only one feature under her belt (*Wedding Bell Blues*) manages to merge elements of comedy and drama.

Kill Me Later establishes its heroine's state of mind in the opening scenes. Selma Blair plays a brooding bank teller who's been carrying on a loveless affair with her boss (D. W. Moffett), but when his wife turns up, pregnant and happy, Blair's emotions flare up. She ascends to the roof of the bank building, climbs on the ledge, and prepares to jump off. Just then the door to the roof opens and a bank robber (Max Beesley), fleeing from policemen who are in hot pursuit, grabs her as a hostage. When she's forced to take off with him, she elicits a promise from the thief: he will kill her later.

Naturally, as they take it on the lam a relationship develops between the two. As we learn more about them we come to understand what has driven Blair to the point of no return, and how a seemingly smart guy like Beesley could commit such a desperate crime. The key to the movie is that each one is determined to shield the other.

Casting is crucial to the success of this film. The female protagonist is a gloomy figure who dresses all in black; if there weren't something inherently interesting or likable about the actress playing her, we wouldn't have any reason to care about her fate. Blair gives us that ability. (Although she's never become a major star, Blair reflects a refreshing intelligence on camera; we sense that the wheels are always turning in her head.)

Beesley has to indicate that his Charlie Anders has something on the ball, even though he's risked everything in a moment of foolish bravado. He, too, gives a thoroughly engaging performance. (His career seemed poised to move up a notch when he won the leading role in *Glitter* the following year opposite pop star Mariah Carey, but the film tanked. He's kept busy since then, mostly on television with recurring roles in such British series as *Bodies, Talk to Me, The Last Enemy, Hotel Babylon,* and *Survivors.*)

Israeli-born actress-turned-director Dana Lustig imposes a flashback/flash-forward structure on this low-budget film, which is fashionable but not essential. It's a character piece, not a caper or a police procedural, despite the presence of those story elements . . . and these particular characters make it worth seeing.

62. KING OF CALIFORNIA

(2007)

Directed by Mike Cahill

Screenplay by Mike Cahill

Actors:

MICHAEL DOUGLAS

EVAN RACHEL WOOD

WILLIS BURKS II

LAURA KACHERGUS

PAUL LIEBER

KATHLEEN WILHOITE

If you were asked to name Michael Douglas's best performance, any number of films might spring to mind: *Wall*

Street, Romancing the Stone, Fatal Attraction, Basic Instinct, or possibly *Wonder Boys,* which won him critical plaudits even though audiences didn't flock to the film.

In my opinion he gives his finest performance in a little film that virtually no one saw called *King of California.* Douglas disappears into the character he's playing, a wild-eyed dreamer quite unlike anyone he's ever brought to life before. Most important, he makes us believe that the guy is real. (He even has an interesting backstory: a jazz bass player, he always played his own brand of music, never bending to popular trends. Douglas studied the bass in order to look convincing for the few moments we see him playing his instrument.)

Just released from a mental institution, Douglas returns home to discover that his teenage daughter (Evan Rachel Wood) has not only grown up but has become self-reliant. Living alone, she's found ways to cope, as a way of protecting herself from the instability of her existence. Even the future of their house is uncertain: it's mortgaged to the hilt and sits at the edge of a brand-new suburban development.

Wood quickly realizes that her father hasn't changed: he's just as crazy as ever. While institutionalized, he's been reading up about the history of Southern California, and is certain that forgotten Spanish treasure is sitting underground not far from where they live, waiting to be discovered. It's just a matter of determining the exact spot and digging.

I won't reveal any more of the story, except to say that Wood is swept up in this Quixote-like quest, against her better judgment. The father-daughter relationship is further explored in flashbacks that deftly counterpoint the present-day adventure. The undercurrent of rampant development (and all it represents) buzzes throughout the proceedings, adding a nice touch of social commentary to the central story.

King of California was written and directed by Mike Cahill, who attended film school at UCLA but got side-tracked from pursuing a career in the movie business. He spent many years writing novels, but when he finally decided to tackle a screenplay, he contacted his old classmate Alexander Payne, who was so impressed with the result that he agreed to coproduce it along with his *Sideways* partner Michael London.

The idea germinated in Cahill's mind for a long time, without his even realizing it. As he said at the time of the film's release, "I have been driving from a small town about ninety miles away from L.A., off and on, for fifteen years or so. I grew up in California and I've been watching the landscape change. I've always thought about all the stuff underneath there that's getting covered up."

What I love about *King of California* is that you're never sure exactly where it's headed—and even when you think you are, it goes further than you'd ever expect. Douglas has a great finale and then the film closes out with a coda that provides one extra smile, as it hearkens back to an idea planted much earlier in the picture.

Sad to say, this movie disappeared without a trace, which may make it difficult for Cahill to get backing for other movies. If people would only give it a chance, I think they might experience the same sense of discovery that appealed to me so much.

63. THE KING OF MASKS

(1997)

Directed by Wu Tianming

Screenplay by Wei Minglun

Based on the story by Chen Wengui

Actors:

CHU YUK

CHAO YIM YIN

ZHANG RIUYANG

ZHAO ZHIGANG

When you can send an e-mail to someone halfway around the globe and receive an instantaneous reply, it's clear that we all live in a global village. Yet I don't think any medium is more powerful than film in fostering our understanding of different cultures and creating empathy for people we might never meet. Every time I see a film from China, for instance, I get more than an interesting story; I learn about deep-rooted traditions and customs that still inform their way of life.

The King of Masks is a simple yet eloquent story, set in the rural world of Sichuan in the 1930s. A lowly street entertainer named Wang (played by Chu Yuk) is getting on in years and has but one asset, the secret technique that enables him to switch masks in the blink of an eye. This art is known as "face changing" and it is wondrous to behold. Even the country's leading actor, who is pampered and praised, bows to the mastery of this humble performer. But Wang despairs that he has no heir to whom he can pass on the ancient ritual and it secrets.

Chinese tradition dictates that he can only bequeath his

assets to a son, so because life is cheap—especially the life of a child during difficult times—he purchases a little boy on the black market, and nicknames him Doggie. How this leads to heartbreak, political gamesmanship, and the true expression of love is what makes this film so magical.

Wu Tianming, who directed *The King of Masks* (from a screenplay by Wei Minglun) is considered one of the founders of modern Chinese cinema. As the head of the Xi'an Film Studio, he served as mentor to such young filmmakers as Chen Kaige and Zhang Yimou. But he was also outspoken, and spent eight years in exile before returning to his homeland to make this beautiful movie. Although the tale is set in the 1930s, its points about social hypocrisy and the value of life are still relevant today, and show that Tianming lost none of his edge during his years away from China.

The beauty of *The King of Masks* is that so much of its story is visual, not verbal, which only underscores its universality. Why it isn't celebrated alongside other contemporary Chinese films is a mystery to me. I think it's a gem.

64. KING OF THE HILL

(1993)

Directed by Steven Soderbergh

Screenplay by Steven Soderbergh

Based on the memoir by A. E. Hotchner

Actors:

JESSE BRADFORD

JEROEN KRABBÉ

LISA EICHHORN

KAREN ALLEN

SPALDING GRAY

ELIZABETH MCGOVERN

JOSEPH CHREST

ADRIEN BRODY

CAMERON BOYD

AMBER BENSON

KRISTIN GRIFFITH

REMAK RAMSAY

KATHERINE HEIGL

When I see a movie I like, I want to spread the word about it. When, on all-too-rare occasions, I see a movie I *love* I become a one-man public relations campaign, urging friends and even strangers to see it. But sometimes fate, and the vicissitudes of the movie business, can work against even the best-reviewed picture.

King of the Hill was the third feature film written and directed by Steven Soderbergh, who burst on the scene in 1989 with his award-winning sleeper *sex, lies, and videotape.* His second film, *Kafka,* was universally considered a failure. (I must say, I disagree; when I first met Soderbergh I told him I was the guy who liked *Kafka* and he replied, "Then you are *the guy* who liked it.")

He rebounded with *King of the Hill,* an exquisite piece of work that won laudatory reviews (including four stars from Roger Ebert) . . . but because its distributor opened it in just a handful of theaters, and it lacked marquee names to draw people in, it lingered for a little while and then vanished. Although it is owned by Universal Pictures (which absorbed the assets of its original distributor), it has never been released on DVD in the United States. I cling to my now-precious laser disc version, and urge anyone else who wants to see it to scan their cable and satellite listings, purchase a used VHS cassette, or find a European-issue DVD online. The film is worth making that kind of effort to see.

The setting is St. Louis in the 1930s at the depths of the Great Depression. Jesse Bradford plays Aaron, a twelve-year-old boy whose family is being pulled apart: his younger brother is sent away to live with relatives, while his mother's consumption forces her (Lisa Eichhorn) to check into a sanitarium. His loving but unreliable father (Jeroen Krabbé) is a salesman who is forever dodging landlords and collection agents. Eventually he lands a job on the road, leaving Aaron to fend for himself. At another time and place, being alone in a residential hotel in the middle of a major city might seem ominous, or threatening, but to a smart, resourceful kid like Aaron, it also presents infinite possibilities.

He talks his way into an exclusive school and concocts fanciful stories about his family. Meanwhile, he receives an education of a different sort from the people he meets on the street and in the hotel, including a woozy prostitute (Elizabeth McGovern) and her mysterious client (Spalding Gray).

I can't think of a film that paints a more vivid portrait of life during the Depression than this one. Its constant ring of truth derives from Soderbergh's brilliant script, expert production design by Gary Frutkoff, and canny casting. Every supporting character is well drawn and well played (by a fine cast including such up-and-comers as Adrien Brody and a young Katherine Heigl), but top honors go to Jesse Bradford. In his review for *Variety,* Todd McCarthy wrote, "As a boy increasingly forced to apply his creativity to his life rather than his imaginative world, Bradford simply gives one of the best pre-teen performances in memory." The promise he showed in this film has borne fruit ever since, in such films as *Happy Endings* and *Flags of Our Fathers,* but there aren't many roles as good as this in any lifetime.

Soderbergh has become one of our most prolific and adventurous filmmakers, alternating personal projects (*Schizopolis, Che, The Girlfriend Experience*) and experimental films (*Full Frontal, Bubble*) with mainstream movies (*Erin Brockovich, Oceans 11,* and its sequels). He has produced a number of worthwhile films and mentored young directors along the way. He's even found time to interview some of his favorite directors, including Mike Nichols and Richard Lester, both in print and on commentary tracks of numerous DVDs.

But from my point of view, there is still one piece of unfinished business, and I still hope to see the day when *King of the Hill* is celebrated as the masterpiece it is.

65. KONTROLL

(2003)

Directed by Nimród Antal

Screenplay by Jim Adler and Nimród Antal

Actors:

SÁNDOR CSÁNYI

SÁNDOR BADÁR

ZOLTÁN MUCSI

ZSOLT NAGY

CSABA PINDROCH

ESZTER BALLA

LÁSZLÓ NÁDASI

PÉTER SCHERER

I f someone pitched you the idea of making a movie about the men who check passengers' tickets on the subway system in Budapest, Hungary, you'd probably roll your eyes in disbelief—or disinterest. But filmmaker's Nimród Antal's vision, and the world he brings to life, make *Kontroll* both fascinating and unique.

Is it science fiction? Not really . . . yet the environment in which the story unfolds, and its cast of characters, somehow don't seem real. The entire film takes place underground, and in this world we discover a separate society made up of misfits, outcasts, and renegades. These ragged but single-minded control agents work for the metro system in teams; they are openly derisive of their superiors and compete with one another for supremacy on their turf beneath the streets. In this setting, even the buzzing hum of fluorescent light fixtures seems ominous.

A series of unexplained murders triggers the story line, just as the recurring appearance of an ethereal young woman in costume provides the hint of a love story.

This cutting-edge, genre-bending movie has elements of action, mystery, fantasy, romance, black comedy, and high drama.

I was lucky enough to see *Kontroll* at the Telluride Film Festival, and later invited the director (who cowrote the film with Jim Adler) to bring his film to my class at USC. My students loved it, as I thought they would.

Antal told us of his upbringing in Southern California, where he always felt slightly out of place; this may explain his affinity for the outsiders who populate *Kontroll*. He later moved back to Hungary and attended the state film school. *Kontroll* was his first feature film, and he never expected anyone to see, let alone appreciate, it outside of Budapest. He was stunned that it attracted attention from film festivals around the world, and delighted when it even won a U.S. distributor.

Despite critical acclaim, *Kontroll* never found its rightful audience. This film is one of a kind, just waiting to be discovered.

66. LA CIUDAD/THE CITY

(1999)

Directed by David Riker

Screenplay by David Riker

Actors:

JOSEPH RIGANO

MATEO GÓMEZ

FERNANDO REYES

MARCOS MARTÍNEZ GARCÍA

MOISÉS GARCÍA

ANTHONY RIVERA

CIPRIANO GARCÍA

LETICIA HERRERA

JOSÉ RABELO

I see a great many films every year. For one to linger in my mind for days is unusual; when a movie stays in my consciousness for years it's downright amazing. Yet I still think about the images and the melancholy mood of *La Ciudad* a decade after seeing it. With no stars in its cast, an unknown director working in black and white, and a foreign language on its sound track, its chances of succeeding in U.S. release were slim, but it did win rave reviews and remains one of the most striking American films of the 1990s.

Writer-director David Riker, a graduate of New York University, had already won a student film award from the Directors Guild of America and a prestigious Student Academy Award when this debut feature reached the public. He and cinematographer Harlan Bosmajian worked together for six years to realize their vision: an omnibus film consisting of four vignettes about the lives of Hispanic immigrants in New York City. They mostly sought out nonprofessionals to fill their cast and worked hard, I'm sure, to put them at ease in front of the camera.

Each segment stands alone, yet they have a cumulative impact as the filmmaker brings heartrending empathy to each character's story. In "Bricks" we enter the world of day laborers where immigrants are subject to the whims and casual cruelty of a stranger whose truck they board in search of work—no questions asked. A man who has no place to leave his son brings him along for the day to clean and load bricks. It seems fairly mundane but, as we discover, that routine can be fraught with drama when something goes wrong on the job.

Concern for a child is the focus of another story about a puppeteer who lives in a station wagon with his young daughter. He knows she is bright and wants to send her to school—but in order to register her he must show a permanent address.

Love—or the dream of love—propels a newcomer from Mexico, a stranger in the concrete jungle, who chances to meet a girl from his hometown. She represents a personification of home . . . if he can only locate her a second time.

Finally, we meet a seamstress who labors in a sweatshop for the sole purpose of sending money home to her child, who is sick. Like the other women at her workplace, she is at the mercy of her uncaring employers, and when a conflict arises she turns to her fellow workers—who, like her, are paralyzed with fear over losing their jobs. Will they stand with her or will she become just another faceless victim?

La Ciudad is not a polemic or a political tract—far from it. It is an eloquent, even poetic, slice of life that finds true drama in the most ordinary lives imaginable, and that is the source of its extraordinary power. That, and the haunting black-and-white images that evoke the great Italian neo-realist films of the 1940s and '50s. (One might also draw a comparison to Dianne Arbus's urban photographs.)

I wish I could say that this extraordinary film launched David Riker on a great filmmaking career, but the only credit I can find for him since this feature's release is as screenwriter of the 2009 release *Sleep Dealer*.

Cinematographer Harlan Bosmajian, on the other hand, hasn't stopped working. He photographed the TV series *Strangers with Candy* and such (mostly New York–based) feature films as *Lovely & Amazing, Shadowboxer, Winter Solstice,* and *Starting Out in the Evening*.

But whatever he and his college collaborator may achieve in the future, *La Ciudad* will always stand out as a singular achievement.

67. LA PETITE LILI

(2003)

Directed by Claude Miller

Screenplay by Julien Boivent and Claude Miller

Based on the play *The Seagull* by Anton Chekhov

Actors:

NICOLE GARCIA

BERNARD GIRAUDEAU

JEAN-PIERRE MARIELLE

LUDIVINE SAGNIER

ROBINSON STÉVENIN

JULIE DEPARDIEU

YVES JACQUES

MICHEL PICCOLI

ANNE LE NY

MARC BETTON

Sexual intrigues and clashing egos are the main ingredients of *La Petite Lili,* but filmmaker Claude Miller (and his screenwriting partner, Julien Boivent) have something more up their sleeve in this intriguing film set in and around a French country house.

For one thing there is the obvious allure of the title character, an aspiring actress played by the sensuous Ludivine Sagnier (who first made an impression on American audiences in the thriller *Swimming Pool*). Then there is great amusement in observing Julien (Robinson Stévenin), a self-serious young man who rejects his parents' bourgeois success and wants to express himself as an experimental filmmaker. Lili becomes his first muse, but she has dreams of her own and isn't afraid to pursue them.

Julien's mother is Mado Marceaux (Nicole Garcia), a longtime movie star who's aware that she isn't getting any younger; her lover is a successful movie director named Brice (Bernard Gireaudeau) who represents everything young Julien despises. Yet Julien's first film, which is screened one night in a barn on the estate, is hopelessly dense and pretentious.

There are other characters in this heady mix, and in time you may recognize the entire setup as a modern-day version of Anton Chekhov's *The Seagull*. But where that durable play engages in debates over literature, this one substitutes filmmaking; that leads to an unexpected coda that the Russian playwright couldn't have anticipated. It's in this final sequence that filmmaker Miller has the last laugh on both his characters and his audience. It's a delicious turn of events that I'd rather not spoil.

La Petite Lili is intelligent, sexy, and satisfying, with a particular appeal to film buffs who will savor the concluding sequence.

68. LA PROMESSE

(1996)

Directed by Jean-Pierre Dardenne and Luc Dardenne

Screenplay by Jean-Pierre Dardenne and Luc Dardenne

Actors:

JÉRÉMIE RENIER

OLIVIER GOURMET

ASSITA OUEDRAOGO

RASMANÉ OUEDRAOGO

When was the last time a movie you watched made you feel as if you'd been punched in the gut—figuratively speaking? *La Promesse* is just such a film. Belgian filmmaking brothers Jean-Pierre and Luc Dardenne, who write and direct together, have a knack of making their fictional movies seem palpably real, so when we identify with a leading character we share their emotions.

In this case the protagonist is a fifteen-year-old boy named Igor (Jérémie Renier) who lives with his father, Roger (Olivier Gourmet). Roger is a no-nonsense kind of guy who has no moral compass or sense of shame. He routinely exploits illegal immigrants by hiring them for construction jobs, then bleeding them dry by renting them poorly heated, overcrowded apartments. Igor is too young and naive to fully understand what's going on. He relates to some of the workers as friends, and when an African man named Hamidou suffers a serious injury at the construction site, he asks Igor to promise that he will look after his wife and child. It is a vow the boy takes seriously. His father, however, can only think of the threat of exposure. He enlists Igor's help in committing an unthinkable act that will change the boy's outlook on life.

La Promesse, like all of the Dardennes' films, is shot on natural locations in Belgium with a handheld camera that follows its characters around as if it were a cinema verité documentary. The directors' rejection of Hollywood moviemaking conventions, and their matter-of-fact approach to even the most dramatic incidents, allows us to draw our own conclusions. If anything, their nonchalance makes the impact of crucial moments even stronger.

The performances in *La Promesse* are extraordinary, and

the Dardennes apparently thought so, too, as they cast Olivier Gourmet in their subsequent films *The Son, Rosetta,* and *The Child,* which also starred a grown-up Jérémie Renier.

La Promesse won citations as Best Foreign Film from the National Society of Film Critics and the Los Angeles Film Critics Association, but it never achieved widespread recognition among American moviegoers. It's never too late to catch up with this brilliant movie.

69. LADY FOR A DAY

(1933)

Directed by Frank Capra

Screenplay by Robert Riskin

Based on the story *Madame La Gimp* by Damon Runyon

Actors:

WARREN WILLIAM

MAY ROBSON

GUY KIBBEE

GLENDA FARRELL

JEAN PARKER

WALTER CONNOLLY

NED SPARKS

NAT PENDLETON

HALLIWELL HOBBES

HOBART BOSWORTH

ROBERT EMMETT O'CONNOR

WARD BOND

IRVING BACON

SAMUEL S. HINDS

When people ask me why I love old movies so much, it's difficult for me to describe in words the way they make me feel, but all their best qualities are embodied in one film that ought to be more celebrated: Frank Capra's *Lady for a Day.* I'm not suggesting that it's forgotten, or that it wasn't appreciated in its day, when it was nominated for four Oscars, including Best Picture, but it doesn't have the reputation of *It Happened One Night,* which Capra and screenwriter Robert Riskin made the following year, or later gems like *Mr. Smith Goes to Washington* and *It's a Wonderful Life.*

One reason for this is that the film was out of circulation for many years, deliberately held back when the director remade it in 1961 as *Pocketful of Miracles.* Decades of exposure on television and in the 16mm market that helped to stoke the reputation of other 1930s movies were denied this one.

I was an adolescent when I fell in love with old movies, but it took me a long time to catch up with *Lady for a Day,* and I'll never forget the experience. My wife and I attended a matinee at the Regency Theater on Broadway and Sixty-seventh Street in Manhattan (now gone, alas) and when it was over we walked home on a cloud.

This is the magical quality that great movies of that era possess: they actually make you feel better. I'm not talking about empty escapism, but a kind of entertainment that lifts your spirits. This is a high form of art, it seems to me, though it is too seldom recognized as such.

Lady for a Day is based on a story by Damon Runyon, the New York columnist and short-story writer whose name has entered the dictionary to describe quaint, colorful characters like the ones who populate the musical based on his work, *Guys and Dolls.*

Veteran actress May Robson plays Apple Annie, a ragged old woman who sells apples on the street, and who is viewed as a kind of good-luck charm by gangster Dave the Dude (Warren William). When Annie needs help, Dave's girlfriend, Missouri Martin (Glenda Farrell), talks him into doing the right thing. It seems Annie has been corresponding with her daughter, who's attending school in Europe, and pretending that she's part of New York society. Now the grown-up daughter (Jean Parker) is coming to the city with her fiancé, and Annie can't bear the thought that she'll be unmasked as a fraud. So Dave and his cronies knock themselves out to give Annie a temporary home in a mansion, and a complete makeover, in order to continue the masquerade in person.

Capra loved actors and always cast his movies well. Warren William was an elegant, somewhat theatrical leading man (referred to in some circles as the poor man's John Barrymore), and Glenda Farrell was the quintessential 1930s wisecracker. They were borrowed from Warner Bros., where they churned out one snappy movie after another in the early 1930s, to star in this Columbia production. *Lady for a Day* is also filled to the brim with familiar character actors including bumptious Guy Kibbee, sourpuss Ned Sparks, big lummox Nat Pendleton, perennial butler Halliwell Hobbes, imperious Hobart Bosworth, eternal Irish cop Robert Emmett O'Connor, and such Capra favorites as Ward Bond, Irving Bacon, and Samuel S. Hinds in smaller roles.

Watching a bunch of hard-boiled mugs turn soft for the sake of doing a good deed is delightful, and Riskin's perfectly calculated screenplay makes us root for Annie to succeed, with the help of seemingly everyone in New York, from a legless beggar to the mayor and governor. Riskin and Capra didn't mind sentiment, but they lace the film with undercurrents of gangland rivalry, political cronyism, and other realities that make the truce (for Annie's sake) that much more ironic—and sweet. *Lady for a Day* is a wish-fulfillment movie that seems to ask, wouldn't life be wonderful if people really did help one another instead of only looking out for themselves?

Such sentiments would be considered unfashionably corny today, but this movie defies convention and plays as a modern fairy tale. It was just the tonic Depression-weary moviegoers sought in 1933, and it still works its magic. Watching it is a joyous experience.

70. THE LAST SHOT

(2004)

Directed by Jeff Nathanson

Screenplay by Jeff Nathanson

Actors:

MATTHEW BRODERICK

ALEC BALDWIN

TONI COLLETTE

TONY SHALHOUB

CALISTA FLOCKHART

TIM BLAKE NELSON

BUCK HENRY

RAY LIOTTA

JAMES REBHORN

JON POLITO

PAT MORITA

JOAN CUSACK

RUSSELL MEANS

IAN GOMEZ

TOM MCCARTHY

W. EARL BROWN

GLENN MORSHOWER

ERIC ROBERTS

ROBERT EVANS

Sometimes the parts of a movie are greater than the whole; when those parts are really good, I tend to be forgiving. *The Last Shot* is a pretty good movie based on a great idea, but it has so many wonderful performances—and inspired moments—that I recommend it without hesitation.

There are few targets as inviting for satire as moviemakers, but writer-director Jeff Nathanson hit on an irresistible premise for *The Last Shot* when he read an article about an FBI sting that involved mobsters, crooked union leaders, and a Hollywood wannabe. He optioned the rights to the true story and then took dramatic license in order to create an entertaining farce. The script was so appealing that he lined up a dream cast to fill his major roles.

Alec Baldwin plays an FBI agent who sees his chance to move up in the ranks by convincing naive would-be filmmaker Matthew Broderick that he's going to finance his movie. In fact, the whole operation is a sting, a setup to trap some crooked Teamsters who shake down moviemakers when they work on location in New England.

The Last Shot opens with a title sequence (by the clever designers at yU+co.) that evokes iconic images of moviegoing, as well as moviemaking, as if to say, "This is going to be fun." And it is. Nathanson's screenplay offers opportunities for a number of talented actors to go to town: Tony Shalhoub is funny as a racketeer, Toni Collette is hilarious as a star with an ego that's out of control, and Joan Cusack is outrageous in an unbilled cameo as an agent with the foulest mouth in town. (I once got to ask her if the character was inspired by anyone in particular; she told me it was a composite drawn from memory.) Even small parts, like the filmmaker's agent, are played by perfectly chosen performers—in this case, Buck Henry.

The ultimate piece of perfect casting is Matthew Broderick as the movie's hapless hero. He captures all of the innocence and determination of a born dreamer.

The Last Shot loses its momentum somewhere along the way, but it made me laugh out loud, and I smile just at the thought of it. That's more than I can say about other more celebrated comedies.

71. LAWLESS HEART

(2001)

Directed by Neil Hunter and Tom Hunsinger

Screenplay by Neil Hunter and Tom Hunsinger

Actors:

DOUGLAS HENSHALL

TOM HOLLANDER

BILL NIGHY

CLÉMENTINE CÉLARIÉ

JOSEPHINE BUTLER

ELLIE HADDINGTON

STUART LAING

SUKIE SMITH

HARI DHILLON

JUNE BARRIE

PETER SYMONDS

In a relentless search to find new ways to present stories—
and impress young audiences with their cleverness in the
wake of movies like *Memento* and *Adaptation*—some filmmakers have begun to resemble contortionists, bending and
twisting their ideas as if to say, "We'd rather die than tell a
story straight through from beginning to end."

Mind you, I have no issue with nonlinear storytelling, so
long as the process enhances the material at hand and isn't
simply being trotted out as a gimmick.

A perfect example of how to do this well is the British
import *Lawless Heart*, written and directed by Neil Hunter
and Tom Hunsinger. At first we're not aware that there is
anything unconventional about the picture: it opens with
the funeral of Stuart, a restaurant owner in a small seaside
town. Among the mourners is Dan (played by the wonderful Bill Nighy), a doleful fellow whose wife was the deceased's sister. Dan is at an emotional crossroads in his life
and extremely susceptible to feminine attention; he shows
particular interest in a Frenchwoman who works at the local
flower shop.

At the end of this vignette, we pick up the same story
from a wholly different point of view. This time the focus
is on Nick (Tom Hollander), Stuart's partner, who's in a
state of shock over his lover's death. Uncertain as to whether
he wants to continue operating the restaurant or return to
London, he invites Stuart's boyhood friend Tim (Douglas

Henshall) to stay with him while he's in town, then finds himself being pursued by a kooky woman named Charlie (Sukie Smith) who seems unconcerned with the fact that he's gay.

The final segment deals with Tim, a hippie-esque character who's been away for years. Being back home fires different emotions in him, including the possibility of settling down.

The beauty of this film is that with each retelling we get to know these characters better and understand the larger context of their actions and decisions. Overlapping incidents, including secrets and deceptions, offer us the satisfaction of putting the pieces of a puzzle together and fitting them all into place.

Yet the filmmakers don't attempt to tie everything up in a neat little package; that's also part of what makes *Lawless Heart* so interesting.

The performances are first-rate across the board, but I confess a special fondness for Bill Nighy, who was just making a name for himself on this side of the pond when *Lawless Heart* turned up. He won the Best Supporting Actor award from the Los Angeles Film Critics Association that year, spurred by his hilarious performance as a sardonic rock star in *Love Actually*. Since that time he has become one of the world's foremost character actors, known to millions as Davy Jones from two *Pirates of the Caribbean* outings. I would put his work in this film against anything else he's done to show his brilliance in balancing comedy and drama within one conflicted character.

72. LEVITY

(2003)

Directed by Ed Solomon

Screenplay by Ed Solomon

Actors:

BILLY BOB THORNTON

MORGAN FREEMAN

HOLLY HUNTER

KIRSTEN DUNST

MANUEL ARANGUIZ

DORIAN HAREWOOD

GEOFFREY WIGDOR

LUKE ROBERTSON

Sometimes when my fellow critics disagree with me, I'm at a loss to explain the difference of opinions. One film that I found absorbing—and quite moving—received negative, even hostile, reviews. *Levity* marked the directorial debut of screenwriter Ed Solomon, whose work up until that time was mostly in a comedic or lighthearted vein (*Bill and Ted's Excellent Adventure, Men in Black, What Planet Are You From?*). Perhaps some people felt he was overreaching with this ultraserious drama—but as I say, I like it. And yes, the title is meant to be ironic.

Billy Bob Thornton plays a man who's spent more than twenty years—in fact, his whole adult life—in prison for a murder he committed during a robbery. Now his time is up. Leaving the safe haven of prison is a daunting prospect, and as he reluctantly returns to the world outside (a world he's never experienced as a grown-up) he feels an aching need to make contact with the sister of the man he killed. He returns to the scene of his crime, cruising the neighborhood hoping to make contact with her (Holly Hunter). But when they do connect, and eventually get to know each other, he can't bring himself to tell her who he is. He is particularly concerned with her teenage son (Geoffrey Wigdor), who's out of control.

Thornton gets a job sweeping up for an enigmatic storefront preacher (Morgan Freeman) who offers him a place to sleep in return for his efforts. Freeman runs a neighborhood shelter and way station for lost souls, one of whom is a footloose rich girl (Kirsten Dunst) who's caught up in a hedonistic existence.

Thornton adopts a deadpan, or minimalistic, approach to his character, but his motivations are clear: he sees an opportunity to redeem himself by reaching out to these young people and stopping them from throwing their lives away.

Levity deals with such issues as forgiveness, redemption, guilt, and the painful truth that some deeds cannot be undone. It isn't upbeat material but it's completely engrossing. Some moviegoers seem to believe that if a movie is serious, that means it's going to be a downer. There's a world of difference between a meaty drama and a depressing experience.

Thornton gives a subtle and superb performance, and he's surrounded by exceptional costars. If you're in the mood for a movie that makes you think, and feel, I strongly recommend it.

73. LOOK BOTH WAYS

(2005)

Directed by Sarah Watt

Screenplay by Sarah Watt

Actors:

JUSTINE CLARKE

WILLIAM MCINNES

ANTHONY HAYES

LISA FLANAGAN

ANDREW S. GILBERT

DANIELA FARINACCI

SACHA HORLER

MAGGIE DENCE

EDWIN HODGEMAN

People often ask me what I look for in a movie, and I explain that I don't have a set of rules or requirements . . . but one thing that always appeals to me is originality, a feeling that I'm watching something fresh and not a rehash of ideas I've seen over and over again. The Australian import *Look Both Ways* has that quality in spades, partly because it's the first live-action feature film by animator Sarah Watt, whose imagination was obviously firing on all engines here. Animation figures in this movie, as it helps the filmmaker picture what's going on in the overactive imagination of her heroine. That's just one of its unexpected—and appealing—ingredients.

Justine Clarke plays Meryl, who pictures disaster lurking around every corner. (Her mood isn't any brighter for having just returned from her father's funeral.) This phobia has made her isolated and very tentative in her relationships. Then, by chance, she bears witness to a real accident involving a train, and finds an odd connection with a news-paper photographer (William McInnes) who's covering the incident and its aftermath. He has just been given a grim medical prognosis. As these two fragile individuals embark upon a relationship, they're forced to work through their hang-ups and connect with each other.

Other characters are woven into the fabric of the story, including a reporter for the same newspaper (Anthony Hayes) who's facing a crisis of another kind in his personal life—the news that his girlfriend is pregnant. He, too, has good reason to ponder the question of life and death, and does so in print, while his editor runs a chilling photo of the train victim's wife just as she hears the news that her husband was killed.

Look Both Ways approaches weighty subjects with a light touch, and that's what makes it special. These characters are dealing with our greatest fear—mortality—yet they have to go on living and making choices as they do. I think we all can relate to that process, one way or another.

The film has a quirky and unpretentious quality that's genuinely refreshing. That's why it won the Discovery Award at the Toronto Film Festival, a poll of seventy-five international film critics, and went on to win the Best Film prize at the Australian equivalent of the Academy Awards.

74. THE LOOKOUT

(2007)

Directed by Scott Frank

Screenplay by Scott Frank

Actors:

JOSEPH GORDON-LEVITT

JEFF DANIELS

ISLA FISHER

MATTHEW GOODE

CARLA GUGINO

BRUCE MCGILL

ALBERTA WATSON

ALEX BORSTEIN

SERGIO DI ZIO

DAVID HUBAND

When a film takes more than a decade to come to fruition, is made with love and care, then disappears from theaters within a couple of weeks—without making a "blip" on moviegoers' radar—that's more than a disappointment. It's a crime.

The Lookout is a sharply observed character study cloaked in the guise of a heist movie. It may well be the best movie I saw in 2007, but because it didn't have lofty ambitions, or make any kind of splash, it wasn't mentioned in most year-end surveys and wasn't an Oscar contender. It did win its creator an Independent Spirit Award for Best First Feature, which must have been a source of great satisfaction for writer-director Scott Frank.

Frank is hardly a newcomer to the movie scene. His screenplays include *Little Man Tate, Minority Report,* and two highly regarded Elmore Leonard adaptations, *Out of Sight* and *Get Shorty*. *The Lookout* is an original work that was intended to be one more writing credit on his résumé. Several major directors were attached to it at various times, and Frank made a number of changes as he worked with such filmmakers as Sam Mendes and David Fincher, in some cases for a year or more. For various reasons, these directors abandoned *The Lookout* for other projects, as did actors Tom Hanks, Leonardo DiCaprio, and Brad Pitt, all of whom were mentioned as expressing interest at various times.

Along the way DreamWorks, which was cofinancing the picture, told Frank that if he ever wanted to direct they'd support him. He finally decided that if there were ever a project he knew by heart, and felt confident enough to direct, this was it. DreamWorks then pulled out. Fortunately, Spyglass Films was still enthusiastic, and told the fledgling filmmaker that if he could make the picture for $12 million (a very low figure by mainstream Hollywood standards), he could cast it himself and make it without interference. And that's exactly what he did.

By eschewing major movie stars, Frank did himself a favor and a disservice at the same time. When I tried touting the movie to friends, they would ask, "Who's in it?" When I replied, "Joseph Gordon-Levitt," their eyes turned glassy. "You know," I said, "the kid from *Third Rock from the Sun*? He's grown up now, and he's a really good actor." They'd nod politely. There was equal lack of recognition for sexy leading lady Isla Fisher, in spite of her scene-stealing performance in *Wedding Crashers*. Mentioning Jeff Daniels helped a little, but I recognized a lost cause when I saw it. Perhaps if the film had had A-list stars above the title it would have attracted an audience.

On the other hand, the casting of *The Lookout* is absolutely perfect, from top to bottom. Gordon-Levitt is one of the most talented actors of his generation, and the fact that he's more interested in challenging roles than in seizing the brass ring of stardom makes me admire him all the more. He's done fine work in such indie films as *Mysterious Skin, Brick, Shadowboxer,* and *Stop-Loss,* although some people still know him best as the second lead in *10 Things I Hate About You* with Heath Ledger and Julia Stiles.

Here, he plays a onetime high school jock, the big man on campus in his Midwestern town, whose life changed in the blink of an eye as the result of a terrible auto accident that took another student's life. With some residual brain damage, he lives the life of a drone, holding down a night job as a janitor at the local bank and rooming with an acerbic fellow (Jeff Daniels) who happens to be blind.

Into his dead-end life comes a live wire (Matthew Goode) who remembers him from school and who, with the help of a sexy accomplice (Isla Fisher), lures him into a daring scheme to rob the bank where he works.

The plotting is sure-handed and unpredictable, but what I like most about *The Lookout* is the way it presents its dramatis personae. Each character is colorful, interesting, and completely fleshed out no matter how briefly he or she appears on screen. A bank guard who has a small but recurring role turns up one night with his pregnant wife in the car at curbside, and even though we see her for only a moment, we know everything we need to know about her and her relationship with her eager husband. That's the mark of a well-written, well-directed, and well-cast movie.

I've recommended *The Lookout* so often that I've been able to take a straw poll of people who've tried it out—and every one of them has thanked me for turning them on to such a terrific movie. I hope it's just the first of many for Scott Frank.

75. LOVE AND DEATH ON LONG ISLAND

(1997)

Directed by Richard Kwietniowski
Screenplay by Richard Kwietniowski
Based on the novel by Gilbert Adair

Actors:

JOHN HURT

JASON PRIESTLEY

FIONA LOEWI

SHEILA HANCOCK

MAURY CHAYKIN

GAWN GRANGER

ELIZABETH QUINN

John Hurt is a character actor of exceptional skill, but he isn't the kind of personality performer one would expect to see carrying a movie. That's part of what makes *Love and Death on Long Island* so delightful: it offers Hurt a bravura role that fits him like a fine glove from Alfred Dunhill. Or, to put it another way, if you were casting the part of a dowdy British author/intellectual who lives alone with his books, barely interacting with the modern world, who would you cast in the part? My point precisely.

Giles De'Ath was once married; he's now a widower, and a housekeeper tends to his basic needs. Left to his own devices, he's fairly hopeless. One day he locks himself out of his house, so he decides to pass the time by going to a movie . . . but he can't even do this right and winds up in the wrong auditorium. Instead of an adaptation of an E. M. Forster novel, he finds himself watching a silly teen comedy called *Hot Pants College II.* (He doesn't even realize his mistake right away.) Just as he is about to leave, his eye falls on the film's handsome star, Ronnie Bostock (played by a well-cast Jason Priestley), and he is transfixed. It is a transformative moment for De'Ath: he is overcome. He begins to obsess about the young heartthrob, acquiring fan magazines and even purchasing a TV set and a VCR in order to watch his other movies. (Among the titles: *Skidmarks* and *Tex Mex.*)

De'Ath has never experienced a feeling quite like this; he analyzes (and justifies) it in intellectual terms, but it is in fact a wholly emotional response. In due course he decides he must meet his idol in person. He flies across the Atlantic and makes his way to the Long Island town where he knows Ronnie lives.

Love and Death on Long Island is based on a book by film critic and novelist Gilbert Adair, and marks the feature-film debut of writer-director Richard Kwietniowski. It is a film of wit, nuance, and constant surprise that manages to be just believable enough to work. Hurt makes the leading character arch, amusing, vulnerable, and utterly human. Priestley does a good job as the hunk, and such reliable actors as Sheila Hancock and Maury Chaykin fill in the supporting cast, but this is John Hurt's showcase and he makes every moment count.

76. MAD MONEY

(2008)

Directed by Callie Khouri

Screenplay by Glen Gers

Adapted from the screenplay *Hot Money*

by Neil McKay and Terry Winsor

Original source material by John Mister

Actors:

DIANE KEATON

QUEEN LATIFAH

KATIE HOLMES

TED DANSON

ADAM ROTHENBERG

ROGER CROSS

STEPHEN ROOT

CHRISTOPHER MCDONALD

FINESSE MITCHELL

MEAGEN FAY

Most January movie releases come from the bottom of the barrel, so I dread going to the movies at the beginning of the year. That's why I was unprepared for the enjoyment I derived from *Mad Money* at the beginning of 2008. I watched it with a preview audience and we all laughed continuously, but my fellow critics tore it to shreds. Sometimes, I swear, people make up their minds not to like a movie before it begins . . . and I stand by my opinion.

Diane Keaton, who's been in far too many substandard comedies in recent years, gives a delightful performance here as a so-called perfect suburban housewife whose life comes crashing down when her husband (Ted Danson) breaks the news to her that they're flat broke. The notion of having to work for a living comes as a shock, all the more so when she learns that she has no marketable skills. So she swallows hard and accepts a janitorial job at the local Federal Reserve Bank, supervised by a hawklike Stephen Root. While observing the procedure for destroying used money, she hatches a daring scheme to "recycle" the worn but perfectly good greenbacks and recruits two other employees to pull it off: a hardworking single mother played by Queen Latifah and a ditzy office worker played by Katie Holmes.

The trick isn't merely to carry out their plan without calling attention to themselves, but to keep at it without spilling the beans to outsiders—or spending any of the money while it's still hot. Easier said than done.

Why did I like *Mad Money*? First off, it made me laugh. I also like that it's smart—just believable enough to make sense and outlandish enough to be entertaining. You'd expect no less from director Callie Khouri, who made her reputation as the writer of *Thelma and Louise*. It's based on a British TV movie, cleverly reinvented for American audiences by screenwriter Glen Gers. And it has a perfect cast. The three leading ladies are absolutely believable, including the much-maligned Katie Holmes, who's both likable and funny. Ted Danson adds a battery of wisecracks as Keaton's sardonic husband.

So, you can trust those other critics who said awful things about this movie, or you can sit back and have a good time, as I did. Your move.

77. THE MALTESE FALCON (1931 VERSION)

(1931)

Directed by Roy Del Ruth

Screenplay by Maude Fulton and Brown Holmes

Based on the novel by Dashiell Hammett

Actors:

BEBE DANIELS

RICARDO CORTEZ

DUDLEY DIGGES

THELMA TODD

UNA MERKEL

ROBERT ELLIOTT

DWIGHT FRYE

It is a truism that remakes of famous movies are seldom as good as the originals. *The Maltese Falcon* was filmed three times by Warner Bros., and while John Huston's 1941 film is the only one that deserves to be called a classic, it's fascinating to compare it to the first screen adaptation made ten years earlier. Huston's is superior in every way, but because he hewed so closely to Dashiell Hammett's groundbreaking detective novel, and so did the original, the 1931 version holds up surprisingly well. It wasn't always easy to see, although it circulated on television for some years under the title *Dangerous Female,* to distinguish it from the Bogart movie. (That wasn't a problem for the 1936 retread, a camouflaged version of the story called *Satan Met a Lady*.)

The 1941 movie marked Huston's directorial debut, and he was on fire. His casting was especially brilliant. Humphrey Bogart cemented his stardom with an unforgettable portrayal of the hard-boiled Sam Spade. Mary Astor, a fading leading lady in real life, was every bit his match as the lying, coquettish Brigid O'Shaughnessy. And imagine sitting in a theater in 1941 and seeing Sydney Greenstreet for the first time in a Hollywood movie as the eloquent criminal mastermind Casper Gutman. Every actor is ideally chosen: Peter Lorre as the sinister, effeminate Joel Cairo; Elisha Cook Jr. as Gutman's shifty gunsel; Jerome Cowan as Spade's hard-luck partner Miles Archer; Gladys George as his sultry widow; and Lee Patrick as Spade's indispensable girl Friday, Effie.

If those performances are seared into your consciousness, as they are in mine, it's especially interesting to see how well director Roy Del Ruth and the Warner Bros. team selected actors almost as colorful—and certainly as appropriate—for those roles. The weak link, you might say, is leading man Ricardo Cortez, a capable actor who has the right tone but none of the shading that made Bogart's Spade so memorable. But Bebe Daniels, a big star of the 1920s, is quite good as the woman who sets the case in motion, Ruth Wonderly.

Irish-born character actor Dudley Digges makes a fine Casper Gutman, every bit as pompous and eccentric (if not as physically imposing) as Greenstreet. Film buffs will remember him from such prominent films as *The Invisible Man, Mutiny on the Bounty,* and *The General Died at Dawn.* Perky Una Merkel, with her honeyed Southern accent, is a great choice as Effie. Beautiful Thelma Todd, who specialized in playing femmes fatales when she wasn't doing comedy with Laurel and Hardy or the Marx Brothers, is an alluring widow Archer.

And if there were an early talkie equivalent of Elisha Cook Jr., who played neurotics to a fare-thee-well, it was Dwight Frye, who gained immortality as the unfortunate Renfield opposite Bela Lugosi in *Dracula* and followed it up as the feeble-minded Fritz in *Frankenstein*. Both of them reached theaters the same year as this *Maltese Falcon*.

The other major point of interest in this adaptation of Dashiell Hammett's groundbreaking detective novel is that it was made prior to the revision of the Production Code in 1934. As a pre-Code movie it is much more raw and racy than the 1941 remake was allowed to be. It's clear that Sam Spade has had an affair with his partner's wife—and that Archer knows it. It doesn't take a detective to figure out that he also sleeps with Ruth Wonderly. When Sam orders Ruth to take off her clothes, to prove she isn't hiding anything, the tone is more lascivious here than in the later film. And references to Wilmer, Casper Gutman's so-called gunsel, are a bit more overt regarding his sexuality.

In terms of staging, camera work, and music the film is relatively primitive. Directors and technicians still hadn't found their footing in talkies, as they would very soon. But for anyone who knows and loves *The Maltese Falcon,* this 1931 effort captures the Hammett story and its milieu surprisingly well, and makes a worthy companion piece to the 1941 classic.

78. THE MAN FROM ELYSIAN FIELDS

(2002)

Directed by George Hickenlooper

Screenplay by Phillip Jayson Lasker

Actors:

ANDY GARCIA

MICK JAGGER

JULIANNA MARGULIES

OLIVIA WILLIAMS

JAMES COBURN

ANJELICA HUSTON

MICHAEL DES BARRES

RICHARD BRADFORD

XANDER BERKELEY

ROSALIND CHAO

JOE SANTOS

TRACEY WALTER

SHERMAN HOWARD

An old friend of mine had a gift for being able to strip every film down to its core. I'd mention a title and he'd say, "Oh, that was the Orpheus legend, except they changed the ending," or "Didn't you recognize that as *King Lear*?" He's no longer alive, or I would consult him on a regular basis, and I wish we'd had a chance to discuss *The Man From Elysian Fields*. Would he have thought of it as a variation on *Faust* or would he have had other ideas? And what would he have made of the title's reference to Greek mythology, where the Elysian Fields were the burial ground for the blessed?

The setting for the story is modern–day Los Angeles, yet

the film seems to exist in a world all its own. Andy Garcia plays a dedicated novelist who lives in Pasadena, and works in a tiny room in an office building at the corner of Hollywood and Vine. He's got just one problem: nobody wants to read his books. He loves his son and his wife, Julianna Marguiles, but he can't pay the bills. It looks as if he's going to have to swallow his pride and find another way to make a living. Just then a mysterious man invites him down the hall to the office of Elysian Fields. He enters the office and meets the owner—played by Mick Jagger. Elysian Fields is a very discreet, high-end escort service.

Garcia is understandably put off by the whole thing, but agrees to give it a try—without telling his wife. His first client is beautiful Olivia Williams, who's married to a feisty but aging Pulitzer Prize–winning author, played to perfection by James Coburn. Before long, Garcia starts working with the writer on what will almost certainly be his final novel. Except he can't tell anyone—and his repeated, unexplained absence puts a strain on his marriage.

It's a great setup, and I'm deliberately withholding details so as not to spoil the film's surprises.

Andy Garcia is excellent as the writer caught in a moral bind, torn between love, responsibility, and sheer temptation—both sexual and professional. James Coburn has one of his best late-in-life roles as the big bear of a man who's in an equally dicey situation, needing help but not eager to accept it—and risking emasculation in the process. The casting of Mick Jagger is equally inspired, as the novelty—along with the rock icon's powerful presence—gives weight to his character. Anjelica Huston contributes fine work in a supporting role as Jagger's client and inamorata.

The Man From Elysian Fields maintains an eerie, almost other-worldly mood as it spins its sinuous tale. The cinematography by Kramer Morgenthau and production design by Franckie Diago help to create this intriguing atmosphere. I could nitpick about details in the story, but I forgive the movie its faults because it won me over so completely.

79. MAN PUSH CART

(2006)

Directed by Ramin Bahrani

Screenplay by Ramin Bahrani

Actors:

AHMAD RAZVI

LETICIA DOLERA

CHARLES DANIEL SANDOVAL

ALI REZA

FAROOQ "DUKE" MUHAMMAD

There is a somewhat cynical theory that there are only seven stories in all the world and every novel, play, or movie is a variation on one of them. If that's true then I have all the more respect for authors, playwrights, and screenwriters who manage to create stories that seem fresh and new. *Man Push Cart* is a perfect example: the daily struggle for survival is as old as mankind itself, but this film reveals the particulars of one man's existence in a way that makes it both unique and memorable.

Has anyone ever stopped to wonder about the lives of the people who sell them coffee and doughnuts from those stainless-steel carts that dot the streets of Manhattan? Probably not . . . but then, filmmaker Ramin Bahrani says he's interested in telling stories about people we don't usually see on-screen. In this case, he blurs the line between reality and fiction by casting a nonprofessional actor (Ahmad Razvi), shooting in natural locations, and lightly imposing a story line on the proceedings. He also shows us just how hard a man like Ahmad works, rising long before the sun to clean and stock his cart, then laboriously pushing his heavy vehicle into place as New Yorkers make their way to work in the morning.

We learn the details of Ahmad's life in bits and pieces. He comes from Pakistan, where he had a wife and child, and enjoyed some measure of success as a rock star with a hit CD. Now he battles his in-laws for glimpses of his son, and clutches at straws for some relief from his onerous routine. An attractive Spanish woman who mans her uncle's newsstand nearby makes friendly overtures to the shy street vendor, while a go-getter who recognizes him from the old country holds out the promise of reigniting his musical career.

The movie's greatest strength is its verisimilitude as it details Ahmad's day-to-day existence. No wonder: Razvi was a real-life pushcart vendor whom Bahrani befriended while he was researching the film, and some of the movie was shot with hidden cameras. Even lifelong New Yorkers may marvel at the view this movie offers of their city, unlike any ever captured before. And nowhere does *Man Push Cart* more closely resemble classic neorealist films like *The Bicycle Thieves* than in a heart-stopping moment when Razvi discovers that someone has taken his cart.

Man Push Cart may have been made quickly and cheaply,

but it wears its micro budget as a badge of honor. The sum of its parts is greater than the whole, because writer-director-editor Bahrani and his cinematographer, Michael Simmonds, achieve something that many multimillion-dollar studio films don't: you can't take your eyes off the screen.

80. MARVIN'S ROOM

(1996)

Directed by Jerry Zaks

Screenplay by Scott McPherson

Based on the play by Scott McPherson

Actors:

MERYL STREEP

ROBERT DE NIRO

LEONARDO DICAPRIO

DIANE KEATON

HUME CRONYN

GWEN VERDON

DAN HEDAYA

HAL SCARDINO

CYNTHIA NIXON

KELLY RIPA

VICTOR GARBER

Mention illness in relation to a film and people assume one of two things: you're talking about a cheesy TV movie or an absolute downer they'd just as soon avoid. Smart folks can see through the euphemistic description of such movies as a "celebration of life."

Yet that well-worn phrase perfectly describes *Marvin's Room,* a moving, unsentimental, and funny adaptation of Scott McPherson's play featuring a powerhouse cast: Meryl Streep, Diane Keaton, Leonardo DiCaprio, Robert De Niro, Hume Cronyn, and Gwen Verdon. There are even some future TV stars in smaller roles: Cynthia Nixon, Kelly Ripa, and the original costar of *Monk,* Bitty Schram.

Streep plays a stressed-out working-class mom whose older son (DiCaprio) is nothing but trouble; he's even set their house on fire. Out of the blue she hears from her estranged sister, who's been taking care of their ailing father in Florida. It seems that she's facing a health crisis of her own and needs a bone-marrow donor, if she can find a proper match. Streep packs up her kids and makes the trip, still wondering why her sister chose to put her life on hold to take care of their elderly dad, who's lost the ability to speak.

To be perfectly clear, *Marvin's Room* isn't about death or disease: it's about family dynamics and life choices. That's what makes it so universal in its appeal. (Indeed, the perpetually angry young DiCaprio establishes a warm rapport with his aunt, whom he's never really known.)

McPherson's screenplay also scores points with its disarming sense of humor, acknowledging the absurdities of life, the indignity of aging, and the unpredictable ways people relate to one another.

Marvin's Room would be worth seeing on any account because of its stellar cast, all of whom are at the top of their game. Streep is her usual superlative self, and DiCaprio fulfills the promise he showed in such earlier films as *This Boy's Life* and *What's Eating Gilbert Grape.* (He made this simple domestic drama in between *Titanic* and *William Shakespeare's*

Romeo + Juliet.) People who only associate Keaton with comedy should savor her warm and assured performance here. Robert De Niro, whose company produced the picture, has an amusing role as a doctor who is slightly off-kilter.

The casting of Hume Cronyn is particularly effective; he never utters a word, yet his presence is strongly felt in every scene he's in. Those moments wouldn't have had nearly the same impact if an unknown—or less skillful—actor had been in his place.

Marvin's Room also marks the feature-film debut of longtime Broadway director Jerry Zaks. The former actor has since lent his talent to a variety of A-list TV sitcoms, but this sensitive movie reveals his great skill at telling a story and getting the very best from his actors.

81. THE MATADOR

(2005)

Directed by Richard Shepard
Screenplay by Richard Shepard

Actors:

PIERCE BROSNAN

GREG KINNEAR

HOPE DAVIS

PHILIP BAKER HALL

DYLAN BAKER

ADAM SCOTT

PORTIA DAWSON

ROBERTO SOSA

An actor works for years to find a part that suits him, and puts him in the spotlight, then, as often as not, works even harder to make people forget the character so he can move on. Pierce Brosnan came to America's attention as the title character in the clever TV series *Remington Steele* in the 1980s and then inherited the daunting mantle of James Bond a decade later. He's fought ever since to find movie vehicles that will let him (and audiences) leave 007 behind.

Greg Kinnear became famous as the snarky host of the television show *Talk Soup* but happily left his TV persona behind when acting opportunities arose. He surprised critics and moviegoers alike with his moving performance in *As Good As It Gets* (1996), which earned him an Oscar nomination, and later played against his all-American looks in the dark biopic *Auto Focus* (2002) as radio and TV star Bob Crane.

In *The Matador,* both Brosnan and Kinnear defy any preconceived ideas we might have about them and the kind of roles we're used to seeing them play. That's one reason the movie works so well. The other is an inspired and thoroughly unpredictable screenplay by director Richard Shepard.

The two characters meet one night in the bar of a Mexico City hotel. Kinnear is a thorough square who's hoping to rescue his faltering business career at an important meeting. Brosnan is there to rub someone out; he's a hit man. They have nothing in common except, as it turns out, a touch of desperation that—away from home and the everyday routine—brings them together. Brosnan even takes his new pal to a bullfight and shows him how he would stage a hit. By the time Kinnear goes home to his wife (Hope Davis) in Denver, he is bursting with stories about his colorful new acquaintance. Then one night, months later, the doorbell rings. It's the hit man, who tells Kinnear, "You are my only friend in the world."

The Matador is a character study played in the key of black comedy. It's dark, quirky, and surprising. Kinnear, Davis, and Brosnan bring their earnest but off-kilter characters to life with great zest and complete conviction. Brosnan is particularly unsparing of his heroic screen image, as if thumbing his nose at James Bond and his trademark sangfroid. Whatever else he does, I'm sure The Matador will remain a benchmark in his career.

82. MATCHSTICK MEN

(2003)

Directed by Ridley Scott

Screenplay by Nicholas Griffin and Ted Griffin

Based on the novel by Eric Garcia

Actors:

NICOLAS CAGE

SAM ROCKWELL

ALISON LOHMAN

BRUCE ALTMAN

BRUCE MCGILL

SHEILA KELLEY

BETH GRANT

FRAN KRANZ

STEVE EASTIN

TIM KELLEHER

JENNY O'HARA

NIGEL GIBBS

Ridley Scott is known for making big, often epic-scale movies such as *Alien, Blade Runner, Black Hawk Down,* and *Gladiator.* When he tackled the subject of the Crusades in *Kingdom of Heaven,* his director's cut ran more than three hours. But every now and then he feels the need to shift gears and make something lighter. Sometimes this doesn't pan out, as anyone who saw *A Good Year* can verify (although I suspect he and Russell Crowe had a great time soaking up the weather, wine, and food of Provence).

However, *Matchstick Men,* which fell between *Black Hawk Down* and *Kingdom of Heaven,* brought out the best in the director: it's different, more intimate material for Scott, with a perfect part for Nicolas Cage (who purchased the screen rights to Eric Garcia's novel in the first place).

If this had just been the story of two con men—an old hand and his younger, somewhat impatient protégé—there would have been sufficient material for an entertaining film. But *Matchstick Men* builds layer after layer on top of that foundation. Cage isn't simply a flawed hero: he's a mess. Highly phobic and obsessive-compulsive, he can't get along without the counsel of his psychiatrist and the pills he prescribes. One day his shrink encourages him to look up the child he had with his ex-wife. The girl is now fifteen years old, and it takes a lot for Cage to work up the nerve to introduce himself . . . but he does.

Bringing a daughter (Alison Lohman) into his world isn't easy. Not only does he have to try to overcome his many personality problems, but he can't be honest with her about what he does for a living—especially since he and his partner (Sam Rockwell) are baiting the trap for a major con. Yet having someone in his life to care about causes real change in his outlook on life, especially when she begins to care about him, too.

I can't go into further detail about Nick and Ted Griffin's screenplay without spoiling its many surprises. Suffice it to say that Scott's eye for detail serves this movie well. The locations around Los Angeles are well chosen and the casting is impeccable (including such reliable and underrated actors as Bruce Altman, as the psychiatrist, and Bruce McGill, as the "mark"). Sam Rockwell is terrific, as always, and Alison Lohman makes an indelible impression as the teenager who slowly warms up to the father she's never known.

As for Nicolas Cage, he is always at his best playing damaged men. His character could be completely off-putting but instead we root for him, especially as he grows into his new role as a father.

Hans Zimmer provides an inventive score, which is supplemented by an eclectic selection of source music. I will admit that *Matchstick Men* goes on a bit longer than it should, but its pleasures are many and its plot twists are clever without being forced.

83. MATEWAN

(1987)

Directed by John Sayles

Screenplay by John Sayles

Actors:

CHRIS COOPER

WILL OLDHAM

MARY MCDONNELL

BOB GUNTON

JAMES EARL JONES

KEVIN TIGHE

GORDON CLAPP

JOSH MOSTEL

JOE GRIFASI

MAGGIE RENZI

DAVID STRATHAIRN

NANCY METTE

JOHN SAYLES

JACE ALEXANDER

KEN JENKINS

I could easily fill a number of spots in this book with the work of John Sayles, one of the most independent of independent filmmakers. Already established as a fiction writer of considerable skill, he hit a bull's-eye with his first attempt at filmmaking, *Return of the Secaucus Seven* (1980). Funding his efforts, in part, by writing (and polishing) mainstream Hollywood movies, he has never compromised his ideals. That doesn't mean every movie he makes is great, but each one aspires to tell a good story and bring interesting, multifaceted characters to the screen. His ear for dialogue is extraordinary; so is his eye for casting the right actor in each part. Such eminent actors as David Strathairn and Chris Cooper have emerged from Sayles's stock company of performers. (A good actor himself, he often appears in his own films, in small roles, and has appeared in other directors' movies, as well. He's wickedly funny as a self-indulgent director in Bertrand Tavernier's *In the Electric Mist*.)

Sayles is unapologetically liberal, but he usually avoids polemics in his screenplays. That's one reason *Matewan* is so effective. The story of a labor struggle in rural West Virginia in the 1920s, it could have dissolved into a series of button-pushing Hollywood clichés. Not here. The good guys and bad guys are clearly defined, but the story has many facets, and no one understands that better than Sayles.

The setting is a poor Appalachian community (pronounced MATE-wan, not Mat-e-wan) where the Stone Mountain Coal Company controls the lives of its residents. With a recent reduction in wages, there have been rumblings of unionism and that won't be tolerated. The company has already integrated Italian immigrants into the community to break the spirit of the locals; now it's trainloads of blacks who are supposed to quell the idea of opposing the bosses (not that they've been warned of the situation ahead of time).

Chris Cooper plays a labor organizer who arrives in Matewan with a mission, fully aware of the powder keg that rests under his feet. He must pacify the various factions and keep them from fighting each other so they can focus their energies on the ultimate goal: speaking with one voice and standing against the bosses.

The dramatis personae of the story range from a teenage preacher (Will Oldham) to a prostitute (Nancy Mette) who took up her profession after her husband died in the mines. There are solid performances from James Earl Jones, as one of the black workers who listens to Cooper with an open mind; Mary McDonnell, as a widow who works as hard as any of the men in town; David Strathairn, as the local police chief; and Josh Mostel, as the mayor. Sayles gives himself a showcase scene as a fire-and-brimstone preacher, and his longtime partner and producer Maggie Renzi is quite effective as one of the Italian women who views her lot in life without an ounce of sentiment.

Matewan gives us a strong sense of time and place. (Sayles even wrote some bogus labor songs for his workers to chant.) Haskell Wexler's vivid, black-and-white cinematography adds to the grittiness of the milieu. But it's Sayles's clear-eyed vision that makes this movie so memorable.

84. MAYBE BABY

(2000)

Directed by Ben Elton

Screenplay by Ben Elton

Based on the novel *Inconceivable* by Ben Elton

Actors:

HUGH LAURIE

JOELY RICHARDSON

ADRIAN LESTER

JAMES PUREFOY

TOM HOLLANDER

JOANNA LUMLEY

ROWAN ATKINSON

MATTHEW MACFADYEN

DAWN FRENCH

EMMA THOMPSON

RACHAEL STIRLING

The ascension of Hugh Laurie to full-fledged American TV stardom on *House* must have amused his loyal fans—and possibly even the actor himself—given his long and prominent career on British television (in such series as

Blackadder, Jeeves and Wooster, and *A Bit of Fry and Laurie*), not to mention the fine work he's done on screen in such movies as *Peter's Friends, Sense and Sensibility, The Borrowers,* and *Stuart Little.* There is also a certain irony in watching this multitalented performer break through in a dramatic role when he built his reputation doing comedy.

Television also brought overdue recognition to Joely Richardson (sister of the late Natasha, daughter of Vanessa Redgrave and director Tony Richardson) when she starred in *Nip/Tuck.* Yet she, too, has a long if spottier résumé, including turns as Lady Chatterley in a 1993 TV movie of the same name, Marie Antoinette in *The Affair of the Necklace,* Wallis Simpson in the TV movie *Wallis & Edward . . .* and a costarring role opposite Hugh Laurie in the Disney studio's live-action version of *101 Dalmatians.*

In 2000 they were again cast as husband and wife in a likable comedy called *Maybe Baby.* It would be difficult to find a more engaging screen couple, so one is immediately drawn into their lives as we learn of their difficulty having a child. If you've ever experienced any of the trials and tribulations they go through in this film, you know it was based on firsthand experience. Indeed, the popular British writer-performer Ben Elton, who also directed *Maybe Baby,* based his screenplay on his autobiographical novel *Inconceivable.*

Laurie plays a BBC television producer whose insufferable boss is played by Matthew Macfadyen. Our hero longs to write screenplays, and finally decides to write about what he knows: the pain, and humor, of a couple trying to make a baby. The only problem is that he can't tell his wife what he's doing, as he is essentially stealing their day-to-day experiences for the sake of a movie. Meanwhile, in her job as a casting director, she faces temptation in the person of a randy, rakishly handsome actor (James Purefoy) who seems unconcerned that she is happily married.

Moments that are plainly, sometimes painfully truthful are balanced against scenes of broad comic exaggeration, with brief but amusing contributions by such eminent comedic actors as Emma Thompson (as a New Age fertility specialist), Rowan Atkinson (as an overly enthusiastic ob/ gyn), Joanna Lumley, and Dawn French, this modest British film calls on the best possible source of comedy and drama: real life.

85. THE MERRY GENTLEMAN

(2009)

Directed by Michael Keaton
Screenplay by Ron Lazzeretti

Actors:

MICHAEL KEATON

KELLY MACDONALD

TOM BASTOUNES

BOBBY CANNAVALE

DARLENE HUNT

GUY VAN SWEARINGEN

WILLIAM DICK

As I repeatedly tell my students, every movie has a saga; sometimes the story of how a film came together is just as interesting as the picture itself. In the case of *The Merry Gentleman* the road to production seemed fairly uneventful at first. Writer Ron Lazzeretti developed the idea for a

dark-tinged romantic thriller and showed it to fellow Chi-
cagoan Tom Bastounes, an actor and producer with whom
he'd worked on an indie feature called *The Opera Lover*.
They secured financing, and their script was good enough
to attract Michael Keaton and the gifted Scottish-born actress Kelly Macdonald to play the leading roles. Bastounes
had already targeted the second male lead for himself.

Lazzeretti was all set to direct his own screenplay when a
ruptured appendix sent him to the hospital. One thing anyone
who works in the film business quickly learns is that a film is
like a house of cards that can collapse in the blink of an eye.
Unexpected bad weather, a sudden injury, an actor changing
his mind: almost anything can throw a promising production
out of whack, or destroy it completely.

In this case, Lazzeretti realized that if he tried to put the
movie on hold until he recovered it might not happen at all.
Then Michael Keaton expressed interest in taking his place
behind the camera.

As an actor Keaton has never shied away from a challenge, and he'd grown very fond of this script, and his character. Although he had never directed a feature film before,
he felt confident about this one, and the completed film
bears that out.

Macdonald plays a vulnerable woman who has fled her
abusive husband and moved to Chicago to start life anew.
She lands a good office job but keeps an arm's length from
even her friendliest coworkers because she doesn't want to
discuss her past—or explain her bruises.

Keaton plays a hit man who, by the very nature of his
profession, is a loner. One night, shortly before Christmas,
he fires on a man in Macdonald's office complex from across

the street. As she leaves the building a short time later, she looks up and catches a glimpse of him on the roof, where he's perched on the ledge, apparently preparing to jump. Her scream catches him off guard and sends him reeling backward.

How these two troubled and intensely private people meet and develop a relationship is the crux of the movie. In a film like this, maintaining the right tone is crucial, and Keaton never makes a false move. Lazzeretti's script has scary scenes and lighter moments as well; they blend together into a seamless whole because we buy into the central characters. Keaton's low-key portrayal of the hit man who hides more than he ever reveals is excellent, and Macdonald (who's an asset to any movie she's in) is superb. Bobby Cannavale is genuinely frightening as Macdonald's husband, and Tom Bastounes brings just the right note of rumpled affability to the role of a Chicago cop who's attracted to Macdonald but clumsy about taking the next step.

The Merry Gentleman, ironically titled after the Christmas holiday that's a backdrop for the story, is an austere but stylish little film noir, and a feather in Michael Keaton's cap—as both actor and director.

86. METROLAND

(1998)

Directed by Philip Saville

Screenplay by Adrian Hodges

Based on the novel by Julian Barnes

Actors:

CHRISTIAN BALE

EMILY WATSON

LEE ROSS

ELSA ZYLBERSTEIN

RUFUS

JONATHAN ARIS

IFAN MEREDITH

AMANDA RYAN

JOHN WOOD

LUCY SPEED

One of the bonuses in looking back over neglected films of the past ten to fifteen years is discovering good performances by actors whose stock has risen during that time. Christian Bale has been acting since he was a boy; as an adult he's shown a penchant for challenging and difficult material, but he's also found a niche in the mainstream thanks to *Batman Begins, The Dark Knight,* and *Terminator Salvation.* Bale was in his mid-twenties when he made *Metroland,* and his serious mien made him a perfect choice to play an ordinary middle-class Brit. (This was before he made a sharp left turn in such films as *Velvet Goldmine, American Psycho,* and *The Machinist.*)

Metroland is a deceptively simple story about a young, happily married man whose oldest friend, a hard-living, no-madic, self-styled poet (Lee Ross), comes to visit after five years and rags his pal about having sold out to suburban life and an office job. Chris (Bale) already finds himself thinking a lot about the past, and his youthful sojourn in Paris, where he hoped to live his life as a photographer. That's where he met his first love, a sexy, straightforwardly honest young woman (Elsa Zylberstein). The continuing presence of his old friend—and the seeming stagnation of his sex life with his wife (Emily Watson)—puts him in a funk, and has him wondering if he didn't give up on too much, too soon.

The film is based on the debut novel by the well-regarded British author and critic Julian Barnes. Some reviewers found the film too facile, and it's notable that a female critic, the *New York Times*'s Janet Maslin, regarded both of the women in the story to be stereotypes. I respectfully disagree. If the French-woman weren't so magnetic—and so radically different from his British wife—the movie wouldn't work. And one couldn't find an actress more innately intelligent than Emily Watson, who makes Chris's spouse a believable, three-dimensional character.

And of course there is a rose-colored hue to Chris's memories of the bohemian life he gave up in Paris: that's the point.

With actors as skillful as Christian Bale, Emily Watson, and Elsa Zylberstein bringing these people to life, *Metroland* digs beneath the surface and examines the truth of hopes, dreams, and reality. It's a straightforward but eminently satisfying film.

87. A MIDNIGHT CLEAR

(1992)

Directed by Keith Gordon

Screenplay by Keith Gordon

Based on the novel by William Wharton

Actors:

PETER BERG

KEVIN DILLON

ARYE GROSS

ETHAN HAWKE

GARY SINISE

FRANK WHALEY

JOHN C. MCGINLEY

LARRY JOSHUA
CURT LOWENS

At this point it may seem as though we've seen as many films with antiwar messages as war movies themselves. Even so, *A Midnight Clear* stands out from the crowd.

When William Wharton's novel was published in 1996 it earned accolades from many critics, one of whom said it belonged on the same shelf as Stephen Crane's *The Red Badge of Courage*. But unlike Crane, when Wharton wrote about men in war he did so from firsthand experience. He was still a teenager when he volunteered for active duty, served in the U.S. Infantry during World War II, and suffered serious wounds during the Battle of the Bulge. He later said that he based *A Midnight Clear* on actual events, and it's not difficult to imagine that his protagonist, Will Knott, is Wharton himself.

In adapting this book for the screen, actor-turned-filmmaker Keith Gordon was determined not only to capture the almost-surreal tone of the book and cast it with young actors, but also to drive home Wharton's observation of a war peopled with soldiers who were barely out of adolescence.

The time is December 1944; the setting is the Ardennes Forest in the dead of winter, where the snow creates an eerie light, and enemy soldiers can seemingly materialize from out of nowhere—and disappear in the blink of an eye. The film focuses on a U.S. intelligence squadron made up of exceptionally bright—but emotionally raw—young men whose assignment is to flush out Germans nearby. Ethan Hawke plays Will, who narrates the film. When a fellow soldier, nicknamed Mother (and played by Gary Sinise, in his feature-film debut) goes mad and runs toward the forest, tearing off his clothes, it's Will who goes after him and brings him back.

The other members of the unit (played by talented actors Frank Whaley, Peter Berg, Kevin Dillon, and Arye Gross, all at the outset of their careers) have no way of knowing that the Germans who hover nearby are just as young and just as scared as they are. In fact, they'd like nothing better than to surrender and bring their suffering to an end— especially as Christmas nears.

A Midnight Clear is a riveting, meticulously crafted drama that was a labor of love for Gordon and his cast, as is evidenced by the stories related by the director and Ethan Hawke on the commentary track of its tenth anniversary DVD release. It had real meaning for them, which helps explain why it resonates so strongly with us in the audience.

88. THE MIGHTY

(1998)

Directed by Peter Chelsom

Screenplay by Charles Leavitt

Based on the novel *Freak the Mighty*

by Rodman Philbrick

Actors:

KIERAN CULKIN

ELDEN HENSON

SHARON STONE

GENA ROWLANDS

HARRY DEAN STANTON

GILLIAN ANDERSON

JAMES GANDOLFINI
MEAT LOAF
JENIFER LEWIS

I don't get cited in movie ad campaigns very often because I don't write good, pithy, enthusiastic quotes. However, I did conduct a one-man promotional campaign for *The Mighty* when it came out in 1998 because I fell in love with the film. I only wish I'd convinced more people to see it.

Charles Leavitt's screenplay is based on a popular juvenile novel by Rodman Philbrick called *Freak the Mighty*. The main characters are a pair of seventh-grade students who are social outcasts, each for a different reason. Kevin (beautifully played by Kieran Culkin) is smart as a whip, but has a degenerative physical disability known as Morquio's syndrome. He can't participate in sports, and most of the kids at school make fun of him. Kevin tends to disappear into a world of his own imagination. Max (Elden Henson), who narrates the story, is an overgrown hulk who's failed seventh grade before and is an object of ridicule for most of his classmates.

One day a teacher assigns Kevin the task of helping Max learn to read. Using his ingenuity, and love of books—and refusing to coddle his reluctant pupil—the smaller boy introduces Max to the legend of King Arthur, inspiring him with tales of the knights of old. In time, they team up to emulate those knights, combining Kevin's brains and Max's brawn. Or, as Kevin puts it, "You need brains and I need legs, and the Wizard of Oz doesn't live in South Cincinnati."

Here is where *The Mighty* really soars, imposing a metaphoric layer onto the real world that has treated these boys so poorly. Empowered by their belief in knighthood and its values, they set out to perform heroic deeds—and we root for them at every turn.

The Mighty could have played out like a soap opera, but it doesn't. The parents and grandparents in the story (played by Sharon Stone, Gillian Anderson, Gena Rowlands, and Harry Dean Stanton) wring their hands, but the boys refuse to wallow in self-pity. (James Gandolfini also appears in a climactic sequence as Max's father.)

Peter Chelsom, who found just the right approach to such unusual fare as *Hear My Song* (1991) and *Funny Bones* (1995), scores another bull's-eye here, and obviously developed great communication with his young actors. *The Mighty* is a very special film.

89. MILLIONS

(2005)

Directed by Danny Boyle
Screenplay by Frank Cottrell Boyce
Based on the novel by Frank Cottrell Boyce

Actors:

ALEXANDER NATHAN ETEL

LEWIS OWEN MCGIBBON

JAMES NESBITT

DAISY DONOVAN

CHRISTOPHER FULFORD

JANE HOGARTH

ALUN ARMSTRONG

ENZO CILENTI

LESLIE PHILLIPS

Audiences are ready, even eager, to accept fantasy in an otherworldly realm, like those depicted in *The Lord of the Rings* or *The Chronicles of Narnia*. They'll even accept utter make-believe in a popcorn movie like *Transformers*. But they're tougher to win over when someone tells a story in which subtler fantastic elements—without large-scale special effects—arc integrated into an everyday setting. Still, every now and then, a picture persuades moviegoers to make that leap of faith, and *Millions* is a great example.

Danny Boyle is now enshrined in movies' hall of fame as the Oscar-winning director of *Slumdog Millionaire,* but he made his reputation with the heart-stopping British film about the underground drug culture, *Trainspotting.* Writer Frank Cottrell Boyce is best known for serious films like *Welcome to Sarajevo* and *Hilary and Jackie.* But it turns out they both have a lighter side, and express that quite nicely in this entertaining fable.

Our heroes are wide-eyed Damien, who's seven, and his nine-year-old brother Anthony, who are uprooted from their gray city dwelling and moved to a shiny new suburban development by their recently widowed father. Damien has an active imagination, but one day while he's playing near the railroad tracks a bagful of money lands right in front of him . . . and it's very real indeed.

His ambitious brother starts figuring out how they can best make use of the money—which is in pound notes, just as England is about to switch (at least, for the purposes of this story) to the euro—but soon two outsiders interfere with his plans. One is a scheming drifter who wants the cash for himself. The other is St. Francis of Assisi, who comes to Damien in a vision and tells him he should share his newfound wealth with the poor.

I would rather not reveal more of the story or the way it is presented. The film addresses issues of ethics and morality, but it's not out to preach, and would never be mistaken for an after-school special.

Millions is a lively and unpredictable mix of unreality and heartfelt emotions, beautifully expressed by its two young actors, Alex Etel and Lewis McGibbon. You'll never guess where the story is heading, which makes *Millions* a charming surprise package for anyone willing to surrender to its charms.

90. MIRRORMASK

(2005)

Directed by David McKean
Screenplay by Neil Gaiman
Story by David McKean and Neil Gaiman

Actors:

STEPHANIE LEONIDAS

JASON BARRY

ROB BRYDON

GINA MCKEE

STEPHEN FRY

Where would contemporary authors, artists, and filmmakers be if they couldn't refer to such universally understood touchstones as *The Wizard of Oz* and *Alice in*

Wonderland? Sometimes I resent the reliance on these age-less creations, but occasionally I think the creators of the new work are clever enough to warrant their own round of applause.

There is no question that celebrated fantasy author Neil Gaiman (*Sandman, Stardust, Coraline, The Graveyard Book*) and his frequent collaborator, artist and graphic designer Dave McKean, turned to L. Frank Baum and Lewis Carroll for inspiration in fashioning both the plot and the look of this movie, but I think the end result can stand on its own quite well.

Stephanie Leonidas plays Helena, an adolescent girl who no longer enjoys life with her parents' perpetually struggling circus, to put it mildly, even though it's her father's labor of love. (He's played by the likable comic actor Rob Brydon.) A talented artist, she escapes into the world of her imagination at every opportunity. Then, when her mother (the wonderful Gina McKee) takes ill after a heated argument, Helena actually steps into the alternate universe she has created. Here, against a wildly fanciful and bizarre backdrop, she finds herself in the unexpected (and uncomfortable) position of potential savior. The world has been cast into a state of darkness and only she can find the means to awaken the slumbering Queen of Light (who, naturally, is also played by McKee). In her travels to the Dark World, our heroine discovers that she has a doppelganger—a "bad" Helena—who personifies all of her worst thoughts and fears.

Stripped down to its barest essentials, this is the story of a quest—a metaphoric one, to be sure—not unlike the journey undertaken by Dorothy in *The Wizard of Oz*. Helena meets many strange and extraordinary creatures along the way, notably a juggler named Valentine (Jason Barry) who becomes her friend and adviser.

Despite its complications the story is fairly simple; what complicates it, and threatens to weigh it down, is the sheer volume of visual invention paraded before us. There's scarcely a "normal" moment once we leave the drab world of the family circus, and it can be overpowering at times. Roger Ebert described the characters as "very strange creatures, some of them with shoes for heads, others weirder than that, who seem by Hieronymus Bosch out of an acid trip."

What keeps the story anchored, it seems to me, is the fact that we identify with Helena and empathize with her guilt over having argued with her mother just before she's rushed to the hospital. Leonidas's likable performance, and McKee's natural warmth, make their characters relatable and remind us that everything else we see is a mirror distortion of the crises both mother and daughter are experiencing.

Dave McKean has won awards and acclaim for his illustrations. For his feature-filmmaking debut he gathered a group of young, eager artists to work with him to design and execute a daunting number of computer graphic images. The results are quite astonishing, all the more so when you learn that they were done by a handful of people working on a minuscule budget.

Even if *Mirrormask* isn't destined to become part of our collective consciousness like *Alice in Wonderland* and *The Wizard of Oz,* I think it's an ideal film for families to share together, if the kids are old enough to digest such a dark story. It may well fire their own imaginations.

91. MOONLIGHTING

(1982)

Directed by Jerzy Skolimowski

Screenplay by Jerzy Skolimowski

Actors:

JEREMY IRONS

EUGENE LIPINSKI

JIRÍ STANSILAV

EUGENIUSZ HACZKIEWICZ

ay *Moonlighting* and most people immediately think of the popular TV series of the 1980s with Cybill Shepherd and Bruce Willis. I wish more people would say, "Oh, you mean that incredible movie with Jeremy Irons?" But thanks to DVD, there is always the chance for people to discover this little-known gem.

Moonlighting is the work of Polish filmmaker Jerzy Skolimowski, who has never achieved the notoriety of his friend Roman Polanski (for whom he wrote the latter's breakthrough feature, *Knife in the Water*), but he has maintained a presence on the international film scene for decades, earning prizes at top film festivals and achieving international recognition for such films as *Le Départ, Deep End, The Shout, Torrents of Spring,* and *The Lightship.*

But to my mind, *Moonlighting* is a masterpiece that stands apart. Skolimowski has often worked in England, and was living in London when Poland's Solidarity movement was wiped out and martial law was imposed in December 1981. He wrote this elliptical movie in response and quickly put it into production.

A gaunt, grim-faced Jeremy Irons gives a marvelous

performance as Nowak, who heads a group of Polish construction workers who have been hired under the table, so to
speak, to renovate a well-heeled government official's home
in London. They have to smuggle their equipment into the
country, as neither Poland nor England would look kindly
upon this scheme. (After all, they're willing to work much
cheaper than a British crew.) They have no work permits,
so for the duration of their time in the UK, they sleep inside
the house. It's up to Nowak—the only one who speaks
English—to provide food and look out for them. When he
walks by a shop window and sees on television news cover-
age of the events back home, he is dumbstruck. He decides
not to tell his cohorts, worried that they may walk off the
job. As fear sets in, and funds run low to sustain himself
and his crew, Nowak becomes increasingly desperate, and
perfects his shoplifting skills. It's all about survival—at least
until the job is finished.

Moonlighting is incredibly suspenseful, but where it might
have been dark and dismal it is ironic and mordantly funny.
Aside from the basic absurdity of the situation, there are
Irons's increasingly daring and outrageous schemes to fleece
his local supermarket and flirt with a neighborhood salesgirl.

Had Skolimowski made a sober or somber parable about
political upheaval in his homeland, the film wouldn't be
nearly as entertaining as it is. *Moonlighting* is affecting precisely because it is so unpretentious—and entertaining.

92. MOUNTAINS OF THE MOON

(1990)

Directed by Bob Rafelson

Screenplay by William Harrison and Bob Rafelson

Based on the novel *Burton and Speke* by

William Harrison and the journals of Sir Richard Francis

Burton and John Hanning Speke

Actors:

PATRICK BERGIN

IAIN GLEN

RICHARD E. GRANT

FIONA SHAW

JOHN SAVIDENT

JAMES VILLIERS

ADRIAN RAWLINS

DELROY LINDO

PAUL ONSONGO

BERNARD HILL

ROSHAN SETH

ANNA MASSEY

LESLIE PHILLIPS

OMAR SHARIF

ROGER REES

Bob Rafelson is one of the most interesting and individual talents in contemporary American film. As cocreator of the faux rock group the Monkees, he produced (and sometimes wrote and directed) their hit TV series, cowrote and directed their inventive feature film *Head,* and then enjoyed his greatest critical and commercial success with *Five Easy Pieces,* starring another *Monkees* writer, Jack Nicholson. He and Nicholson continued to collaborate over the decades, on *The King of Marvin Gardens, The Postman Always Rings Twice, Man Trouble,* and another of this book's selections, *Blood and Wine.* Among his other notable films are *Stay Hungry* and *Black Widow,* but nothing in Rafelson's portfolio would lead anyone to expect a film as grand, or far-reaching in its ambitions, as *Mountains of the Moon.*

This handsomely mounted saga, photographed by the great Roger Deakins, turns back the clock to a time when the English-speaking world was captivated by daring explorers like Sir Richard Burton. At a time when travel was arduous and methods of communication primitive, he didn't hesitate to leave Victorian England, and his wife, behind to embark on bold, dangerous expeditions. (He had many other talents and interests, including linguistics and a fascination with erotica that inspired him to translate the Kama Sutra.) This film focuses on his search for the source of the Nile River in the mid-1800s. Patrick Bergin, who should have springboarded to stardom on the strength of this performance, is a charismatic Burton, with Iain Glen equally well cast as John Hanning Speke, the ambitious dilettante who accompanies him.

Historians have speculated about the relationship between these two disparate men—one a genuine adventurer, the other an opportunist—who eventually became bitter enemies. Each man also flirted with homosexual desire for the other, although to what degree, we'll never know.

Because the screenplay for *Mountains of the Moon* is based in part on the men's surviving journals, there are vivid, eye-filling details of their exploits in Africa. Their groundbreaking exploration of that continent is a major element of the film. It is also inspired by a biographical novel written by William Harrison, who collaborated with Rafelson on the script, so we cannot take everything we see as the gospel. But what makes this film so special is that it manages to embrace the sweep of an epic with the compelling details of a highly personal story. It isn't an old-fashioned "boys' adventure" like *King Solomon's Mines,* but a realistic drama about the hardships these men faced on their journeys, and the equally trying problems they had to confront upon their return.

It certainly captures the spirit of its time, when men like Burton defied the constraints of Victorian behavior and Speke sought personal gain in a way that seems curiously modern.

93. MRS PALFREY AT THE CLAREMONT

(2005)

Directed by Dan Ireland

Screenplay by Ruth Sacks

Based on the novel by Elizabeth Taylor

Actors:

JOAN PLOWRIGHT

RUPERT FRIEND

ZOE TAPPER

ANNA MASSEY

ROBERT LANG

MARCIA WARREN

MILLICENT MARTIN

LORCAN O'TOOLE

MICHAEL CULKIN

TIMOTHY BATESON

CLARE HIGGINS

EMMA PIKE

The problem with many films about elderly characters is that they strive—often much too hard—to be cute and endearing. What sets *Mrs Palfrey at The Claremont* apart from the crowd is that it succeeds without condescending to its characters or, for that matter, its audience.

The film's strongest asset is its leading lady, the formidable Joan Plowright. This veteran actress is not above chewing some scenery, as she's shown in a number of Hollywood movies, but here she exercises admirable restraint. Mrs. Palfrey is a lonely widow who moves to London to distance herself from her grown daughter and be closer to her grandson. The only problem is that she hasn't consulted the young man, who doesn't return her calls. So it is that the proudly independent woman checks into the Claremont, a residential hotel where the other residents immediately start sniffing her out.

Then, through happenstance, Mrs. Palfrey meets a nice young man named Ludovic (Rupert Friend) who helps her at an awkward moment and quickly befriends her; in time their relationship deepens. And, in an amusing turn of events, Mrs. Palfrey is obliged to explain away Ludo's presence by pretending that he is her grandson.

If you refuse to accept the premise that a man in his twenties could express genuine friendship for a woman in her seventies, this is not your kind of story. Indeed, this is a wish-fulfillment movie, with only one foot firmly planted in the real world—but it's just real enough to win us over, especially in the skilled hands of Plowright, Friend, and such fine actors as Anna Massey, Robert Lang, and Millicent Martin. (Mrs. Palfrey's grandson is played by Lorcan O'Toole, son of Peter O'Toole.)

The screenplay is based on a novel from the 1950s by Elizabeth Taylor (the author, not the movie star), adapted by Ruth Sacks, who was in her seventies when she wrote the script. The director is considerably younger: Dan Ireland, cofounder of the Seattle International Film Festival, who made an impressive directorial debut with *The Whole Wide World* (1996). His evocation of a dowdy residential hotel is perfect, as is his handling of the mostly senior cast. And if the film never soars to the heights of Noël Coward's *Brief Encounter,* which Mrs. Palfrey cites as her all-time favorite, it does provide eminently satisfying entertainment, and a great showcase for its glowing star.

94. MY FIRST MISTER

(2001)

Directed by Christine Lahti

Screenplay by Jill Franklyn

Actors:

LEELEE SOBIESKI

ALBERT BROOKS

DESMOND HARRINGTON

CAROL KANE

MARY KAY PLACE

JOHN GOODMAN

MICHAEL MCKEAN

RUTANYA ALDA

'm a sucker for Albert Brooks. That may explain why I was more enthusiastic about *My First Mister* than some other critics, but I don't intend to apologize for liking this movie. I think it's charming.

Buoyed by an Academy Award for Best Short Subject (*Lieberman in Love*) the gifted actress Christine Lahti made her feature directing debut with this genteel story about a very odd couple, written by Jill Franklyn, whose most prominent credit before this film was the "Yada Yada" episode of *Seinfeld*.

The talented Leelee Sobieski plays seventeen-year-old Goth girl Jennifer, whose divorced mother (Carol Kane) has all but given up on trying to communicate with her. It can't be easy: Jennifer is obsessed with dark images and music and has punctured her body in a variety of unappealing ways. Then one day she happens upon an uptight, punctilious, forty-nine-year-old clothing salesman named Randall (Brooks) and something clicks. It isn't sexual, as the film makes plain. She senses in him not just loneliness but an individuality that she can relate to and respect.

Randall is divorced and leads a quiet, orderly existence, but Jennifer makes it her mission to loosen him up and expose him to all sorts of new experiences. At the same time, he inspires her to clean up her act and lose the heavy mascara and mourning clothes.

None of this would be remotely convincing if we didn't like the two actors and believe them in these roles. Brooks (who is underrated as an actor) has a steady stream of funny lines that aren't simply wisecracks but utterances that perfectly suit his character. When she insists that he get a tattoo, he says to the artist, "I want the smallest tattoo you have.

Can you give me a dot, or a period?" Sobieski, who is meant to be off-putting at first, becomes sympathetic as we learn about the influences that have shaped her young life. The more time these two people spend together on-screen, the more we accept their unusual friendship: they truly bring out the best in each other. (We also get to meet Jennifer's father, played in broad comic fashion by John Goodman.)

The film has been criticized for surrendering to predictable plot turns, and if that makes me a sentimentalist, so be it. I cared enough about these people that I invested in them emotionally. *My First Mister* is a sweet, likable movie.

95. THE MYSTERY OF PICASSO

(1956)

Directed by Henri-Georges Clouzot

With:

PABLO PICASSO

CLAUDE RENOIR

HENRI-GEORGES CLOUZOT

Many great artists cannot explain how they do what they do, regardless of their medium. Asking a great sculptor how he achieves his results is akin to questioning a composer about his inspiration for the music that seemingly pours out of him.

In the 1950s, French filmmaker Henri-Georges Clouzot, best remembered for such thrillers as *Diabolique* and *The Wages of Fear,* convinced his friend Pablo Picasso to join him in an experiment. Clouzot set a camera on one side of a translucent canvas and had Picasso paint on the opposite

side. The astonishing result allows us to watch the spontane-
ous creation of one picture after another, stroke by stroke.
No questions are asked or answered, but we do have the rare
privilege of witnessing a genius at work.

In the middle of the film, there's a break where we get
to see the filmmaking setup, and watch the (shirtless) artist
from the other side of the easel. Clouzot even reveals some
of his trickery; although the creation of a painting seems
continuous, in fact he would stop the camera from time to
time and (seamlessly) pick up where he and the artist left off.
Inspiration was not a free-flowing process even for a genius
like Picasso.

Not so incidentally, the cinematographer, whom we see
in behind-the-scenes footage, is Claude Renoir, nephew of
the great filmmaker Jean Renoir—and great-nephew of the
illustrious painter Pierre Auguste. Claude worked with his
uncle on such films as *Grand Illusion, The River,* and *Elena
and Her Men.* It isn't known whether Renoir or Clouzot
came up with the idea of expanding the film from a stan-
dard frame to wide screen, but the transition is pleasing to
the eye and must have been especially impressive in 1956
when CinemaScope was still fairly new.

The score for *The Mystery of Picasso* is by another formidable Frenchman, George Auric, who collaborated with
Jean Cocteau for many years (on such classic films as *Blood
of a Poet, Beauty and the Beast,* and *The Testament of Orpheus*)
and whose other credits on both sides of the Atlantic include *The Wages of Fear, Lola Montes, Roman Holiday,* and
The Innocents.

We don't necessarily come away from this film with a
greater understanding of Pablo Picasso or the intangible

thought process that produces great works of art. On the other hand, we do see how an artist can change his mind in the middle of a painting, and come to realize that the piece as a whole is greater than the sum of its parts, as unrelated brush strokes eventually coalesce into a finished work.

The Mystery of Picasso was awarded a Special Jury Prize at the Cannes Film Festival in 1956. More than half a century later, it remains a mesmerizing film.

96. NINE LIVES

(2005)

Directed by Rodrigo García

Screenplay by Rodrigo García

Actors:

GLENN CLOSE

ROBIN WRIGHT PENN

HOLLY HUNTER

SISSY SPACEK

KATHY BAKER

AMY BRENNEMAN

ELPIDIA CARRILLO

DAKOTA FANNING

LISA GAY HAMILTON

MOLLY PARKER

MARY KAY PLACE

AMANDA SEYFRIED

STEPHEN DILLANE

WILLIAM FICHTNER

JASON ISAACS

JOE MANTEGNA

IAN MCSHANE

SYDNEY TAMAIIA POITIER

AIDAN QUINN

MIGUEL SANDOVAL

LAWRENCE PRESSMAN

Filmmaker Rodrigo García is fascinated by women, as anyone can tell who has seen *Things You Can Tell Just By Looking at Her, Ten Tiny Love Stories,* and *Nine Lives.* Perhaps it's because multiepisode films are considered a tough sell that these cinematic collections of short stories aren't better known; it can't be for lack of star power.

Nine Lives is especially satisfying not only because the writing is so good and the casting so strong but because García developed a particular style of shooting (with his cinematographer, Xavier Perez Grobet) to tell each story in one continuous take! These extended shots run anywhere from ten to fourteen minutes, yet they never seem like just a gimmick; García makes the storytelling technique seem organic.

The stories themselves all deal with women at a crossroads in their lives. A married woman (Sissy Spacek) is about to have an adulterous affair in a motel room. A teenage girl (Amanda Seyfried) wants to leave home to go to college but feels anchored by her parents' dependency on her. A woman (Kathy Baker) tries to prepare herself emotionally for a breast-cancer operation. A mother (Glenn Close) bonds with her daughter (Dakota Fanning) as they visit a cemetery. A divorcée (Amy Brenneman) is unexpectedly drawn to her ex-husband as his second wife is about to be buried.

Robin Wright Penn plays a woman who reconnects with an old boyfriend while wheeling a shopping cart around a supermarket. Elpidia Carrillo plays a convict in prison who is on edge as she awaits a visit from her daughter. Holly Hunter has an embarrassing fight with her boyfriend while they're visiting friends. Lisa Gay Hamilton plays a woman scarred by sexual abuse who seeks a kind of sanctuary in the backyard where she grew up.

Some of these stories dovetail but there is no attempt to tie them all together. García's writing is too graceful to succumb to such a contrivance; he is focused on his characters and the tiny details that create drama in an everyday world.

He also has a great gift for casting, and obviously some of the best actresses in the business want to work with him. They all give uncommonly fine performances and bring out the best in their male costars (Ian McShane, Jason Isaacs, Aidan Quinn, Joe Mantegna, William Fichtner, Stephen Dillane).

With a cast like that and the quality of writing on display, *Nine Lives* should already be well known to movie lovers. Perhaps García's success as the creator, executive producer, frequent writer, and director of the acclaimed cable TV series *In Treatment* will pique some people's interest in seeing this excellent film.

97. NOTHING BUT THE TRUTH

(2008)

Directed by Rod Lurie

Screenplay by Rod Lurie

Actors:

KATE BECKINSALE

MATT DILLON

VERA FARMIGA

EDIE FALCO

ALAN ALDA

DAVID SCHWIMMER

NOAH WYLE

ANGELA BASSETT

COURTNEY B. VANCE

PETER COYOTE

JAMEY SHERIDAN

FLOYD ABRAMS

PRESTON BAILEY

JULIE ANN EMERY

MICHAEL O'NEILL

KRISTEN SHAW

KRISTEN BOUGH

ROBERT HARVEY

ANGELICA TORN

ROD LURIE

Writer-director Rod Lurie is fascinated by the worlds of journalism and politics, as evidenced by such films as *The Contender, Resurrecting the Champ,* and the short-lived television series *Commander in Chief,* which featured Geena Davis as the first female president of the United States. He managed to combine his interests in *Nothing But the Truth,* a hard-hitting film that takes its inspiration from real-life events but puts its own spin on them.

Kate Beckinsale gives an exceptional performance as a Washington, D.C., newspaper reporter who pursues a story that shows the U.S. government has acted improperly in creating an international incident. In the process she reveals that a fellow mom at her daughter's school (Vera Farmiga) is in fact an operative for the CIA. Beckinsale runs with the volatile story but pays a heavy price for her exclusive: government special prosecutor Matt Dillon sees that she's thrown in prison for refusing to reveal her source.

Beckinsale's editor (Angela Bassett) and the newspaper's lawyer (Alan Alda) do everything they can, but the prison term drags on for days, then weeks, then months. Meanwhile her apolitical husband (David Schwimmer) tries to understand how she can make their young son suffer a wrenching emotional separation for the sake of a principle.

We, too, have cause to wonder if the reporter's decision is the right one as the drama unfolds. Filmmaker Lurie shows us both sides of the story before landing a wallop with his final revelation.

Obviously, Lurie based his screenplay on the real-life story of *New York Times* reporter Judith Miller and former spy Valerie Plame, but this film isn't just a camouflage of the facts. It has its own story to tell, and it does so with intelligence and verisimilitude. The cast couldn't be better; Beckinsale hasn't had a role this good in years, and once again Vera Farmiga deserves "most valuable player" consideration.

This is the kind of movie that is bound to stimulate discussion and debate, as it did when my wife and I first saw it. What's more, we found that it had staying power . . . yet what lingered in our minds wasn't the issue of journalistic ethics but the choices Beckinsale's character made as a mother and a wife. Any movie that has you thinking and talking about it afterward is easy to recommend.

If you're wondering why you're not familiar with this film, given its provocative subject matter and high-profile cast, it met the same fate as Brian Goodman's *What Doesn't Kill You* (which Rod Lurie coproduced) in December 2008. It played just one week in theaters before its distributor went out of business. These worthy films never had a chance; if not for DVD they might have vanished altogether.

98. OCTOBER SKY

(1999)

Directed by Joe Johnston

Screenplay by Lewis Colick

Based on the book *Rocket Boys* by Homer H. Hickam Jr.

Actors:

JAKE GYLLENHAAL

CHRIS COOPER

LAURA DERN

CHRIS OWEN

WILLIAM LEE SCOTT

CHAD LINDBERG

NATALIE CANERDAY

SCOTT MILES

CHRIS ELLIS

If there's anything that can hurt a movie nowadays it's the perception that it's "nice" or "sweet." Those words, which once were considered compliments, are now seen as a liability by Hollywood, which believes that young audiences will reject anything that doesn't have edginess, or at least attitude.

They're not entirely wrong. Having taught at USC for more than a decade, I've gauged my students' response to movies old and new; they readily embrace cynicism but have a harder time when a film is openly emotional or free of irony. I have also learned that many of them don't actually approach life with such a hardened attitude—but peer pressure makes them think they should. If I show them a film that's nice or sweet and I prepare them for it by giving them permission to drop their defenses, they often respond with enthusiasm.

I can't imagine anyone, young or old, who wouldn't respond to *October Sky,* yet it was considered a long shot in the commercial marketplace because it's about teenagers who *aren't* cynical. Lewis Colick's screenplay is based on the autobiography of Homer Hickam Jr., whose life changed when he saw the Soviet satellite *Sputnik* in the evening sky one night in 1957. Although he was a poor math and science student, he was genuinely inspired by *Sputnik* and became passionate about rocketry. He banded together with three smart classmates and soon they were building their own backyard rockets.

What gives this real-life story depth and dimension is the surrounding story. The film takes place in Coalwood, West Virginia, where coal is the only business and the local mine is every young man's destination. Homer (well played by Jake Gyllenhaal, just on the verge of stardom) is the son of a mine foreman (Chris Cooper) who fully expects his son to follow in his footsteps and has no patience for his often-foolhardy experiments. The father could have been played as an out-and-out villain, but the script, and Cooper's fine performance, make clear that he's just a stubborn man whose job pressures leave him no room for softheartedness.

Even the encouraging schoolteacher, nicely played by

Laura Dern, is defying her principal by urging Homer and his friends to aim high—and escape the dead-end destiny of their classmates.

What could have emerged as a series of platitudes remains grounded by Colick's script and Joe Johnston's sensitive direction. But the real lynchpin of this movie is Gyllenhaal's unabashed—and infectious—enthusiasm as the boy who refuses to abandon his dream.

Best of all, under the closing credits of *October Sky* we see vintage home-movie footage of the real-life Homer Hickam Jr. and friends as they conduct their rocketry experiments. Cynics please note: Hickam realized his dream and spent his life working for NASA. The reason this heartfelt movie works so well is that it isn't espousing a hollow sentiment. Hollywood couldn't have invented a happier ending.

99. OFF THE MAP

(2004)

Directed by Campbell Scott

Screenplay by Joan Ackermann

Based on the play by Joan Ackermann

Actors:

JOAN ALLEN

SAM ELLIOTT

VALENTINA DE ANGELIS

J. K. SIMMONS

JIM TRUE-FROST

AMY BRENNEMAN

Had the filmmakers known that the name of their film would prove ironic—not only describing its characters but the fate of the film itself—they might have sought another title. Nevertheless this absorbing drama gives first-rate actors roles they can sink their teeth into.

The location plays a crucial role in that story, just as it apparently did in the production of the film. New Mexico has mystical qualities that can't be explained, only experienced, and the movie goes a long way toward capturing that feeling.

Amy Brenneman appears in a framing scene before the story proper gets under way and we learn that she is the central character, now grown up. At the age of eleven, Bo Groden (wonderfully brought to life by Valentina de Angelis) is mature beyond her years because she has had to take on adult thoughts and responsibilities, given that her father (Sam Elliott) is paralyzed by depression and her mother (Joan Allen) has her hands full trying to keep the family together—and fed.

They live so far "off the map" that the Internal Revenue Service has never explored their curious income tax filings until now. A buttoned-down IRS agent (Jim True-Frost) shows up one day, parched by the sun, but instead of carrying out his assignment he becomes part of their extended family. Another perpetual presence in their lives is an old friend of Elliott's (played by that indispensable character actor J. K. Simmons) who survives on a monthly veterans' pension and a regular dose of antidepressants. His dry sense of humor fills in a lot of conversational gaps and gives young Bo someone to relate to.

This could be the basis for a short story or sketch, but

it makes sense as a feature-length film because writer Joan Ackerman has created such fully developed, if quixotic, characters.

Only a mature, sensitive director could strike the right note with such material, and Campbell Scott does just that. (Better known for his work as an actor, he also codirected the much-loved movie *Big Night* starring Stanley Tucci and Tony Shalhoub.) He fully captures the environment as well as the people in it, and that is no small feat. *Off the Map* is a sleeper well worth discovering.

100. ONCE WERE WARRIORS

(1994)

Directed by Lee Tamahori

Screenplay by Riwia Brown

Based on the novel by Alan Duff

Actors:

RENA OWEN

TEMUERA MORRISON

MAMAENGAROA KERR-BELL

JULIAN (SONNY) ARAHANGA

TAUNGAROA EMILE

CLIFFORD CURTIS

RACHAEL MORRIS

PETE SMITH

I can't think of many movies that have affected me as *Once Were Warriors* did when I first saw it. The characters' emotions are so naked, so raw that they cut like a knife—and their physicality is genuinely frightening at times. I can't recommend the film as lighthearted entertainment, but I can promise you an experience you will never forget.

Long before Peter Jackson made a name for himself and reinvigorated his country's film industry, a handful of New Zealanders made their mark on the world stage. Riwia Brown adapted the novel by Alan Duff which hit home with readers in his homeland. Successful TV (and television commercials) director Lee Tamahori chose it as his first foray into feature films, and while he's had a major-league career ever since, making Hollywood movies (*Mulholland Falls, Die Another Day, xXx: State of the Union*), this remains his finest work to date. Perhaps it isn't incidental that his father is Maori.

Once Were Warriors offers a portrait of a wildly dysfunctional Maori family living in suburban Auckland. While on the surface the husband and wife seem to have assimilated into mainstream society, their heritage weighs heavily on them. They were expelled from their tribe years ago when Beth (Rena Owen) forsook her noble bloodline by marrying Jake (Temuera Morrison). The only question, eighteen years and five children later, is why she stays with him: he thinks nothing of holding a nonstop party in their home, and when he's roaring drunk he beats his wife without mercy. Yet we also see that the two of them enjoy partying—when they're both liquored up—and making love.

The children have problems of their own and their own ways of coping. The oldest boy has joined a gang, while the oldest girl has moved in with her boyfriend, who lives in an abandoned car.

It's difficult to put into words why this film is so powerful, or why in spite of its grim nature it's a must-see. The answer lies in its brutal honesty, showing how even the moodiest people can experience good times—and then turn on a dime, especially when alcohol is involved. Its other shining virtue is its extraordinary performances, by Owen and Morrison. They are so overpoweringly great it seems unjust that they haven't been celebrated ever since the picture's release and rewarded with other roles worthy of their talent. (They've both continued to work, mostly in New Zealand, but ironically, their latter-day fame has come from associations with *Star Wars*: Morrison played Jango Fett in *Episode II* and Commander Cody in *Episode III* of the George Lucas saga and has voiced other characters in subsequent animated films. Owen played Nee Alavar in *Episode II* and has lent her voice to other animated *Star Wars* films.)

Once Were Warriors is a shattering drama: once seen, never forgotten.

101. ONE FINE DAY

(1996)

Directed by Michael Hoffman

Screenplay by Terrel Seltzer and Ellen Simon

Actors:

MICHELLE PFEIFFER

GEORGE CLOONEY

MAE WHITMAN

ALEX D. LINZ

CHARLES DURNING

JON ROBIN BAITZ

ELLEN GREENE

JOE GRIFASI

PETE HAMILL

ANNA MARIA HORSFORD

SHEILA KELLEY

ROBERT KLEIN

AMANDA PEET

BITTY SCHRAM

HOLLAND TAYLOR

RACHEL YORK

BARRY KIVEL

GEORGE MARTIN

MICHAEL MASSEE

The movie industry is sometimes accused of being out of touch with its audience in the heartland. I don't think you have to go to Middle America to find that disconnect; in fact, I think many people in Hollywood itself have an identity crisis. They act hard-boiled and cynical because letting down their guard would be unwise . . . and I think they've transmitted those feelings to much of their audience. TV shows and movies encourage us to be cool, but underneath the facade many people adopt, I think we're just as vulnerable as we ever were and, as hit movies prove again and again, we long for a happy ending.

In spite of having two major stars in its cast, *One Fine Day* never found its audience because moviegoers perceived it to be too sweet, and parents didn't latch on to the fact that it's a perfect film to share with their family.

In fact, this chaste romantic comedy is about bringing two fragmented families together.

George Clooney plays a brash, divorced New York City newspaper columnist who's been saddled—at the last minute—with the responsibility of taking his five-year-old daughter Maggie (an adorable Mae Whitman) to school. Through a series of mix-ups with a schoolmate (Alex D. Linz) and her mom, a divorced architect played by Michelle Pfeiffer, the kids miss going on a field trip, and the already-bickering grown-ups are stuck taking care of them on a particularly hectic day in their careers.

The clever script sets up a believably antagonistic relationship between cocky Clooney and hardheaded Pfeiffer from the moment they meet, and fills the fast-moving story with enough detail over the course of the day that we don't have a chance to dwell on why they can't get along. By the time they finally have a chance to breathe, late in the day, and begin to soften, it's persuasive and fun to watch.

All along, the two kids act just like real kids, and when, near the end of the film, they actually root for their parents to get together, it's wonderfully endearing.

One couldn't hope to find a more attractive couple than Clooney and Pfeiffer, who play off each other with the kind of panache we usually associate with films of the 1940s. This was just Clooney's second starring vehicle after his career kicked into high gear on television's *E.R.,* and he shows what star quality is all about. Pfeiffer, who also produced the movie, has never been more likable.

One Fine Day is overdue for recognition as a romantic comedy that hits the bull's-eye.

102. OWNING MAHOWNY

(2003)

Directed by Richard Kwietniowski

Screenplay by Maurice Chauvet

Based on the book *Stung* by Gary Ross

Actors:

PHILIP SEYMOUR HOFFMAN

MINNIE DRIVER

MAURY CHAYKIN

JOHN HURT

SONJA SMITS

IAN TRACEY

ROGER DUNN

JASON BLICKER

CHRIS COLLINS

Theatergoers and avid movie buffs didn't need the Academy of Motion Picture Arts and Sciences to tell them that Philip Seymour Hoffman is a great actor, but I suppose winning an Oscar (for his brilliant portrayal of author Truman Capote in *Capote*) makes it official. A true man of the theater, Hoffman doesn't shun or disdain movies in any way, but stardom doesn't interest him: good parts do, whether they're in mainstream fare like *Mission: Impossible III* or daringly offbeat projects like *Synecdoche, New York*.

One of my favorite Hoffman performances flew under the radar in 2003. In *Owning Mahowny* he plays a nerdy assistant bank manager in Toronto who manipulates bank funds to fuel his gambling addiction. He is so methodical—and so understated—that no one suspects what's going on, including his boss, his colleagues, and even his girlfriend

(Minnie Driver). He is perpetually in debt to his bookie (Maury Chaykin) but can't stop himself; all he can do is raise the stakes, to increase the sense of danger. When he's done all he can, betting on the horses and major-league baseball teams, he moves to the next level and schedules secret weekend trips to Atlantic City—juggling the bank's books as he goes.

Mahowny is an invisible man to most people—even his car is nondescript—but there is one man who is keenly interested in him: a wily casino manager, superbly played by John Hurt (who starred in director Richard Kwietniowski's earlier film, *Love and Death on Long Island*). It's his job to "read" the people who frequent his establishment, but Mahowny proves to be something of a riddle. He gambles like a high roller but doesn't act like one. Nothing can deter or distract him from his single-minded purpose—not even a hooker who is sent to his room gratis. For a time the film becomes a battle of wits between the gambler and the manager, albeit an oblique one because it isn't waged out in the open.

The suspense in *Owning Mahowny* doesn't derive from wondering if the protagonist will be caught, but how and when . . . and how he will react when his house of cards collapses. If you happened to read journalist Gary Ross's nonfiction book *Stung,* about the real-life 1982 case that inspired the film, you may already know the answers, but I don't think being familiar with the facts could remove the drama from this expertly made movie.

There are other good films about gamblers and the nature of their addiction, but they usually deal with highs and lows. This one focuses on a guy who keeps his emotions completely bottled up, even to his supposed fiancée. (The most revealing moment in the film is a conversation he has with a psychiatrist in which he quantifies the excitement he feels when he is gambling.) Only an actor of extraordinary ability and range could play a man like this, and maintain our interest in him. That man is Philip Seymour Hoffman.

103. THE PAINTED VEIL

(2006)

Directed by John Curran

Screenplay by Ron Nyswaner

Based on the novel by W. Somerset Maugham

Actors:

EDWARD NORTON

NAOMI WATTS

LIEV SCHREIBER

DIANA RIGG

TOBY JONES

ANTHONY WONG

SALLY HAWKINS

When I read that someone was making a new screen adaptation of W. Somerset Maugham's 1925 novel *The Painted Veil,* I couldn't help asking myself why. It was filmed before with Greta Garbo, back in 1934, and it's not one of her most memorable films. MGM remade it as *The Seventh Sin* in 1957 with Eleanor Parker and that didn't make a big impression either. But I didn't reckon with the determination of actor Edward Norton, who fell in love with the book as a young man and spent years trying to get this movie made. He even persuaded Naomi Watts to costar with him and coproduce the picture. Once I saw it I understood what Norton had in mind all this time. It's a beautiful and moving story.

The movie begins in London. Norton plays an utterly unglamorous bacteriologist who falls in love with Watts on sight and impulsively asks her to marry him. She says yes, mostly in order to get away from her overbearing mother. But when they move to Shanghai, she has an affair with a married man from the British consulate (Liev Schreiber). Feeling both betrayed and emasculated, Norton decides to punish her by volunteering to help with an outbreak of cholera in a remote part of China and insisting that she come along. How she deals with the experience, and comes to appreciate her husband, is the core of the story.

Edward Norton is not the kind of actor who shows up for work and reads his lines. He insists on getting involved in the writing process, as he did here with Ron Nyswaner, expanding Maugham's story and exploring how a relationship as badly broken as this one can be mended, and even prevail. That emotional journey is what makes the movie so compelling.

The Painted Veil is also literally beautiful, shot on location in China (by Stuart Drysburgh) and filled with extraordinary sights that frame the story. Alexandre Desplat's exquisite score perfectly supports the emotions on screen, and the well-matched stars are surrounded by other good actors like Liev Schreiber (who found in Watts a real-life mate); Diana Rigg, as a mother superior; and the remarkable Toby Jones, who plays a cynical British functionary stationed in the Chinese outback. (It's the kind of part

George Sanders used to play so often—and did, in the 1957 version of the story.)

I approached this movie with great skepticism and came out a believer. It's rare to see a love story that has real substance, as this one does. *The Painted Veil* defies the glib category "period piece" by virtue of a sincere presentation that makes it immediate and relevant.

104. PARADISE NOW

(2005)

Directed by Hany Abu-Assad

Screenplay by Hany Abu-Assad and Bero Beyer

Actors:

KAIS NASHEF

ALI SULIMAN

LUBNA AZABAL

AMER HLEHEL

HIAM ABBASS

ASHRAF BARHOUM

One of the most enjoyable aspects of attending a film festival is being touted on which movies to see by friends, colleagues, and perfect strangers you chance to meet. At the Telluride Film Festival in 2005, my wife and I read the description of *Paradise Now* and decided it sounded too grim. Then a friend we trust took us aside and said, "You simply must see it." My wife said, "I'm Jewish, and this was made by a Palestinian director. Is it just going to upset me?" He said, "No. Give it a try." We did, and two hours later we were proselytizing to our friends to see it, too.

Paradise Now went on to earn an Oscar nomination as Best Foreign Language Film, and won an Independent Spirit Award, but people didn't go out to see it. I understand: it's a story about two suicide bombers, and that isn't exactly inviting. But the old truism about not judging a book by its cover definitely applies in this case.

Palestinian filmmaker Hany Abu-Assad isn't a propagandist; he's a humanist who tells a moving story of two young men who think they're doing the right thing, until fate forces them to think again. As the clock runs down, the tension grows in this expertly crafted drama.

The story begins in the West Bank of Palestine, where two lifelong friends, Said and Khaled, are persuaded by a dedicated group of extremists to volunteer to make a suicide run to Tel-Aviv. For their own safety and the well-being of the mission, they cannot know when it will take place until the last minute. Then, one day, they receive the word: it is time to prepare. They are shaved and outfitted with black suits, the better to pass themselves off as Jewish settlers on their way to a wedding. They videotape messages of martyrdom. They say good-bye to family and friends without actually saying good-bye. Then rounds of high explosives are taped to their bodies.

But as they make their way across the border something goes wrong and they are separated. What will happen now? Can the mission be saved? And what happens if they have second thoughts?

A great movie can engage and entertain you while making you think, and that's what Abu-Assad achieves in this remarkable movie, which he wrote with Bero Beyer. They create nail-biting suspense by setting their plot in a specific time frame, with the clock (almost literally) ticking, but they still take the time to flesh out their characters and give them three dimensions, even a sense of humor.

What struck me most about the movie is its sure-footed storytelling. What's more, when I spoke to Abu-Asad in Telluride he told me that he was tired of seeing low-budget films made on digital video with jerky, handheld camera work, so he set out to make a contemporary film in a traditional way. The camera work is solid and traditional, and the results are exemplary. *Paradise Now* is a great movie that will stay with me for many years to come.

105. PETER'S FRIENDS

(1992)

Directed by Kenneth Branagh

Screenplay by Rita Rudner and Martin Bergman

Actors:

KENNETH BRANAGH

EMMA THOMPSON

RITA RUDNER

STEPHEN FRY

HUGH LAURIE

IMELDA STAUNTON

ALPHONSIA EMMANUEL

TONY SLATTERY

ALEX LOWE

RICHARD BRIERS

PHYLLIDA LAW

There's something about the concept of a reunion that automatically triggers a series of emotions in all of us. We have wistful thoughts of what might have been, the road not taken, lost love, and so on. No wonder filmmakers love this premise: it's foolproof.

Some critics complained that *Peter's Friends* bore a strong resemblance to *The Big Chill,* especially with the use of pop music on the sound track, but then, that popular film played very much like John Sayles's debut feature *Return of the Secaucus Seven.* No one has a patent on the idea; it's what you do with it that counts.

The screenplay for *Peter's Friends* was written by that clever stand-up comedienne, Rita Rudner, and her husband, Martin Bergman. Even if you don't think their movie ranks as great cinema, you'll have to admit the one-liners are very, very funny.

Rudner also plays one of the leading characters in the ensemble. The setting is an English country manor, where Peter (Stephen Fry) has invited his college pals and their significant others for a weekend reunion after ten years' time. He has recently inherited the manor house and revels in playing host to his friends. They are a theatrical lot and their individual personalities don't take long to identify.

Emma Thompson, for instance, is a lonely woman with low self-esteem who has put snapshots of herself around her home so the cat won't be upset during her absence. Hugh Laurie and Imelda Staunton have lost a child, so they are paranoid about their new baby's well-being at every waking moment. Alphonsia Emmanuel plays a woman with a huge (and indiscriminate) sexual appetite, and Tony Slattery plays a married man who is her latest lover. Kenneth Branagh (who also directed the film) plays a sharp-tongued writer who once dreamed of greatness but settled for success in television. And Rita Rudner plays his wife, a pampered Hollywood TV star who isn't used to deprivation—like not having a television set.

Although the general tone of the movie is light, there is a serious undercurrent, as all the characters deal with mortality, some more directly than others. (One aspect of the story threatens to make the film a period piece, but certainly bespeaks a major concern of its time.)

It's also interesting to look back at the movie's leading players at this point in their lives. Branagh had come onto the world stage just three years earlier with his stunning *Henry V,* while his then-wife Emma Thompson was still a budding star (except in the UK, where she had already headlined her own popular TV show). That's her mother, Phyllida Law, playing the straight-faced housekeeper.

Stephen Fry and Hugh Laurie were making names for themselves, primarily on television, where they were starring in the delightful series *Jeeves and Wooster.* Their sketch show, *A Bit of Fry and Laurie,* and other successes would follow. Imelda Staunton was busy building her reputation on stage, screen, and television, soon to become one of England's leading actresses (and, in 2005, an Oscar nominee for *Vera Drake*).

Rita Rudner never had the screenwriting career this film seemed to promise. She and Bergman wrote another ensemble piece, *A Weekend in the Country,* which he directed, but it didn't get the same attention as *Peter's Friends.* She has continued performing and is a fixture in Las Vegas. (She's also penned some very funny books, including two novels.) Perhaps someday, if we're lucky, she'll write another movie.

106. PHOEBE IN WONDERLAND

(2008)

Directed by Daniel Barnz

Screenplay by Daniel Barnz

Actors:

ELLE FANNING

FELICITY HUFFMAN

PATRICIA CLARKSON

BILL PULLMAN

CAMPBELL SCOTT

IAN COLLETTI

PETER GERETY

MADDIE CORMAN

MACKENZIE MILONE

AUSTIN WILLIAMS

TEALA DUNN

BAILEE MADISON

MAX BAKER

MADHUR JAFFREY

For some filmmakers, a screening at the Sundance Film Festival is a prize in itself. For others, it opens the door and offers promise but doesn't guarantee success. First-time director (and writer) Daniel Barnz was nominated for the Grand Jury Prize in 2008 for *Phoebe in Wonderland,* but struggled to find a distributor for the movie, which received only a desultory release in theaters before going to DVD.

The movie has its flaws, but it offers a rich, emotional experience and exceptional performances. A film that good shouldn't go begging for an audience.

Nine-year-old Elle Fanning plays the title role. Phoebe

is an unusual child by any standards, smart beyond her years yet often combative with her sister and even her schoolmates. Her mother (Felicity Huffman) worries that she isn't doing a good enough job of juggling parenthood and her work on a thesis about Lewis Carroll's *Alice in Wonderland*. Her husband (Bill Pullman) thinks she stresses out too much. Meanwhile, Phoebe retreats into the world of her imagination.

Then a flamboyant new drama teacher (Patricia Clarkson) encourages Phoebe to channel her imagination into a performance as Alice in the school play, and for the first time, the little girl feels at peace. But her victory is a fragile one, because the tiniest thing can rattle her and shake her entire world.

I won't reveal more details of the story or the nature of the young protagonist. Suffice it to say that it's a highly complex, multilayered character, and Fanning manages to convey all of her nuances. A key scene with her mother is emotionally draining, and brutally honest; I don't know when I've seen another moment quite like it on-screen. Christophe Beck's delicate score supports and highlights the many subtle changes of mood that punctuate the story.

A week after its debut at Sundance, Daniel Barnz brought his film to my class at USC. I was worried that it might turn off my students, who aren't used to dealing with such raw emotions, but they embraced the picture as I did, even with its shortcomings. (Some of the storytelling is choppy, and a dorky school principal, played for comedy by the talented Campbell Scott, seems oddly out of place.) I, for one, would rather see an imperfect movie with great moments and memorable performances than a film that's consistent, or slick, but mediocre.

Barnz also confided how he, an utter novice, got Felicity Huffman to appear in his film: he learned that she lived in his neighborhood, knocked on her door, and asked if she'd be willing to read the script. She did, and told him how much she loved it, but said she'd understand that in the process of financing he might want somebody more bankable. Two weeks later she was cast in *Desperate Housewives* and *Transamerica,* for which she got an Oscar nomination. Suddenly, having her attached to *Phoebe* had real significance.

107. THE PLEDGE

(2001)

Directed by Sean Penn

Screenplay by Jerzy Kromolowski

and Mary Olson-Kromolowski

Based on the novel by Friedrich Dürrenmatt

Actors:

JACK NICHOLSON

ROBIN WRIGHT PENN

BENICIO DEL TORO

VANESSA REDGRAVE

TOM NOONAN

PATRICIA CLARKSON

MICHAEL O'KEEFE

AARON ECKHART

COSTAS MANDYLOR

HELEN MIRREN

MICKEY ROURKE

SAM SHEPARD

LOIS SMITH

HARRY DEAN STANTON
PAULINE ROBERTS
EILEEN RYAN

Any filmmaker who fails to tie up the loose ends of his story in a neat little package risks alienating his audience. Sean Penn takes that chance in *The Pledge* and still provides powerful, provocative entertainment, thanks to a fascinating narrative and an exceptional cast. Still, I suppose it's understandable why the movie never caught on in spite of its marquee names.

Penn is drawn to dark and difficult material, as he indicated with his first directorial efforts, *The Indian Runner* and *The Crossing Guard,* as well as his most celebrated work, *Into the Wild. The Pledge* remains a particular favorite of mine because it tells such a compelling story and provides Jack Nicholson with one of his richest and most demanding parts.

The movie opens as Nevada police detective Nicholson is celebrating his retirement with friends and colleagues . . . but the partying is cut short when a report comes in about the rape and murder of a young girl nearby. Although his cronies remind him that he's off the hook, Nicholson insists on checking out the brutal crime, and when the girl's distraught parents turn to him for assurance that he will track down the rapist/killer he gives them his word.

Although officially retired he cannot pry himself away from this puzzling case—and refuses to abandon the pledge he made to those parents. The local cops are convinced that a Native American man they've arrested is the culprit. Nicholson believes they're wrong, and thinks they're settling for a convenient solution to the crime.

In time his sniffing leads him to another part of the state where he decides to settle in, purchasing a gas station and convenience store. Here he starts a new life and develops a relationship with a waitress (Robin Wright Penn) and her daughter. But the case is never far from his mind.

The Pledge takes its time (not unlike its protagonist), allows us to drink in the snowy atmosphere of its setting, and introduces us to a vast array of characters played by such notable actors as Helen Mirren, Benicio Del Toro, Vanessa Redgrave, Mickey Rourke, Aaron Eckhart, Patricia Clarkson, Sam Shepard, Lois Smith, Tom Noonan, and Penn's mother, Eileen Ryan.

What it doesn't do is offer stock characters or easy answers to its riddling central mystery. Jerzy Kromolowski and Mary Olson-Kromolowski adapted their screenplay from the novel by noted Swiss author Friedrich Dürrenmatt. It's been filmed several times before, in Germany (as *In Broad Daylight,* in 1958 and as a 1997 TV movie), and in England (as *The Cold Light of Day,* in 1995), but its European sensibilities never attracted an American filmmaker until Sean Penn came along. *The Pledge* is the kind of movie that stays with you, precisely because it poses as many questions as it answers—and because Jack Nicholson makes such a lasting impression.

108. PRICELESS

(2006)

Directed by Pierre Salvadori
Screenplay by Benoît Graffin

Actors:

AUDREY TAUTOU

GAD ELMALEH

MARIE-CHRISTINE ADAM

VERNON DOBTCHEFF

JACQUES SPIESSER

At one time Hollywood turned out romantic comedies by the carload and made it seem effortless. Box-office figures show that audiences still crave this form of entertainment but most recent examples of the genre, with such attractive stars as Sandra Bullock, Hugh Grant, Kate Hudson, and Matthew McConaughey, are a sorry lot indeed. It's enough to turn any critic into the oldest of fogies, complaining that "they don't make 'em like they used to." And it's true.

In most romantic comedies the setup is fairly clear: we know the man and woman are going to get together at the end. The question is how, and the challenge facing the filmmaker is hiding the various story contrivances underneath a veneer of engaging byplay and action. Think of Cary Grant and Irene Dunne in *The Awful Truth,* or Jean Arthur and Joel McCrea in *The More the Merrier.* They made it look so easy.

One of the best examples of this genre I've seen in a long time has all the attributes of a great Hollywood movie— but it was made in France. If I were to cite one quality that sets it apart from most of its homegrown competition, it's conviction. The actors seem to believe in the characters they're playing, and as a result, so do we.

The actors in this case are unusually skilled. This marks the first time Audrey Tautou has had a chance to play comedy—let alone a glamorous character—since her career breakthrough in the title role of *Amélie*. Gad Emaleh, on the other hand, is a French favorite in comedy films, only one of which, Francis Veber's *The Valet*, has made any impression in the United States.

Director Pierre Salvadori, who cowrote the film with Benoit Graffin, understands that the best comedy seems genuine, not artificial. We're introduced to Emaleh as a hardworking staff member at an elegant resort hotel on the Riviera. He'll do anything for a guest, without complaint. Late that night, he's helping to straighten out the cocktail bar, wearing dress clothes instead of a servant's uniform. Tautou, who's sleeping with an older man in a room upstairs, slips away and goes to the bar, where she mistakes Emaleh for a fellow guest—and winds up sleeping with him in a vacant guest room! When she learns the truth she is positively horrified; you see, she's a full-time golddigger, and has no use for a working stiff who can't support the expensive lifestyle to which she's grown accustomed. At the same time, her sugar daddy kicks her out.

This all occurs in the opening moments of the film; what happens next is as delightful as it is unpredictable. Emaleh is smitten with Tautou and is determined to win her, but she cannot—will not—allow sentiment or feelings to interfere with her "career." How the lowly servant gets the upper hand in the situation is great fun to watch.

Salvadori also knows that he is taking us in the audience

on a wish-fulfillment tour of how the other half lives, so *Priceless* gives us a generous slice of the good life that wealthy people enjoy in the south of France, in its shops, restaurants, and hotels.

Hollywood could learn a lot from a movie like *Priceless*. They haven't fared terribly well transforming European hits into American remakes, but they might take some lessons in the art of crafting a superior romantic comedy.

109. PRISONER OF PARADISE
(2003)

Directed by Malcolm Clarke and Stuart Sender
Narrated by Ian Holm

More people than ever are seeking out documentary films, finding their brand of truth-is-stranger-than-fiction more stimulating than many Hollywood concoctions. If a producer were to dramatize the life of Kurt Gerron, the subject of Malcolm Clarke and Stuart Sender's *Prisoner of Paradise,* he might be accused of exaggeration, yet this jaw-dropping story is absolutely true.

How did a man who was once among the most popular actors in Germany not only wind up in a concentration camp—but find himself being ordered to direct a propaganda movie that would show the world a whitewashed vision of life inside its walls? Those are just the extremes of Kurt Gerron's life story; the rest of it is just as interesting.

Gerron was a star of cabaret and theater during the Weimar years who extended his fame by appearing on-screen in a series of prominent character roles. You may have seen him in such enduring films as Josef von Stern-berg's *The Blue Angel* and G. W. Pabst's *Diary of a Lost Girl.* He eventually moved behind the camera and directed a string of successful movies with such leading actors as Dolly Haas, Peter Lorre, Willy Fritsch, Magda Schneider, Luise Rainer, and Hans Albers.

He led a full, rich life and enjoyed the fruits of his labors. But he also ignored the warnings of friends that as a Jew he was no longer safe in Germany. While others fled to London, Paris, and the United States, he couldn't bear to leave: life was too good to walk away. Then it was too late.

Clarke and Sender chose to make their film at just the right time, when a handful of Gerron's friends and cowork-ers were still alive. Hearing their vivid firsthand accounts of Berlin in the late 1920s and early 1930s, the intoxicating world of cabaret, the rise of Hitler, and the reality of life at Theresienstadt—the "showplace" of concentration camps—makes all the difference in the world. The filmmakers even found home movies of Gerron enjoying his weekend estate in the country with friends from the world of show business.

Ian Holm narrates *Prisoner of Paradise,* a chilling docu-mentary I don't think I'll ever forget.

110. THE PRIZE WINNER OF DEFIANCE, OHIO

(2005)

Directed by Jane Anderson

Screenplay by Jane Anderson

Based on the memoir by Terry Ryan

Actors:

JULIANNE MOORE

WOODY HARRELSON

LAURA DERN

TREVOR MORGAN

ELLARY PORTERFIELD

SIMON REYNOLDS

NORA DUNN

Iake a well-received book, select the ideal woman to write and direct its screen adaptation, and choose two perfect stars (Julianne Moore and Woody Harrelson) to head the cast. The result ought to be at least modestly successful, but *The Prize Winner of Defiance, Ohio,* failed miserably at the box office—in part because its studio promoted it as a nostalgic comedy, which it isn't, and audiences didn't fall for the ruse.

What it *is* is infinitely more interesting than a retread of an *Ozzie & Harriet* episode: the true story of a woman who managed to raise ten children during the 1950s, in spite of a ne'er-do-well husband, by using her wits to enter jingle contests and winning a constant stream of prizes and cash.

If, like me, you're old enough to remember those twenty-five-words-or-less contests, you'll enjoy reliving the period when sponsors demanded more of a contestant than mere luck in a random drawing. Back then companies asked ordinary people to send in slogans, endorsements, and rhymes, and smart women like Evelyn Ryan (who gave up her ambition to become a journalist) sustained their families this way. That's the amazing saga that Evelyn's daughter Terry Ryan chronicled in her book.

But there are other facets to the story. The first involves Evelyn's alcoholic, self-destructive husband, a charmer (at times) whose male pride affects every aspect of the family's existence and leads to some heartbreaking scenes.

He is not the only man whose vanity and condescending attitude toward women—especially housewives—affects the leading character. Writer-director Jane Anderson doesn't need to exaggerate the situation because anyone of a certain age can confirm these facts of American life in the 1950s (and beyond).

What keeps *The Prize Winner of Defiance, Ohio,* on track is the indomitable spirit of Evelyn Ryan, played to perfection by Julianne Moore. She knows her place and doesn't try to buck the system; instead she works within it, enduring every hardship and setback for the sake of her ten loving children. Nor is she a plaster saint: she suffers mightily but can't afford to drown herself in tears because life in the Ryan household must go on.

With Edward T. McAvoy's impeccable production design, Jonathan Freeman's cinematography, and Hala Bahmet's costume design in perfect harmony, filmmaker Anderson transports us to another time and place— occasionally breaking the fourth wall to comment on some of the absurdities of the baby-boom era.

The Prize Winner of Defiance, Ohio, will serve as a revelation to younger viewers and a time trip for those who lived through the period. It vividly illustrates how unfair some things were (within my lifetime) and how far we've come. Most of all it provides engaging and thoughtful entertainment about real people who are worth getting to know.

111. QUEEN OF HEARTS

(1989)

Directed by Jon Amiel

Screenplay by Tony Grisoni

Actors:

VITTORIO DUSE

JOSEPH LONG

ANITA ZAGARIA

EILEEN WAY

VITTORIO AMANDOLA

IAN HAWKES

TAT WHALLEY

One day in 1999, on assignment from *Entertainment Tonight,* I went to Grauman's Chinese Theater on Hollywood Boulevard to cover the hand-and-footprint ceremony for Sean Connery. The event was also a promotion for his newest film, *Entrapment,* so his costar Catherine Zeta-Jones was there along with their director, Jon Amiel. At a quiet moment I approached the filmmaker to tell him that his BBC miniseries *The Singing Detective* was the greatest show I'd ever seen on television, and that I was also an enormous fan of his first feature film, *Queen of Hearts.* He thanked me and said with a smile, "You know, sometimes I think if those are the only two credits I have on my headstone I won't have done too badly."

Queen of Hearts is too fundamentally offbeat to have won over a mass, mainstream audience, but it does have fervent admirers, and I am one of them. Everyone I know who *has* seen it seems to feel the same way.

I've tried to imagine how the concept was pitched to the BBC, but I can't. Tony Grisoni's screenplay is so idiosyncratic it offers no point of comparison to any other movie. It opens as a kind of romantic adventure, with Danilo and his beloved Rosa managing to foil her mother, Sibilla, and his father, Vittorio Duse, on what was to be her wedding day. Mama has arranged for her to marry the butcher's son, Barbariccia, but Danilo and Rosa outwit their parents and make a daring getaway.

They settle in England, with the perpetually furious Mama Sibilla, and while Danilo is working as a waiter a vision comes to him: he learns the secret of winning at cards from a talking pig, and winds up scoring enough money to open his own café in the East End of London. Over the years the life of the café is intertwined with Danilo and Rosa's growing family. Eventually, Danilo's aging father joins them. Then one day Barbariccia turns up, still hungering for revenge—and Rosa.

This could be the outline for a melodrama or a farce, but *Queen of Hearts* is neither. As narrated by the couple's ten-year-old son—who is as British as his parents are Italian—it has the quality of a fable or a tall tale that has been passed down from one generation to another. The movie embraces fantastical elements and larger-than-life emotions but does so with wit and charm. I can't think of another family saga quite like it.

With its boisterous picture of *la famiglia* and its dreamlike quality, *Queen of Hearts* is a singular piece of entertainment.

112. QUINCEAÑERA

(2005)

Directed by Richard Glatzer and Wash Westmoreland

Screenplay by Richard Glatzer and Wash Westmoreland

Actors:

EMILY RIOS

JESSE GARCIA

CHALO GONZÁLEZ

J. R. CRUZ

ARACELI GUZMÁN-RICO

JESUS CASTAÑOS-CHIMA

DAVID W. ROSS

JASON L. WOOD

As a working critic I get invited to many more films than I have time to see. Every publicist tries to write a persuasive press release, so I've learned to trust my instincts when reading about a film that hasn't yet been reviewed to decide if it's worth my time. Something about the description of a small-scale film called *Quinceañera* piqued my interest and, in fact, the picture actually exceeded my expectations.

An intimate story is set against the backdrop of Echo Park, an older area of Los Angeles that became a Latino enclave years ago when Anglos moved out to the suburbs. Now Echo Park is undergoing another transition as upwardly mobile couples—many of them gay—are discovering the still-affordable neighborhood and renovating its vintage houses.

Newcomer Emily Rios plays Magdalena, whose family is eagerly preparing for her traditional fifteenth birthday party celebration—her quinceañera. But an unexpected piece of news interrupts their plans: it seems she's pregnant. She swears she hasn't had sex, but her stern and stubborn father, a storefront preacher, won't believe her, so she moves in with her kindly great-grand-uncle Tio (Chalo González), who's also taken in her black-sheep cousin Carlos (Jesse Garcia). Carlos is experiencing a different kind of awakening with a gay man who's just moved into the neighborhood.

The film deals with many forms of culture clashes—and coming together—in an ever-changing world. Its creators, Richard Glatzer and Wash Westmoreland, were inspired to make *Quinceañera* by what they experienced in real life as newcomers to Echo Park. They prevailed upon their friends and neighbors to help out with advice, use of locations, and recommendations of people to fill the various roles in their script. Because they were making a nonunion movie, they had to find individuals who had talent but didn't belong to the Screen Actors Guild. Luck was on their side, not only with the young leads but with the film's oldest performer, Chalo González, who has charm and charisma to spare as the kindly Uncle Tio.

The movie has an unmistakable air of honesty about it that's positively disarming. It offered me one of my most enjoyable and enlightening moviegoing experiences in 2006.

The little-movie-that-could also garnered a formidable array of honors. It won both the Grand Jury Prize and the Audience Award—an impressive one-two punch—at the

Sundance Film Festival. Its writer-directors and producer Anne Clements won the John Cassavetes Award for low-budget filmmaking at the Independent Spirit Awards. It also won GLAAD and Humanitas Awards, reflecting the broad societal swath it covers so effectively.

113. RAISING VICTOR VARGAS

(2003)

Directed by Peter Sollett

Screenplay by Peter Sollett

From the short film *Five Feet High and Rising* by Peter Sollett

Original short story by Peter Sollett and Eva Vives

Actors:

VICTOR RASUK

JUDY MARTE

DONNA MALDONADO

WILFREE VASQUEZ

ALTAGRACIA GUZMAN

MELONIE DIAZ

SILVESTRE RASUK

At one time, New York's Lower East Side was a Jewish ghetto, a simmering part of the city's melting pot and the source of many stories, plays, and movies. But times change. The neighborhood is still home to an immigrant community, as we learn in *Raising Victor Vargas,* but these people come from the Dominican Republic.

Raising Victor Vargas won rave reviews in 2002 because it's not like any other movie in recent memory: an unusual

story with colorful characters and performances that reso-
nate because they seem so genuine. That's because writer
and director Peter Sollett worked with his cast of mostly
nonprofessionals to achieve that special quality.

Victor (Victor Rasuk) is a self-styled Don Juan in his
neighborhood, but in truth he's just a cocky kid who's being
raised—along with a brother and a sister—by his loving if
naive, Old World grandmother. When Victor's reputation is
besmirched, he feels pressure to prove himself and sets his
sights on Judy, the most beautiful girl at the neighborhood
swimming pool. She has no interest in him whatsoever, but
she doesn't reckon with Victor's determination—and his re-
fusal to take no for an answer.

These people aren't one-dimensional stereotypes: they
live and breathe, and we see them in their natural element.
The film is as much a portrait of a neighborhood and its
culture as it is about its leading characters. It dodges typical storytelling formulas and shows how relationships can
develop by accident, coincidence, and, in some cases, sheer
persistence.

Filmmaker Peter Sollett first explored these concepts in a
short subject called *Five Feet High and Rising* (2000), which
won awards at the Cannes, Sundance, and South by South-
west Film Festivals. That inspired the writer-director to
expand his material to feature length, with the same young
actor in the leading role. Victor Rasuk has worked steadily
ever since, in such films as *Lords of Dogtown, Bonneville, Stop-
Loss,* and *Che,* but I don't think he'll ever forget his experience playing Victor Vargas—not once, but twice. He told me
that when he started working with Peter Sollett, any time
he felt a line or an action wasn't believable he would speak

up, and the director encouraged that kind of interaction. It shows.

Raising Victor Vargas feels intimate and real at every turn. I couldn't take my eyes off the screen. There are no movie stars or special effects here, but there is a particular kind of magic in a low-budget film that can win you over so completely.

114. RESURRECTING THE CHAMP

(2007)

Directed by Rod Lurie

Screenplay by Michael Bortman and Allison Burnett

Story by Michael Bortman and Allison Burnett

Source material by J. R. Moehringer

Actors:

SAMUEL L. JACKSON

JOSH HARTNETT

KATHRYN MORRIS

ALAN ALDA

TERI HATCHER

DAVID PAYMER

PETER COYOTE

HARRY J. LENNIX

RACHEL NICHOLS

DAKOTA GOYO

We've all become so accustomed to movies following formulaic patterns that when a filmmaker throws us a curve we often don't know how to respond. Because *Resurrecting the Champ* is based on a true story it doesn't conform to

Hollywood conventions, and that's what makes it so interesting. Just when a "typical" studio movie would be building up to a happy ending, this one gets really interesting.

The source material for the film is an article by Pulitzer Prize–winning journalist J. H. Moehringer that appeared in the *Los Angeles Times* magazine. A compelling first-person narrative, it told how the reporter noticed a homeless, boozy black man who hung around a sports stadium in Santa Ana, California, attracting the attention of passersby with his colorful chatter. Moehringer took an interest in the man and his stories and came to discover that he was a long-forgotten prizefight champion named Bob Satterfield. In piecing the story together he hoped to help "The Champ" back on his feet and, at the same time, land himself a great story.

Samuel L. Jackson gives one of his best performances as the aging street person whose pride was washed away years ago. Josh Hartnett is also credible as the ambitious reporter who sees a golden opportunity to propel his career to the next level. (I am deliberately withholding more information about the plot.)

The movie works because it is built on the foundation of reality. It never sacrifices credibility in spinning its tale, but viewers should not confuse it with a documentary. Much of Hartnett's story (about unresolved issues with his famous father and an awkward separation from his wife and son) is fictional. Screenwriters Michael Bortman and Allison Burnett deftly weave this material into the larger fabric of the piece in a way that balances nicely with the saga of "The Champ."

Director Rod Lurie is a former journalist and has a good feel for newspaper stories (as he proved again with *Nothing*

But the Truth). His dramatization of Hartnett's ambition, hubris, and dressing-down at the hands of his editor (Alan Alda) and his wife (Kathryn Morris) play out in believable fashion and help flesh out what could have been merely an interesting vignette about a down-and-out boxer.

115. RESURRECTION

(1980)

Directed by Daniel Petrie

Screenplay by Lewis John Carlino

Actors:

ELLEN BURSTYN

SAM SHEPARD

RICHARD FARNSWORTH

ROBERTS BLOSSOM

CLIFFORD DAVID

PAMELA PAYTON-WRIGHT

LANE SMITH

EVA LE GALLIENNE

LOIS SMITH

E llen Burstyn has given many fine performances, but I have a special place in my heart for her work in *Resurrection,* which earned her an Academy Award nomination, her fifth following *The Last Picture Show, The Exorcist, Alice Doesn't Live Here Anymore*—which earned her the gold statue—and *Same Time, Next Year.* (She earned another nomination twenty years later for *Requiem for a Dream.*) Consider the caliber of those movies and then note that Ms. Burstyn names *Resurrection* as her personal favorite of all the pictures she's made.

It was written by Lewis John Carlino, who has penned such screenplays as *Seconds, The Mechanic, The Sailor Who Fell From Grace With the Sea, I Never Promised You a Rose Garden,* and *The Great Santini.* (Many of those are adaptations, but this film is an original work.) It was directed by Daniel Petrie, whose many credits include such lauded TV movies as *Eleanor and Franklin, Sybil, the Dollmaker,* and *My Name Is Bill W.,* and whose features range from *Lifeguard* to *Rocket Gibraltar.* When Janet Maslin reviewed *Resurrection* for the *New York Times* in 1980 she opined that "they have outshone their past work to a remarkable degree; this is a movie that really seems to have brought out the best in everyone who worked on it."

The critics who didn't care for *Resurrection* were those who couldn't buy into its story, about a woman who is in a terrible car accident and undergoes a near-death experience. Sometime later she has an encounter with a man (Richard Farnsworth) during a trip through the desert—and shortly thereafter discovers that she has the ability to heal people through the laying on of hands.

Burstyn's character, Edna, doesn't question how she came to acquire this gift. (Was it her own brush with death? Did it have something to do with that man in the desert?) She bestows it willingly on others through love, but her new boyfriend (Sam Shepard) urges her to acknowledge her connection to God.

What the movie captures so well is the concept of belief—a kind of wish fulfillment that old Hollywood movies trafficked in so effortlessly. By 1980 a seemingly permanent cynicism had begun to set in, to the point where it's very difficult to sell a modern audience on even the kind of lighthearted fantasy several generations grew up on in movies like *Topper, Miracle on 34th Street,* and *Harvey.*

Earlier movies about faith healers, like Frank Capra's *The Miracle Woman,* were generally concerned with commercialism and fraud. Burstyn's character is the real thing, and that's what sets this movie apart.

The film is beautifully designed (by Paul Sylbert) and photographed (by Mario Tosi) and flawlessly cast. One of its many other assets is the presence of the legendary stage actress and teacher Eva Le Gallienne, who was then eighty-one years old; she was so effective she earned an Academy Award nomination as Best Supporting Actress. But in spite of a strong supporting cast, the movie rests squarely on Burstyn's shoulders. If we don't believe her, the whole thing collapses. As it happens, we *do* put our faith in her, and she is incandescent.(Incidentally, *Resurrection* was not a great success, and it's difficult to find on video, but it made a deep impression on people who did see it. Burstyn told me that people talk to her about it all the time. It was remade for television in 1999 with Dana Delany in the leading role.)

116. SAFE MEN

(1998)

Directed by John Hamburg

Screenplay by John Hamburg

Actors:

SAM ROCKWELL

STEVE ZAHN

MICHAEL LERNER

HARVEY FIERSTEIN

MARK RUFFALO

JOSH PAIS

PAUL GIAMATTI

CHRISTINA KIRK

ALLEN SWIFT

I enjoyed *Safe Men* when I first saw it in 1998 because I like offbeat little comedies. Since that time, a number of people connected with it have gone on to greater success and recognition, which gives the movie marquee value it didn't possess the first time around. That list begins with Paul Giamatti, who'd made a big impression in Howard Stern's *Private Parts* the year before, and was on his way to becoming a major player. Here he plays a racketeer's hench-man called Veal Chop, and takes a backseat to the movie's well-cast stars, Sam Rockwell and Steve Zahn. Mark Ruf-falo also makes an appearance as a safecracker, two years before he became a so-called overnight sensation in *You Can Count on Me* opposite Laura Linney.

Then there's *Safe Men*'s writer and director, John Ham-burg. This was his first feature film, and while it was made on a small budget, it's clearly the work of a skillful comedic mind. Hamburg went on to write *Meet the Parents* and its sequel *Meet the Fockers,* two of the most successful comedies of all time.

But I still prefer the quiet sensibility of *Safe Men,* the story of two show-business wannabes who are mistaken for burglars and drafted into the mob life in Providence, Rhode Island. How anyone could think these goofballs are profes-sional anythings—let alone burglars—is not quite clear, but local Jewish mobster Michael Lerner (who wears a warm-up suit most of the time) is convinced, and so is his archrival, played by Harvey Fierstein. With such characters making nonstop threats, our two heroes have no choice but to try to carry out three robberies, even though they're utterly incapable of doing anything right.

I can only recommend this film if you share my weakness for quirky, off-kilter comedies that produce smiles and chuckles rather than belly laughs. I especially like this cast, from top to bottom. Any one of them brightens up a movie; having them all in the same film is an embarrassment of riches.

117. SCARECROW

(1973)

Directed by Jerry Schatzberg

Screenplay by Garry Michael White

Actors:

GENE HACKMAN

AL PACINO

DOROTHY TRISTAN

EILEEN BRENNAN

ANN WEDGEWORTH

RICHARD LYNCH

One of the problems with mainstream Hollywood movies is that they're afraid of taking their time or lingering on an image. Stillness is verboten. Perhaps that's why the opening scene of *Scarecrow* stands out in sharp relief. Director Jerry Schatzberg holds the camera on a continuing shot of a hill along the side of the road as a character (whom we don't yet know) makes his way toward us. The sky is dramatic, the composition of the shot (by the great cinematographer Vilmos Zsigmond) is compelling, and we can't help wonder what's about to happen.

What happens is that we meet our main characters, who are hoping to hitch a ride on that road: Lion, played by Al Pacino, and Max, played by Gene Hackman. They're drifters who wind up traveling together, learning about each other and uncovering a variety of peccadilloes as they hit the road. Max has recently completed a prison stretch and is saving his money to buy a car wash, which represents his ticket to success. Lion is a sailor who yearns to see the child who was born while he was away at sea. Max is the dominant character who's always ready to pick a fight—and does—while Lion is a natural clown who has a knack for disarming tension and confrontations. The two misfits forge a prickly friendship that ultimately is based on mutual need.

Remember that both Pacino and Hackman were still fairly new to moviegoers when this film came out. Both were New York stage actors who got their big breaks during an amazing period in American cinema. Hackman had been working in television and films without much notice when he galvanized audiences in *Bonnie and Clyde* (1967). His performance as Buck Barrow earned him his first Academy Award nomination as Best Supporting Actor, and his career was off and running. Pacino had only appeared in three movies before *Scarecrow,* but the second was *The Godfather* (1972), which changed the lives of everyone connected with it.

Scarecrow is a road movie crossed with a character study, and the two stars catch lightning in a bottle. (Hackman was later quoted as saying that this was his all-time favorite role.) But the film was a flop, and certainly did nothing for the screen career of Garry Michael White, who has fared much better in the world of theater.

Virtually every filmmaker I meet expresses admiration for American films of the early 1970s—with good reason—but *Scarecrow* is unjustly forgotten among the many gems of that period. It holds up beautifully today and is still awaiting rediscovery.

118. SEVEN MEN FROM NOW

(1956)

Directed by Budd Boetticher
Screenplay by Burt Kennedy

Actors:

RANDOLPH SCOTT

GAIL RUSSELL

LEE MARVIN

WALTER REED

JOHN LARCH

DONALD BARRY

STUART WHITMAN

How can a seemingly simple Western be as multilayered, resonant, and thoroughly satisfying as *Seven Men From Now*? Even if I had the answer, I suspect it wouldn't take me very far if I were trying to make a film just like it today. Simplicity, like wit, is no longer valued in Hollywood.

The beauty of *Seven Men From Now* is that it accomplishes so much without fanfare. It seems like a fairly straightforward story about a loner (Randolph Scott) who is out to avenge the death of his wife. We meet him as he is tracking down the men responsible. Along the way he teams up with a good-hearted if ineffectual homesteader (Walter Reed) and his beautiful wife (Gail Russell), who are traveling by Conestoga wagon. He also encounters a mean-spirited gunman (Lee Marvin) who's a natural-born tease with a gift of gab.

Anyone who accepts the stereotype of Randolph Scott as a square-jawed, one-dimensional hero clearly hasn't seen this film, or the others that followed in a remarkable out-pouring of creative energy by young screenwriter Burt Kennedy and director Budd Boetticher. Theirs was an inspired collaboration, to put it mildly: *Buchanan Rides Alone, The Tall T, Comanche Station,* and *Ride Lonesome* are all superior character-driven Westerns, made on modest budgets but yielding rich results.

The key word in describing *Seven Men From Now* is subtext. Scott and Russell form a bond, yet nothing is ever directly expressed of the longing they clearly feel for each other. As for the bad guy, he's bad, all right, but Lee Marvin's performance is outrageous. One doesn't expect laugh-out-loud moments involving a character who is clearly a heartless villain. Kennedy and Boetticher were confident enough of their story, and their actors, to permit this colorful supporting actor (who was not yet a star) to walk away with virtually every scene he's in. (It also says something about Randolph Scott that he wasn't threatened by the younger actor.)

Boetticher and veteran cinematographer William Clothier also took the time to craft beautiful—and meaningful—compositions. There is a scene of Scott bunking down for the night underneath the wagon, with Russell just above him, that's unforgettable.

Seven Men From Now sparkles with sharp writing, expert playing, and confident direction . . . and it manages to tell its story in just seventy-eight minutes!

The film was out of circulation for several decades, along with other films produced by John Wayne's Batjac company. It was finally restored by the UCLA Film and Television Archive in 2000, and watching it that summer at UCLA, with Kennedy and Boetticher in attendance, was a memorable experience. The director accompanied it to film festival showings in New York and Europe, which must have been enormously satisfying. Within a year both he and Kennedy had gone to their final reward.

I was asked to introduce the film at that year's Telluride Film Festival and happily complied. On my way to its second showing, I ran into French filmmaker Barbet Schroeder and said, "Didn't I already see you at the screening yesterday?" He replied, "I'm going again; I have so much to learn from it!"

119. SHADOWBOXER

(2006)

Directed by Lee Daniels

Screenplay by William Lipz

Actors:

HELEN MIRREN

CUBA GOODING JR.

STEPHEN DORFF

VANESSA FERLITO

JOSEPH GORDON-LEVITT

MO'NIQUE

MACY GRAY

redibility is in the eye of the beholder. I can't count the number of times I've found a movie's story line— or premise—so preposterous that I couldn't watch it with a straight face. At the same time, I've accepted some outlandish plot twists that other critics have rejected out of hand. There is no "right" or "wrong" in cases like this, only the opinion of the viewer.

Shadowboxer was dismissed by many reviewers as being outlandish and unbelievable. But I found myself in its thrall, possibly because I'm such a fan of Helen Mirren. I was willing to accept every implausibility because the picture created and maintained a fascinating mystique. Is it realistic? No . . . and I don't think it's trying to be. Is it intriguing to enter the world of unreality that the film creates? Absolutely.

To my mind, Helen Mirren is reason enough to watch any film. Here, she plays a hit man—or hit woman, if you prefer—who is dying of cancer. She lives and works with a younger partner, played by Cuba Gooding Jr. Theirs is a highly unusual relationship that's both personal and professional, which is revealed one layer at a time as the movie progresses. Despite his devotion to her, he is completely unprepared for her to make the decision she does when confronted with an assignment to shoot a pregnant woman (Vanessa Ferlito).

Stephen Dorff costars as Ferlito's brutally violent husband, and other small roles are filled by such familiar faces as Joseph Gordon-Levitt, Mo'Nique, and Macy Gray.

Shadowboxer marks the directorial debut of Lee Daniels, an entrepreneur whose producing credits include such challenging dramas as *Monster's Ball* and *The Woodsman*.

While he took his lumps for this ambitious blend of crime caper and love story, he couldn't have asked for more committed performances from his stars. (He fared considerably better with his next film, *Precious,* based on the novel *Push* by Sapphire, in 2009.)

If you reject stylized storytelling, or have no stomach for violence, you might skip this recommendation.

If you reject stylized storytelling, or have no stomach for violence, you might skip this recommendation. But if you like Mirren and Gooding, and are willing to give them some rope, you just might find yourself drawn into this unusual film.

120. SOMETHING NEW

(2006)

Directed by Sanaa Hamri

Screenplay by Kriss Turner

Actors:

SANAA LATHAN

SIMON BAKER

MIKE EPPS

DONALD FAISON

BLAIR UNDERWOOD

WENDY RAQUEL ROBINSON

ALFRE WOODARD

GOLDEN BROOKS

TARAJI P. HENSON

EARL BILLINGS

JOHN RATZENBERGER

Here's a movie that lives up to its name, offering something new—and refreshing—in the discouraging field
of romantic comedies. It's bad enough that so many films
in this genre seem contrived and mechanical, but far too
often I get the feeling that the stars and filmmakers don't
really believe in what they're doing. If they don't, how
can we?

Something New is a happy exception to that pattern, and
not just because of its racial twist. Sanaa Lathan (who made a
big impression on me in the 2000 movie *Love and Basketball*)
is excellent as Kenya McQueen, an educated and successful
businesswoman from an upwardly mobile black family in
Los Angeles. She would never think of linking herself with
a white man—"It's not a prejudice, it's just a preference," she
says—until she finds herself attracted to landscape architect
Simon Baker (star of television's *The Mentalist*), whom she's
hired to redo her garden.

The movie scores because it gets the details right.
Screenwriter Kriss Turner is a veteran of TV comedy series
like *The Bernie Mac Show* and *Everybody Hates Chris,* but
she goes beyond sitcom slickness and imbues her characters
with three dimensions. Throughout the movie she tweaks
our expectations and sensibilities by showing what Lathan
has to endure to maintain her relationship with Baker. That
includes the open skepticism of her girlfriends and the outright disbelief of her family, especially her wise-guy brother,
played by Donald Faison.

Music-video director Sanaa Hamri realizes all the potential in a screenplay that's as much about upward mobility
as it is about love. Unlike so many comedies that portray
contemporary singles, this one isn't dumb. You're not just

waiting for the characters to go through the motions and get together for that final clinch. *Something New* feels genuine to me. It has smarts and it has charm.

Perhaps it was their lack of star power—in movie-marquee terms—that kept this movie from being more successful, or perhaps mainstream audiences still shy away from an interracial romance. If you ask me, Lathan and Baker make an exceptionally attractive couple.

121. SON OF RAMBOW

(2008)

Directed by Garth Jennings

Screenplay by Garth Jennings

Actors:

BILL MILNER

WILL POULTER

JULES SITRUK

JESSICA STEVENSON

NEIL DUDGEON

ANNA WING

ED WESTWICK

Some movies are considered a tough sell because they don't have a hook that advertising and marketing people can latch on to. This British import had one, but apparently moviegoers didn't understand it . . . and stayed away. What's more, the film was held back from release for one full year after Paramount acquired it at the Sundance Film Festival in 2007. Reportedly much of that time was spent in legal discussions to make sure the star and creators of *First Blood* (the movie that introduced Sylvester Stallone as Rambo) wouldn't sue over this offbeat homage.

Son of Rambow is, in fact, a quirky coming-of-age movie about two alienated boys in the early 1980s. Will Proudfoot (Bill Milner) has led a sheltered life, as his family is part of a strict religious sect that forbids such worldly diversions as television; what's more, his mother has to raise him and his siblings on her own. As a result, he finds his only escape is through drawing. One day at school he chances to meet an arrogant bully named Lee Carter (Will Poulter) who sees in Will a perfect new patsy. Enjoying the attention, Will readily submits to Lee's demands.

It turns out that Lee also lives in a fractured household with his older brother; the parents are forever traveling and pay no attention to their children. But unlike Will, Lee goes to the movies and the new film *First Blood* has taken his fancy. So he borrows his brother's home-video camera and decides to stage his own version of the action yarn—with Will as his star and stuntman.

Writer-director Garth Jennings and his producing partner Nick Goldsmith drew on their own experiences for this story. Jennings was one of those kids who tried to imitate *First Blood* by making movies with his friends, using the first generation of home-video equipment. He later transformed his youthful flights of fancy into a career, cofounding the production company Hammer & Tongs with Goldsmith in 1999. They built a reputation for creating visually arresting music videos and television commercials. The partners were ready to make their feature-film debut with *Rambow* when the opportunity arose to take on a major studio movie, *The*

Hitchhiker's Guide to the Galaxy. Son of Rambow became their second feature, made on a much smaller scale, with more modest ambitions.

Jennings's screenplay captures the innocence and wonder of adolescence, as well as the adventure of amateur moviemaking. Perhaps his greatest success was finding precisely the right boys to play his main characters. Bill Milner is perfect as Will—wide eyed and vulnerable—while Will Poulter is entirely believable as the bullying Lee, who hides his insecurities under a mask of cockiness.

Son of Rambow isn't quite like any other film I can recall about boyhood, yet its central themes of isolation, friendship, and wanting to be accepted are universal and timeless. Like many other films about growing up, I suspect it speaks most eloquently to adults who can remember the joys and sorrows of their own experiences.

122. SONGCATCHER

(2001)

Directed by Maggie Greenwald

Screenplay by Maggie Greenwald

Actors:

JANET MCTEER

AIDAN QUINN

PAT CARROLL

JANE ADAMS

GREGORY COOK

IRIS DEMENT

E. KATHERINE KERR

EMMY ROSSUM

DAVID PATRICK KELLY

Luck plays a part in any career. Filmmaker Maggie Green-wald has made exceptional movies that anyone would be proud of, but bad luck has hindered their release and kept her from receiving the attention she richly deserves.

Songcatcher received a Special Jury Prize at the 2000 Sundance Film Festival for "outstanding ensemble perfor-mance" by its cast, and Greenwald was nominated as Best Director. With that kind of send-off, this indie film should have been a shoo-in for success. Unfortunately, the film's distributor was swallowed up by another company before the end of that year, and the new firm didn't get behind the picture. (Almost the exact same thing happened to *The Kill-Off,* which earned Greenwald a Best Director nomination at Sundance a decade earlier, in 1990.)

I spent the better part of a year touting *Songcatcher* to anyone who would listen . . . and many who did told me how much they enjoyed the film. That didn't surprise me; it's a richly textured, highly entertaining picture with an array of wonderful performances.

Acclaimed British actress Janet McTeer, who earned an Oscar nomination for *Tumbleweeds* (1999), again plays an American character in this story of an independent-minded woman who teaches music at a New England conservatory. When she is passed over for a promotion, she decides to visit her sister, who is running a one-room schoolhouse in Appalachia. As a musicologist, she is overwhelmed by the amount of folk music that surrounds her, and makes it her business to notate these songs for posterity. In the process, the proper, straitlaced New Englander begins to soften as she gets to know these good-hearted backwoods people.

The supporting cast is first-rate, with Jane Adams as McTeer's closeted sister, teenage Emmy Rossum as her niece, Aidan Quinn as a mountain man who becomes her love interest, and comedienne Pat Carroll as an earth-mother type who is a lynchpin in her quest to learn about indigenous folk music of the region.

Songcatcher combines the best qualities of a character study and a period piece, and enables us to share the sense of discovery that stimulates its main character. It's an alto-gether remarkable film and a vivid piece of Americana.

123. SPRING FORWARD

(2000)

Directed by Tom Gilroy
Screenplay by Tom Gilroy

Actors:

NED BEATTY

LIEV SCHREIBER

CAMPBELL SCOTT

IAN HART

PERI GILPIN

BILL RAYMOND

CATHERINE KELLNER

HALLEE HIRSH

Ned Beatty has appeared in scores of movies since he made his unforgettable debut in 1972's *Deliverance,* in-cluding such heavy hitters as *Nashville, All the President's*

Men, Superman, and *Network* (which earned him an Oscar nomination as Best Supporting Actor), but when I met him at the Independent Spirit Awards in 2006 and told him how much I love *Spring Forward* (1999), he seemed genuinely pleased. He told me that it meant a lot to him, too, adding that he and costar Liev Schreiber stayed in touch and hoped to work together again.

I was happy to get that reaction because it confirmed my belief that *Spring Forward* was a labor of love. The first feature film written and directed by New York–based actor Tom Gilroy, it earned strong reviews and some attention on the film festival circuit, though its quiet nature guaranteed that it wasn't destined to be a mass-audience favorite. Yet actors Beatty and Schreiber recognized something special in Gilroy's screenplay—just as viewers lucky enough to have seen it have come away richer for the experience.

The story takes place over the course of four seasons. Murph (Beatty) works for the parks department in a suburban Connecticut town. Paul (Schreiber), who's just served time for armed robbery, is assigned to help him as part of a program to rehabilitate ex-convicts. The two men couldn't be more different, yet over the course of a year their relationship grows and deepens. We learn about their backgrounds, their failings, and their hopes. Murph becomes a surrogate father for Paul, who acquires wisdom from the experiences he's shared with the older man. And, as it turns out, Paul has something to offer Murph as well. (I'm deliberately being vague about all of this, as I don't want to give away too much.)

Spring Forward is a character study based almost entirely on conversation, but the settings, the work the two men do while they talk, the change of seasons, and the people they chance to encounter all figure in the cumulative effectiveness of the piece. I suppose the same material could be performed onstage, but I don't think it would have the same impact.

Subtlety isn't a quality much admired—or sought—in Hollywood, but it's one of this film's assets. To find a movie that dodges clichés and creates two striking and memorable characters is cause for celebration.

124. STARTING OUT IN THE EVENING

(2007)

Directed by Andrew Wagner

Screenplay by Andrew Wagner and Fred Parnes

Based on the novel by Brian Morton

Actors:

FRANK LANGELLA

LAUREN AMBROSE

LILI TAYLOR

ADRIAN LESTER

JESSICA HECHT

MICHAEL CUMPSTY

JOEL WEST

The best film I saw in 2007 was my first screening at that year's Sundance Film Festival in January. For the rest of the year I kept telling people about *Starting Out in the Evening,* and while some other critics agreed with me, the movie never received its just due. Just one year later its star, Frank Langella, was nominated for an Oscar for his brilliant performance as Richard Nixon in *Frost/Nixon* . . . but in my opinion he deserved equal recognition for his work in this picture.

Langella plays Leonard Schiller, a onetime literary lion whose glory days are behind him; he's been forgotten by everyone except his old colleagues and admirers. A naive but determined and outspoken grad student, played by Lauren Ambrose (of *Six Feet Under* fame), seeks him out because she's writing a thesis about him and wants to know more about the elusive novelist. He's a very private person and doesn't want her intruding on his life—at first—but gradually begins to thaw. The relationship between master and pupil becomes challenging and complex as the two gradually open up to each other.

Lili Taylor adds to her gallery of great performances as Langella's daughter, who, at the age of forty, is still trying to figure out what she wants from life, including whether she wants to continue seeing her ex (Adrian Lester).

Starting Out in the Evening is a stoic, classically crafted film, and a beautifully observed character study; these aren't two-dimensional figures but real people. Langella's performance, as a man who is a model of self-containment, is incredibly expressive; his every gesture has meaning. The film also makes wonderful use of Manhattan, interiors as well as exteriors, to capture the flavor of their lives. Harlan Bosmajian's lighting is exceptional.

Director Andrew Wagner studied film at NYU, and was later a directing fellow at AFI. Both of his student films were showered with prizes. He sold a number of screenplays and received acclaim for his first small-scale film as writer-director, *The Talent Given Us*. For this more ambitious follow-up he adapted Brian Morton's novel with Fred

Parnes. In a just world, *Starting Out in the Evening* would be much better known, and so would its principal creator.

125. STARTUP.COM

(2001)

Directed by Chris Hegedus and Jehane Noujaim

When a documentarian decides to profile an individual, or bear witness to a project that's about to unfold, he or she takes an enormous chance, gambling that the time and money invested will yield interesting results. What if the venture collapses or the subject turns out to be a flake?

Chris Hegedus and Jehane Noujaim gambled when they set out to chronicle a promising Internet enterprise. They couldn't have foreseen that their story would blossom into an incredible saga with personal ramifications worthy of the best fiction. That's why *Startup.com* is so riveting: you couldn't make up a story this good.

The protagonists are Kaleil Isaza Tuzman and Tom Stern, who have been best friends since high school. Now, in their early twenties, they believe they've hit on a surefire idea for a company called govWorks.com, which will simplify ordinary citizens' dealings with municipal governments. Kaleil is the front man, a glib, persuasive fellow who knows how to pitch the idea to potential investors. He also becomes an appealing media figure, the exemplar of a modern-day entrepreneur. Tom is better suited to working in the trenches, supervising the often-daunting technical challenges of the business as it goes through a series of growing pains. There is another partner who becomes a third wheel at a certain stage of the story.

The movie spans a year and a half, from mid-1999 to the end of 2000, as the company tries to strike a balance between pie-in-the-sky promises and the reality of running a day-to-day operation.

Paralleling the mounting drama of whether or not these young partners can make a success of their venture is the evolving personal relationship between them. It doesn't take long to see that they are moving and growing in different directions. Their goals and philosophies diverge—even their attitude toward family and the women in their lives— and one can sense that this is creating a fault line in their company's foundation.

Startup.com doesn't take sides in the conflicts that arise, allowing each viewer to ask himself questions about personal goals, ethics, and morals, and test his resolve, as the people on-screen are forced to do over and over again. What's more important, loyalty or success? If you had to choose between losing a friend and losing a strategic business alliance, what would you do? Because each person will answer these questions differently, each one will take something different away from the experience of watching the movie. I defy anyone to find a fictional film as compelling as this.

126. STATE OF THE UNION

(1948)

Directed by Frank Capra

Screenplay by Anthony Veiller and Myles Connolly

Based on the play by Howard Lindsay and Russel Crouse

Actors:

SPENCER TRACY

KATHARINE HEPBURN

ANGELA LANSBURY

VAN JOHNSON

ADOLPHE MENJOU

LEWIS STONE

RAYMOND WALBURN

MARGARET HAMILTON

CARL (ALFALFA) SWITZER

CHARLES LANE

IRVING BACON

TOR JOHNSON

I suppose it's symptomatic of human nature that every generation thinks it's the first to experience life's great lessons. It's one of the reasons I enjoy watching old movies; they may not always present an accurate picture of "real life," but they do reflect the attitudes and mores of their time.

That's why I love Frank Capra's *State of the Union,* which goes behind the scenes of a presidential campaign and reveals that little has changed over the years where politics is concerned.

There are other good reasons to see the film: it teams Spencer Tracy and Katharine Hepburn for their fifth time (although Hepburn was a last-minute replacement for

Claudette Colbert). The costarring cast is just as strong. Van Johnson had become America's favorite boy-next-door in the mid-1940s, but here he plays a cynical columnist (with a nonstop arsenal of wisecracks) and shows what a fine comedic actor he could be. Movie veteran Menjou is perfection itself as a smooth political operator who knows how to throw the bull—and when to talk turkey.

Then there's Lansbury, who as usual was cast as a woman older than her years—and nailed the part decisively. She was twenty-two years old when she took on the role of a cold-blooded newspaper publisher and kingmaker who decides that her lover (self-made—and very much married—industrialist Tracy) should be the next president of the United States. It's one of her all-time juiciest parts and one of her best performances. Early in the film we see how she inherits not only the job but the power that comes with it from her father, played by Lewis Stone. (This foreshadows the fabled career of Katherine Graham, who later inherited ownership of the all-powerful *Washington Post* from her husband.)

Ironically, critics in 1948 decried the movie's casting, declaring that both Lansbury and Johnson were too young to be credible in their roles. Here's at least one instance in which time has been kind to a film. Lansbury and Johnson don't seem young at all by today's standards of eternal youth.

The most relevant aspect of *State of the Union* to modern viewers is the key dramatic conflict of the story: Tracy is an honest man who genuinely wants to do good for his country, but he quickly learns that being a viable candidate means having to make compromises—and get into bed with people you don't like.

Frank Capra took a drubbing from critics for watering

down Howard Lindsay and Russel Crouse's Broadway play, and injecting it with Hollywood tropes and comedy shtick. Yet those ingredients, corny as they may seem at times, still work today. I screened this film for my USC students, who aren't accustomed to watching "old movies." Before we began I tried to set the film into historic context, explaining that it came out during a volatile presidential campaign year when Harry Truman (a piano-playing haberdasher from Missouri) was in the White House, radio was the dominant communication medium but television was making its way into American homes, most people traveled by train, and the worst insult one could hurl at someone was that he was a Communist. I also explained that Van Johnson wasn't just a wiseguy but what they used to call a "wolf." And I noted that while this film might seem dated in some respects, in other ways it was surprisingly progressive: its depiction of a man having a mistress, and even Tracy citing the name of Crispus Attucks in a list of great Americans (not a common occurrence in 1940s America).

It took my twenty-somethings time to get into the rhythm of the film—so different from modern movies in every way—but by the homestretch they were so in tune with the movie that they laughed at every cutaway Capra built in for laugh reaction in the climactic scene (with character actor Irving Bacon tending bar—and doing broad "takes"). Capra's sense of an audience still held up after sixty years.

There's also a pearly moment when Tracy, about to deliver his ultimate campaign speech via a television hookup in his home, makes eye contact with two workmen nearby. One of them just stares at Tracy and chews gum. The guy is clearly thinking, "What makes you think you're better than anyone else?" Capra holds the shot for a long, long time because it conveys more than any dialogue possibly could, and though this same workman later voices his feelings in a speech, it's that cinematic moment—something you couldn't achieve on a stage without the benefit of close-ups—that does the job.

State of the Union may not be a perfect movie but it is wonderfully entertaining, and most certainly a time capsule worth exploring.

127. THE STEEL HELMET

(1951)

Directed by Samuel Fuller
Screenplay by Samuel Fuller

Actors:

GENE EVANS

ROBERT HUTTON

STEVE BRODIE

JAMES EDWARDS

RICHARD LOO

SID MELTON

In spite of such vivid, realistic, and revisionist films as *Saving Private Ryan* and *Flags of Our Fathers,* which depict scenes of violence that Hollywood muted in the 1940s and '50s, the war movies made by the late, great Sam Fuller still stand out today. His autobiographical infantry saga of World War II, *The Big Red One,* is perhaps the most famous, but he was one of the few Hollywood filmmakers to address the Korean War, and *The Steel Helmet* is still one of the best of its kind. His own experiences in combat informed all of Fuller's work, and perhaps that's why this film still holds up so well.

Gene Evans, a virile character actor who became Fuller's alter ego on-screen, gives a gritty performance as Sergeant Zack, a no-nonsense infantryman who survives a massacre with the help of a boy he nicknames Short Round. Eventually the two of them hook up with a medic and fall in with a patrol that digs in at a Buddhist temple.

The Steel Helmet was ahead of its time in so many ways. It offers an utterly unsentimental look at war and features a multiracial cast, including James Edwards (one of Hollywood's first black actors to be cast in serious roles) and Richard Loo (who spent many years playing Japanese stereotypes) as a Japanese-American soldier. There's also a character who was a conscientious objector during World War II. These were highly unconventional concepts for a Hollywood movie of this time, but Fuller was nothing if not gutsy, and he found in theater-owner-turned-producer Robert Lippert an ally who was willing to back him without interference, so long as he brought in his movies on a tight budget. It's no-frills filmmaking and it runs just eighty-five minutes, but it packs a punch.

The Steel Helmet also celebrates the incredible pluck and determination of the ordinary American GI, and the way good soldiers lean on each other for support and survival. No one ever accused Sam Fuller of being subtle, but his rat-a-tat-tat dialogue still crackles after all these years. I think *The Steel Helmet* is one of the most underrated war movies of all time.

If you like this lean, mean movie you might want to explore Fuller's other movies, including his early works (*The Baron of Arizona, I Shot Jesse James, Park Row, Pickup on South Street*) as well as his later Westerns and melodramas (*House of Bamboo, Run of the Arrow, Forty Guns, Shock Corridor, The Naked Kiss*). And if you want to immerse yourself in a really great story, I encourage you to read his autobiography, *A Third Face: My Tale of Writing, Fighting and Filmmaking*. You'll soon discover that Fuller was just as colorful as the characters he brought to life on-screen.

128. STILL CRAZY

(1998)

Directed by Brian Gibson

Screenplay by Dick Clement and Ian La Frenais

Actors:

STEPHEN REA

BILLY CONNOLLY

JIMMY NAIL

TIMOTHY SPALL

BILL NIGHY

JULIET AUBREY

HELENA BERGSTROM

BRUCE ROBINSON

RACHAEL STIRLING

I don't know if rock 'n' roll should last a lifetime," says a young woman who's spent the last twenty years pining for the musician she loved, before he self-destructed. But, given the chance to help keyboard player Stephen Rea reunite their '70s band, Strange Fruit, she jumps in whole-heartedly. And so do we in the audience. I was rooting for *Still Crazy* from the opening scene. Not only does it have an irresistible premise, but it features many of my favorite British actors.

In the case of the rock 'n' roll band Strange Fruit, it's been twenty years since they performed together, and that last concert was an utter disaster (lightning struck the out-door stage). The band's former keyboard player (Stephen Rea) now services condom-dispensing machines, so when the son of that fateful concert's promoter approaches him about a reunion, he's game. For one thing, he's got noth-ing to lose, and besides, he's never completely abandoned his love for rock 'n' roll. He looks up the band's intrepid girl Friday (Juliet Aubrey) and together they go in search of the former musicians who have fallen off the show-business map. One is a roofer (Jimmy Nail), one is a gardener (Tim-othy Spall) who's on the lam from tax authorities, another (Bill Nighy) tries to keep up a good front as a wealthy (if henpecked) retiree who lives in a Gothic castle . . . and one apparently died of a drug overdose. The guy who's most enthusiastic about hitting the road again is, of course, the band's erstwhile roadie (Billy Connolly).

At this point the movie could go in any direction, from farce to tragedy. *Still Crazy* is essentially a comedy, but it has just the right amount of bittersweet in its makeup and surprise in its plotting. What's more, the music is actually good.

Having recently made two "straight" musical biopics, *The Josephine Baker Story* and *What's Love Got to Do with It*, Brian Gibson was a fortuitous choice to helm this film. The screenplay was penned by Dick Clement and Ian La Frenais, the most durable and prolific writing team in recent history. Their TV and movie credits, spread over four decades, include much-loved British comedy series like *Porridge,* features ranging from swingin' '60s fare like *Otley and The Touchables* to *Flushed Away* and *The Bank Job,* and one of the greatest movies ever written about a band, *The Commitments.* They know both comedy and character and fill this film with both commodities; the former bandmates aren't stick figures but colorful people with a variety of peccadilloes. Of course, having them played by the likes of Bill Nighy, Timothy Spall, and Billy Connolly doesn't hurt.

129. STONE READER

(2003)

Directed by Mark Moskowitz
Screenplay by Mark Moskowitz

A good documentary can take unfamiliar subject matter and make you interested in it. This film goes one step further: it purports to tell us what it's going to be about, which seems interesting enough, but evolves into something much larger in scope, and even more captivating than its core topic.

Director Mark Moskowitz takes another risk by making himself an integral part of the movie. This has worked well for others (like the poster boy for personal filmmaking, Michael Moore), but it can also backfire if we don't care for the person on-screen, or if he seems to intrude on the material.

In this case, filmmaker and film are completely intertwined. Moskowitz, who makes political-campaign TV commercials for a living, is an avid, lifelong reader. One day, while rearranging the books on the shelves of his New England home, he comes upon a novel called *The Stones of Summer,* which he read when it was new in the early 1970s and he was a teenager. He had trouble getting through it then, but after revisiting it he becomes convinced that it is a masterpiece, a profound, evocative book about its times. Like any devoted bibliophile he checks to see what else Dow Mossman has written and finds, to his surprise, that this was his only published novel. What's more, he can't find out anything about the author—even if he's still alive.

To disappear from the public eye in the Internet era isn't easy, so Moskowitz undertakes a quest, not only to find Mossman, if he can, but to figure out how and why such a talented writer fell off the map, and why his book wasn't more celebrated. But beyond that well-defined goal, he decides to explore the very nature of reading, and why we feel so connected to certain books we encounter over the course of our lives.

If you love books, chances are you won't mind the fact that Moskowitz meanders far and wide, not only interviewing people directly involved with *The Stones of Summer* and leading literary lights but old friends and new acquaintances he makes along the road—book critics, editors, authors, and fellow readers—all of whom are happy to relate their thoughts about life and literature.

Does the filmmaker ever track down Dow Mossman? I'm reluctant to tell you, although the film is less a mystery/suspense tale than a meditation on reading and writing. All

I know is that I reveled in every moment of *Stone Reader* because, like Moskowitz, I've been in love with books since childhood, and there are very few films that celebrate that special relationship.

130. SWEET LAND

(2005)

Directed by Ali Selim

Screenplay by Ali Selim

Based on the story *A Gravestone Made of Wheat* by Will Weaver

Actors:

ELIZABETH REASER

TIM GUINEE

ALAN CUMMING

JOHN HEARD

ALEX KINGSTON

NED BEATTY

LOIS SMITH

ROBERT HOGAN

PATRICK HEUSINGER

STEPHEN PELINSKI

PAUL SAND

JODIE MARKELL

KAREN LANDRY

I love watching a film I know nothing about and having the sense of making a discovery. That's how I felt when I saw *Sweet Land,* which has gone on to win rave reviews and film festival honors. It's the work of a first-generation

American named Ali Selim, who expanded a short story into a beautifully nuanced movie about a German mail-order bride who shows up in rural Minnesota in the days following World War I, only to find herself ostracized by her future husband's community, and even the local priest. Not only is the Norwegian populace a tight-knit, clannish group, but anti-German sentiments are still strong in the wake of the armistice. How will this newcomer ever fit in, and how will her husband-to-be ever reconcile his own feelings and the pressure being brought to bear on him?

Sweet Land is a film of subtlety and silence as much as dialogue and exposition. Much is told with a glance or a gesture, and the performances of leading lady Elizabeth Reaser as Inge, leading man Tim Guinee as Olaf, and such fine actors as Alan Cumming, John Heard, and Ned Beatty are exemplary. You really feel as if you're experiencing this story with them as Reaser stubbornly refuses to give up on her tiny stake in the American dream.

Writer-director Selim grew up hearing his father's stories of emigrating from Egypt to Minnesota in the early 1950s and I'm sure they informed his worldview even though the time and circumstances are different in this particular story. Selim and producers James Bigham and Alan Cumming (the same) won the Best First Feature prize at the Independent Spirit Awards, where Elizabeth Reaser was nominated as Best Actress. If there were any justice, she would have had an Oscar nomination as well: if you can find another performance as challenging, expressive, and wide ranging among the films of 2005, I'd be shocked. She barely speaks, and when she does, it's in the German language. Reaser has done other good work on television (where she was featured as a car-crash victim in

Grey's Anatomy and starred in the short-lived *The Ex List*) and the big screen, but I'm sure more people will know her as the matriarch of the vampire family in the *Twilight* movies than will ever see her in *Sweet Land*. That's their loss.

How does a first-time feature-film director cast so well and realize all the colors and emotions in his screenplay? I don't know, but sometimes the fates smile on a movie and this is one glorious example. I'm especially fond of the way Selim described his film in an article he wrote: he says it's about moving beyond tolerance to acceptance. That's as lovely and profound as the movie itself.

131. THE TAO OF STEVE

(2000)

Directed by Jenniphr Goodman

Screenplay by Duncan North, Jenniphr Goodman, and Greer Goodman

Source material by Duncan North

Actors:

DONAL LOGUE

GREER GOODMAN

DAVID AARON BAKER

KIMO WILLS

NINA JAROSLAW

AYELET KAZNELSON

At one time, sloth or laziness might have seemed an un-likely quality for the leading character of a movie, but the emergence of the slacker has changed that perception.

There are many examples of slacker heroes but the one I like best is played by that likable actor Donal Logue, who's best known for his work on such TV series as *Grounded for Life* and *Life*. He is the star of a disarming little comedy called *The Tao of Steve.*

Logue plays Dex, who teaches school for a living but spends most of his time lounging around his Santa Fe, New Mexico, house in a bathrobe, expounding on his philosophy of life to his roommates. Dex may not look like much, but he gets all the women he wants because of his patented approach, which is inspired by cool people he admires, like Steve McQueen (not to mention Steve McGarrett and Steve Austin). Dex can talk for hours about his rules of engagement for dealing with the opposite sex—and he's not just idle bluster, because despite his slovenly appearance he is a veritable chick magnet.

But Dex's theories disintegrate when he spots an attractive woman named Syd, played by Greer Goodman. For once he's caught off guard and forgets to put his famous game plan into play: he becomes just like the rest of us, awkward and tongue-tied. Worst of all, he violates his cardinal rule by allowing her to sense that he's actually interested in her.

The Tao of Steve is smart and funny, with a fresh take on the eternal challenge of male-female relationships. It revels in its engaging dialogue and banter.

It's interesting to note that this entertaining movie was written by the actress who plays Syd, Greer Goodman, in collaboration with her sister Jenniphr, who directed it, and Duncan North, who presumably brought a male point of view to the writing of the screenplay. I can't picture anyone else but Donal Logue in the leading role; he was awarded a Special Jury Prize for Outstanding Performance in this film at the Sundance Film Festival.

The Tao of Steve is one of those tiny movies that's built a loyal following through repeated showings on cable TV. I'll bet if the filmmakers published Dex's words of wisdom in booklet form they could make a bundle through TV infomercials. (But remember, it was *my* idea.)

132. TASTE OF CHERRY

(1997)

Directed by Abbas Kiarostami

Screenplay by Abbas Kiarostami

Actors:

HOMAYOUN ERSHADI

ABDOLRAHMAN BAGHERI

AFSHIN KHORSHID BAKHTIARI

SAFAR ALI MORADI

I must confess that I was a latecomer to the work of celebrated Iranian filmmaker Abbas Kiarostami; now I'm a devotee. He is a master storyteller who opens our eyes to the humanity of his native culture while exploring universal emotions and conflicts.

Taste of Cherry is one of his most provocative films. He wastes no time with preliminaries, pulling us immediately into the agitated world of its main character, Mr. Badii (Homayoun Ershadi, who a decade later would do such a wonderful job as Baba in *The Kite Runner*). A well-dressed man, he drives a Range Rover around the outskirts of Tehran, a look of desperation on his face. The reason: he is looking for someone who will promise to bury him after he commits suicide.

He is willing to pay a handsome sum, but suicide is a sin, and one by one, the people he tries to convince turn him down. The man who finally agrees to perform the task turns out to be something of a philosopher.

Kiarostami tells us precious little about Mr. Badii, yet we learn a great deal about the people he meets during his frantic search . . . and we acquire a tangible sense of place as he drives from the bustling city to its arid outskirts and back again.

As Stephen Holden wrote in the *New York Times,* "Mr. Kiarostami, like no other filmmaker, has a vision of human scale that is simultaneously epic and precisely minuscule. While each of the men Mr. Badii approaches is a vivid, autonomous individual with a rich personal history and an innate sense of dignity, each is also seen as part of the human anthill."

The movie asks us to ponder what life is about—and what it's worth. Mr. Badii seems to have attained some level of success but it clearly hasn't brought him happiness. The security guard at a construction site whom he accosts could surely use the money he is offering, but he refuses to have anything to do with his outrageous scheme. A soldier responds the same way.

In this contemplative context, Kiarostami deliberately confounds the viewer by leaving the outcome of his story to our imagination. It is a curious ploy that caused a number of critics to denigrate the film, in spite of its reception at the Cannes Film Festival, where it won the Palme d'Or. I can neither defend nor explain the finale, but I also cannot allow it to undermine all that has preceded it. *Taste of Cherry* is a haunting film with moments that have stayed with me for years.

133. THE THIRD MIRACLE

(1999)

Directed by Agnieszka Holland

Screenplay by Richard Vetere and John Romano

Based on the novel by Richard Vetere

Actors:

ED HARRIS

ANNE HECHE

ARMIN MUELLER-STAHL

MICHAEL RISPOLI

CHARLES HAID

JAMES GALLANDERS

CATERINA SCORSONE

BARBARA SUKOWA

JAMES GALLANDERS

JOHN-LOUIS ROUX

KEN JAMES

I honestly don't know how actors do what they do. They endure constant rejection, and then, if they're lucky and achieve some measure of success, they have to choose between commercial projects that will pay the rent and keep them in the public eye, and smaller, more personal films that offer deep-down satisfaction. The smart ones find a way to navigate between both worlds, as Ed Harris does.

Still, I'm sure it's frustrating when someone puts his heart and soul into a movie that nobody sees. Sometimes, when I mention such a film during an interview, I feel as if I've touched a raw nerve, reminding the actor of something that once meant a great deal but didn't pay off. While I was talking to Ed Harris about *National Treasure: Book of Secrets*, I brought up *The Third Miracle* and said I was sorry that it had flown under the radar. "That was a really nice movie," he said, and smiled when he mentioned the name of its director, Agnieszka Holland. "My last film with Agnieszka was *Copying Beethoven* . . . it didn't even *get* to the radar. But *The Third Miracle* was a really nice film." Then, after a pause, he added, "I'm very proud of that film, actually," as if warming to the memory of it.

Based on a novel by Richard Vetere, *The Third Miracle* deals with a priest (Harris) who is assigned to investigate a supposed miracle in a working-class Midwestern neighborhood. The priest is having his own spiritual crisis, and moves warily into the community, where he meets the daughter (Anne Heche) of the woman for whom the statue serves as a memorial. The woman was beloved in her church parish, and the congregation is convinced that she was a saint. As he prepares a case for Vatican review, the priest's own faith—and unconventional behavior—are called into question, especially by a rigid archbishop (Armin Mueller-Stahl) from Europe.

Vetere adapted his novel for the screen, with John Romano; they couldn't have asked for a more sympathetic director than the Polish-born Holland, who has dealt with religious subject matter before, and whose films are always thoughtful and mature. With full-bodied characters and a story laced with nuance and surprise, I found *The Third Miracle* completely absorbing, from start to finish: one of those rarities nowadays, a movie for adults.

134. THUMBSUCKER

(2005)

Directed by Mike Mills

Screenplay by Mike Mills

Based on the novel by Walter Kirn

Actors:

LOU (TAYLOR) PUCCI

TILDA SWINTON

VINCENT D'ONOFRIO

KELLI GARNER

KEANU REEVES

BENJAMIN BRATT

VINCE VAUGHN

CHASE OFFERLE

People often ask me what I look for in a film. I don't have any preset checklist but I can tell you that one quality I especially admire is originality. To find that trait in a coming-of-age story is especially rare, which is just one reason I have such regard for *Thumbsucker,* a deeply felt story of a teenage misfit layered with humor in its depiction of the off-kilter grown-ups who surround him.

Had I been familiar with the writings of Walter Kirn when I first saw this movie, I wouldn't have been so surprised. Since then I've sought out Kirn's other novels (like *Up in the Air*) and now I'm a dedicated fan. He has a keen eye for the follies and foibles of American life, and that's what attracted Mike Mills to the property.

This is Mills's first feature but he's hardly a newcomer. His short subjects and documentaries (*Architecture of Reassurance, Deformer, Paperboys*) have won acclaim and prizes at film festivals around the world, but even they are something of a sideline. Mills is a world-class graphic designer whose work encompasses fine art, commercials (for Levi's, the Gap, and Nike, among others), music videos (for such performers as Air, the Beastie Boys, and Yoko Ono), books, CD covers, and even fabric for Marc Jacobs.

Getting the backing to direct your first feature would be daunting enough for anyone, but Mills decided to write the screenplay as well. He showed the finished script to actress Tilda Swinton. She liked it so much she not only agreed to appear as the young hero's loving but distracted mother but signed on as executive producer as well. That helped attract a number of other major names to this modest movie, including Vincent D'Onofrio, who plays the boy's dense but hardworking father; Keanu Reeves, as his New Age orthodontist; Vince Vaughn, as his debate team coach; and Benjamin Bratt, as a TV star on whom Swinton has a desperate crush. Kelli Garner, who plays the hero's sexy schoolmate, appeared in Mills's first short subject when she was just fifteen.

But it's newcomer Lou Pucci on whose shoulders the movie really rests. He hits just the right note as suburban misfit Justin Cobb, who's just trying to find himself but seems to be misunderstood by everyone around him—including his kid brother. Even his tentative relationship with Garner is awash in awkwardness.

Mills told me that when he started working on this project he thought Elijah Wood might be good for the leading role, but it took so long to complete that the actor outgrew the part. Then he began the grueling task of auditions, and no one seemed right. Lou Pucci was the last person he saw; he was nervous, having just survived his first-ever airplane trip, and he seemed to embody the character Mills was trying to put on-screen. Pucci went on to win a Special Jury Prize for this performance at the Sundance Film Festival.

Thumbsucker sets itself apart from most coming-of-age movies with an ironic tone that veers between comedy and drama and keeps us slightly off balance. The look of the film is also striking, which shouldn't come as a surprise given Mills's graphic arts background. He chose a burgeoning suburban neighborhood in Oregon for his location because he liked its unfinished appearance, and decided to film in wide screen—a counterintuitive decision for an intimate story that pays off handsomely.

Incidentally, when *Thumbsucker* made the rounds of the film festival circuit it was often on the same program as a movie called *The Chumscrubber,* which caused some degree of confusion, not the least because Pucci also appears in that film (albeit in a supporting role, billed as Lou Taylor Pucci).

Still, with so many solid names in its cast and good reviews behind it, I thought *Thumbsucker* would have a shot at success in theatrical release. It didn't . . . yet it remains one of my favorite unsung films of the decade.

135. TRISTRAM SHANDY: A COCK AND BULL STORY

(2006)

Directed by Michael Winterbottom

Screenplay by Frank Cottrell Boyce

(billed as Martin Hardy)

Based on the novel *The Life and Opinions of Tristram Shandy, Gentleman* by Laurence Sterne

Actors:

STEVE COOGAN

ROB BRYDON

JEREMY NORTHAM

RAYMOND WARING

DYLAN MORAN

KEELEY HAWES

KELLY MACDONALD

SHIRLEY HENDERSON

STEPHEN FRY

NAOMIE HARRIS

IAN HART

ROGER ALLAM

GILLIAN ANDERSON

BENEDICT WONG

GREG WISE

RONNI ANCONA

The concept of a film-within-a-film isn't new but it always offers interesting possibilities, if the creators don't become consumed by their own cleverness. *Tristram Shandy: A Cock and Bull Story* risks being hoist on its own petard in just this way and avoids it—through sheer audacity.

The ostensible premise here is that a film troupe is shooting an adaptation of clergyman Lawrence Sterne's ribald, notoriously "unfilmable" 1760 book *The Life and Opinions of Tristram Shandy, Gentleman* on location in and around a magisterial estate in England. The cheeky British comic actor Steve Coogan plays Tristram (as well as his father) but, in alternate moments, portrays "himself," an insufferable, ego-driven boor of an actor who is constantly parrying with his quick-witted protégé Rob Brydon. (It's helpful—but not necessary—to know that Coogan achieved TV stardom in the UK on a series called *I'm Alan Partridge.* Before long even the uninitiated viewer gets the gist of Brydon's merciless ribbing.)

Director Michael Winterbottom, who's better known for such serious films as *Welcome to Sarajevo* and *A Mighty Heart,* suddenly and seamlessly takes us from eighteenth-century scenes to chaotic, often hilarious antics that are going on just outside the frame, as it were. The trials of making a costume movie on location under a tight budget, while accommodating the needs (and egos) of the many cast and crew members, are vividly depicted in this fast-paced frolic. It's dizzying at times, but not in an off-putting way; we absorb some of the inner movie's content, and certainly its tone and point of view, while we're marveling at the bedlam surrounding it.

The ingenious screenplay was written by Frank Cottrell Boyce, who worked with Winterbottom before on a number of films including *Butterfly Kiss, Welcome to Sarajevo, The Claim,* and notably *24 Hour Party People,* which showcased Steve Coogan as Tony Wilson, the man who popularized the Manchester music scene in the 1970s. Coogan spoke directly to the camera in that film, which may have given Boyce and Winterbottom the inspiration to further expand the notion of breaking the "fourth wall," as they do here.

A fine supporting cast includes Jeremy Northam, Shirley Henderson, Keeley Hawes, Kelly Macdonald, Naomie Harris, Ian Hart, Roger Allam, Stephen Fry, and Gillian Anderson, whose hiring for the film-within-a-film becomes a key story point. Everyone seems to share Coogan's fearlessness in being portrayed in less-than-idealized terms—and that's part of the fun.

136. TUMBLEWEEDS

(1999)

Directed by Gavin O'Connor

Screenplay by Gavin O'Connor and Angela Shelton

Story by Angela Shelton

Actors:

JANET MCTEER

KIMBERLY J. BROWN

JAY O. SANDERS

LOIS SMITH

LAUREL HOLLOMAN

MICHAEL J. POLLARD

NOAH EMMERICH

GAVIN O'CONNOR

ometimes the stars align just right and a small, indepen-
dently made movie not only turns out well but receives the
acclaim it deserves. *Tumbleweeds* enjoyed that kind of reception
in 1999, earning writer-director Gavin O'Connor the Filmmakers Trophy at the Sundance Film Festival and its leading
lady, Janet McTeer, a host of honors including an Academy
Award nomination. Her young costar, Kimberly J. Brown,
won an Independent Spirit Award for Best Debut Performance.

McTeer could hardly be classified as an unknown, as she
won a Tony Award two years earlier for her performance as
Nora in Ibsen's *A Doll's House* on Broadway, but she was still
a new face to most Americans who couldn't have guessed
that she was British from her convincing performance as
a Southerner in this film. Had we known her better we
might have been more aware, which wouldn't have been to
her advantage or ours.

McTeer plays a woman named Mary Jo who's constantly
packing her bags and moving, mindless of the damage she's
inflicting on her daughter, Ava. Her latest spur-of-the-
moment jaunt has brought them to San Diego, where the
weather is great and the possibilities seem as bright as the blue
sky that greets them. But Mary Jo is forever in search of a guy
who will take care of her, and that usually leads to trouble.

She thinks she's found one this time in the person of a
truck driver and all-around good guy named Jack. Before
long she and Ava move in with him and Ava adjusts to life
at yet another new school where—for once—she senses an
opportunity to shine in the play they're about to put on. But

trouble always seems to lurk around the corner for Mary Jo as she repeatedly makes the same mistakes and refuses to confront her culpability in those choices.

Tumbleweeds is a well-written drama that serves as a showcase for a gallery of fine performances—including such stalwart supporting actors as Jay O. Sanders and Michael J. Pollard as well as the film's director (and cowriter) Gavin O'Connor as the truck driver, proving once again that you can't size up a person by appearance alone.

137. TUVALU

(2000)

Directed by Veit Helmer

Screenplay by Veit Helmer and Michaela Beck

Actors:

DENIS LAVANT

CHULPAN HAMATOVA

PHILIPPE CLAY

TERRENCE GILLESPIE

DJOKO ROSSICH (ROSIC)

Whimsy is not a commodity one finds very often in modern cinema. And there are few insults as searing as the critical putdown "forced whimsy." But when I stumbled onto the German film *Tuvalu,* I was charmed by its distinctively quirky qualities. It is definitely one of a kind.

Unlike some attempts at creating a unique look and feel, this film, directed and cowritten by Veit Helmer, seems organic. It is mostly silent, with sound effects, music, and occasional verbal utterances, and styled in black-and-white wide screen with the look of hand tinting one associates with the early work of Georges Méliès.

Tuvalu has a dreamlike quality, as well, because its links to reality are so tenuous. The setting for most of the action is a once-grand, now-crumbling bathhouse that stands in the middle of nowhere, a surviving relic in a devastated city. Our hero, Anton (played by Frenchman Dennis Lavant), yearns to spend his life at sea, but struggles valiantly to keep the establishment going despite a paucity of customers, a stubborn plumbing system, falling plaster, and myriad other challenges. Anton is driven to succeed for the sake of his father, who is blind, and who—thanks to his resourceful son—believes that the bathhouse is still thriving and serving a large and happy clientele.

Anton's brother Gregor does not share his sibling's devotion to the bathhouse, or their father, and does his best to sabotage the operation, as a developer is interested in buying the property. In the process, he also torpedoes Anton's budding romance with a lovely creature named Eva who has brought her father to the bathhouse.

Critics invoked such names as Buster Keaton, Jacques Tati, and Franz Kafka to describe *Tuvalu,* and the movie certainly owes a debt to them and many others, including Rube Goldberg. But in creating an odd, even bizarre, fairy tale for grown-ups, Helmer marks his own territory. The casting, the settings (including a real-life bathhouse in Sofia, Bulgaria), the use of music and visual effects all contribute to a unique and gloriously odd creation. Clearly, this is not for all tastes, but *Tuvalu* caught my fancy and kept me engaged from start to finish.

138. THE TV SET

(2007)

Directed by Jake Kasdan

Screenplay by Jake Kasdan

Actors:

DAVID DUCHOVNY

SIGOURNEY WEAVER

IOAN GRUFFUDD

JUDY GREER

FRAN KRANZ

LINDSAY SLOANE

JUSTINE BATEMAN

LUCY DAVIS

M. C. GAINEY

PHILIP BAKER HALL

ANDREA MARTIN

WILLIE GARSON

KATHRYN JOOSTEN

Hollywood has turned the camera on itself almost from the beginning of the silent era, taking us behind the scenes of movies in stories as varied as *A Star Is Born, Singin' in the Rain,* and *The Stunt Man.* Examinations of the television industry are more scarce, the shining example being *Network,* which was written by a veteran of TV's golden age, Paddy Chayefsky. Some viewers saw that film as a parable, others as a cautionary tale, but there were moments in it that rang painfully true to people in the know.

I don't think you have to work in the television industry to relate to Jake Kasdan's movie *The TV Set,* even though he wrote his screenplay after being in the trenches of network TV. Anyone who's ever had a difficult, stubborn, or capricious boss should understand full well what these characters are going through—and why they deserve our utmost sympathy. The people in this story have to suffer, but they do so in the service of a clever, funny film.

David Duchovny plays a successful TV writer who's just created a new series that's close to his heart, as it was inspired by his late brother. The show is his baby, and he's very protective of it, so when network boss Sigourney Weaver wants to start making wholesale changes—and doesn't like his casting ideas—he begins to chafe. Ioan Gruffud, better known as one of the *Fantastic Four,* tries to smooth things over; he's just come to Hollywood from England to be Weaver's number-two man at the network, and he finds himself caught between his own intelligent ideas and his need to survive in the new job.

We go through the process of watching a TV series come to life, and see just how things can go wrong along the way. And we come to empathize with Duchovny and his plight—not wanting to be so stubborn that he kills the project, but not wanting to compromise on the things he really cares about. Most of all, we see how tough it is to deal with a boss like Weaver, who's used to getting what she wants, all the time. Her characterization is lethally funny, and frighteningly true.

Writer-director Jake Kasdan cut his teeth on the TV series *Freaks and Geeks,* which was critically praised but barely eked out one season on the air. If virtue is its own reward, he and his colleagues can take comfort in knowing they created something special that still has a loyal following. But I have a feeling he put a lot of himself into the Duchovny character in this bittersweet comedy.

139. TWO FAMILY HOUSE

(2000)

Directed by Raymond De Felitta
Screenplay by Raymond De Felitta

Actors:

MICHAEL RISPOLI

KELLY MACDONALD

KATHERINE NARDUCCI

KEVIN CONWAY

MATT SERVITTO

MICHELE SANTOPIETRO

LOUIS GUSS

ROSEMARY DEANGELIS

VICTOR ARNOLD

DOMINIC CHIANESE

RICHARD B. SHULL

We've all seen movies about cockeyed dreamers and ne'er-do-wells. What sets *Two Family House* apart is that it feels authentic—and there's a good reason. It was based on bona fide family lore that Raymond De Felitta was smart enough to fashion into a movie.

The people seem real, and De Felitta cast just the right people to play them—not stars but familiar actors who perfectly embody these characters. You'll know Michael Rispoli the moment you see him, from *The Sopranos* and dozens of movies and television shows. A number of *Sopranos* players populate the cast, which is only natural for a New York–based movie about Italian-Americans. (Casting directors Sheila Jaffe and Georgianne Walken also worked for that TV series and knew the ethnic talent pool quite well.)

Rispoli plays Buddy Visalo, or Uncle Buddy, as he's referred to by the movie's narrator. Buddy is a good-hearted guy who happened to marry the wrong woman. He could have had a singing career in the years following World War II but his wife Estelle (Katherine Narducci) found the prospect embarrassing. In fact, she finds everything about her husband embarrassing, especially his dream of opening a neighborhood bar where he can sing to his customers.

So Buddy pursues another "crackpot" idea. He buys a two-family house on Staten Island, planning to put his bar on the ground floor and rent out the upstairs apartment. Then he discovers that someone's already living up there. He's a mean drunk (Kevin Conway) and his young Irish wife (Kelly Macdonald) is his number one victim. She's also pregnant, but not with his child. Buddy insinuates himself into the woman's life and this takes him on an unexpected path.

Everything Buddy does comes from the heart, which is why this movie never falters. Its characters seem true and so do their actions, even if they aren't always logical or predictable. If you haven't noticed, real life isn't always logical or predictable.

Two Family House is a crowd-pleaser. It won the Audience Award at the Sundance Film Festival, though it's probably too "good-hearted" to have appealed to a jury accustomed to dark, difficult material.

Writer-director De Felitta went on to make another

warmly entertaining film about offbeat family relations, *The Thing About My Folks* with Paul Reiser and Peter Falk, and another ensemble piece set in a specific part of New York, *City Island*. But I wouldn't be surprised if *Two Family House* remains his primary calling card for many years to come.

140. TWO LOVERS

(2009)

Directed by James Gray

Screenplay by James Gray and Richard Menello

Actors:

JOAQUIN PHOENIX

GWYNETH PALTROW

VINESSA SHAW

ISABELLA ROSSELLINI

ELIAS KOTEAS

MONI MOSHONOV

JULIE BUDD

NICK GILLIE

JOHN ORTIZ

The first great film I saw in 2009, *Two Lovers* is a vivid romantic drama that's meant to express larger-than-life emotions. When he brought his film to my class at USC, writer-director James Gray explained that he wanted to emulate the films of the 1970s that exposed their characters so nakedly you almost felt uncomfortable. In this instance, I actually felt exhilarated.

I also knew that despite its marquee value *Two Lovers* had failed to attract a major distributor and would never reach a wide audience in theatrical release.

Joaquin Phoenix plays a fragile young man who has moved back in with his parents at their Brighton Beach apartment in Brooklyn after a failed suicide attempt. It's here that he chances to meet a new neighbor, played by Gwyneth Paltrow. She doesn't mind spending time with him, but she's self-absorbed and represents trouble with a capital *T.* That doesn't stop him from falling in love with her, almost to the point of obsession. She represents glamour, adventure, the good life in Manhattan and beyond . . . even danger. Then his family introduces him to a "nice girl" from the neighborhood, played by Vinessa Shaw. Unlike Paltrow, she actually likes him and is happy to pursue a real relationship. (It doesn't hurt that her father is also doing business with Phoenix's dad.)

Phoenix tries juggling the two women who represent opposing forces in his life. One woman is dangerous but alluring; the other is sweet and safe. *Two Lovers* deals with fate and the choices we make.

Gray knows this isn't typical story fodder for a contemporary film, and acknowledges that the raw emotions his actors convey lack the layering of irony and cool that today's audiences are accustomed to. Yet that's precisely what sets *Two Lovers* apart. One scene is accompanied by Henry Mancini's lush orchestral piece "Lujon," from the early 1960s. It is used to convey Phoenix's feelings about the glamour of Manhattan at night, and it's perfect. Throughout the story, Gray finds ways to share his character's swirling emotions.

Like Gray's other films (*Little Odessa, The Yards, We Own the Night*), this one has an almost operatic quality, and even utilizes opera on the sound track. *Two Lovers* is infused with cinematic homages, as well, some more obvious than others. (*Vertigo* is clearly an influence.)

I can't imagine two actors who could inhabit the leading roles better than Phoenix and Paltrow, and they are ably supported by Shaw and Isabella Rossellini—who, I have to admit, wouldn't have been my first choice to play a Jewish mother. But, like everything else in the movie, she hits just the right notes.

141. WAKING THE DEAD

(2000)

Directed by Keith Gordon

Screenplay by Robert Dillon

Based on the novel by Scott Spencer

Actors:

BILLY CRUDUP

JENNIFER CONNELLY

HAL HOLBROOK

MOLLY PARKER

JANET MCTEER

PAUL HIPP

SANDRA OH

LAWRENCE DANE

ED HARRIS

If you were an active moviegoer in the early 1980s, you may remember Keith Gordon as the youthful star of

such films as *Dressed to Kill* and *Christine;* he also played
the young Joe Gideon in flashback scenes of Bob Fosse's
All That Jazz. Later that decade he fulfilled a longtime
ambition to direct, piloting his own adaptation of Robert
Cormier's novel *The Chocolate War.* Since then he has
brought his unique sensibilities to a handful of finely tuned
dramas including *A Midnight Clear, Mother Night,* and my
favorite, *Waking the Dead.*

Reviews were mixed for this ambitious film, which demands that the viewer make a leap of faith. I was willing to
do so and was amply rewarded . . . but then I've always been
a sucker for films that integrate fantastic and/or mystical
elements into an everyday narrative.

The action moves back and forth in time, setting its
story in motion during the early 1970s. Billy Crudup plays
a straight-arrow Coast Guard officer who's on a fast track to
a political career when he meets an idealistic Jennifer Connelly. She goads him about his "easy" life and easier choices,
and while they never quite see eye to eye politically they do
fall in love.

But their relationship is star crossed, as we learn from
latter-day scenes in which Crudup is now running for Congress, backed by a Chicago politico (Hal Holbrook) and engaged to his niece. Yet he cannot get over his passion for
Connelly and won't let go of the chance of seeing her again,
even if logic says that isn't possible.

I won't reveal the story's many twists and turns, except to
say that they unfold against a credible backdrop of college-
age idealism and backroom politics. Because Crudup and
Connelly are so well cast and believable, we root for them
and want their love to survive somehow. (Please note that

the film is based on a novel by Scott Spencer, who also wrote *Endless Love,* another story of obsession.)

As a former actor Gordon makes a special connection with his cast. I once told Jennifer Connelly how much I liked this film and she revealed that it meant so much to her that she went through an actual mourning process when shooting was completed.

Waking the Dead offers a highly charged, emotional experience that speaks to one's heart more than one's mind— yet it never sacrifices intelligence for the sake of sentiment. That's why I admire it so much.

142. THE WEATHER MAN

(2005)

Directed by Gore Verbinski

Screenplay by Steven Conrad

Actors:

NICOLAS CAGE

MICHAEL CAINE

HOPE DAVIS

MICHAEL RISPOLI

NICHOLAS HOULT

GEMMENNE DE LA PEÑA

GIL BELLOWS

JUDITH MCCONNELL

When a studio is in doubt about a film's marketability, they will invariably sell it as a comedy, even if it isn't. Thus good movies are torpedoed by their own advertising campaigns.

The Weather Man is a bittersweet, even melancholy, ru-
mination about the American dream of success. Because it
has a recurring gag in which angry people hurl food and
drinks at Nicolas Cage on the street, that was the dominant
visual "message" in all of its previews and commercials. It
made a smart film look dumb, thereby keeping intelligent
moviegoers away while failing to win over the low-comedy
audience it sought to bamboozle. (People can usually smell
a scam like this a mile away.)

The film marked a comeback for a gifted writer named
Steve Conrad, who made a splash by selling his first screenplay, *Wrestling Ernest Hemingway,* to a major studio in his
early twenties. In the years following that film, he soured
on Hollywood and moved away with his family. When he
wrote another solid script a decade later, he approached the
producer who'd bought *Hemingway,* Todd Black; he liked it
and got Nicolas Cage to star. Gore Verbinski, who'd gone
from directing music videos and commercials to great success with such gargantuan productions as *Pirates of the Caribbean,* also responded to the screenplay and broke away from
a string of blockbusters to give this special project the TLC
it deserved.

Cage plays David Spritz, a sad-faced fellow who doesn't
like people very much—especially strangers who recognize
him as the local TV "weather guy" in Chicago. He's made
it on a major-city station and now has a chance of advancing
to a network morning show in New York, but this upward
career trajectory can't compensate for the unhappiness that
pervades his personal life. His ex-wife (Hope Davis) considers him a loser, he has a strained relationship with his
two children, and worst of all, he feels he hasn't earned the

respect of his father, a renowned, prize-winning author (Michael Caine).

How Dave Spritz deals with all of this and manages to find some measure of self-esteem is the crux of the story. It isn't a comedy, but it does traffic in the irony of American life. Dave is an all-too-recognizable character, and while at times he seems to be his own worst enemy we still root for him, hoping that somehow he can overcome his self-imposed obstacles and find a path to happiness.

With his hangdog expression and low-key delivery, Nicolas Cage is perfect in the leading role. (When producer Black submitted the script, he received a call from the actor's agent summoning him to Cage's home that same evening . . . and as Cage walked into the room to greet him he said, "Hi, I'm Dave Spritz." Black knew then and there that Cage was committing to the film—and the character.)

Because it doesn't deal in platitudes and formulaic storytelling I suppose *The Weather Man* is never destined to win over a mass audience, but I think it's a terrific movie and a credit to everyone connected to it.

143. WELCOME TO SARAJEVO

(1997)

Directed by Michael Winterbottom

Screenplay by Frank Cottrell Boyce

Based on the book *Natasha's Story* by Michael Nicholson

Actors:

STEPHEN DILLANE

WOODY HARRELSON

MARISA TOMEI

EMIRA NUSEVIC

KERRY FOX

GORAN VISNJIC

JAMES NESBITT

EMILY LLOYD

JULIET AUBREY

GORDANA GADZIC

IGOR DZAMBAZOV

We've all seen stories about war correspondents—good ones, too—but this one is unique. It's based on the experiences of British TV reporter Michael Nicholson, but that alone wouldn't set it apart. Being true doesn't necessarily make a movie good. What gives this film its cachet is that it dares to paint its emotional, real-life drama against a backdrop of journalists at work, sharing the battle-worn cynicism that is their stock in trade.

Director Michael Winterbottom shot his film on location just months after a cease-fire was declared in 1996, giving it a feeling of actuality that's often harrowing. The time is 1992 and the place is Sarajevo, under siege from Serbs who are protesting Bosnia's newly won independence by bombing the city and shooting innocent people in the streets.

This was the first time I'd taken note of British actor Stephen Dillane. (Since making this film he's played Karenin in an acclaimed TV miniseries of *Anna Karenina,* Leonard Woolf in *The Hours,* Merlin in *King Arthur,* British golf champion Harry Vardon in *The Greatest Game Ever Played,* and Thomas Jefferson in the popular HBO miniseries *John Adams.*) He is perfect in the role of Michael Henderson, a well-known TV reporter who rushes in where angels fear to tread with an intrepid team at his side: a cameraman, producer, and driver (played by Croatian-born Goran Visnjic). One day they encounter a woman who is somehow managing to operate an orphanage dangerously close to the fighting. Henderson sees an opportunity to put a human face on a war that the public back home is tiring of. In the process he becomes emotionally involved and decides to rescue one young orphan: he will take a girl named Emira back to his home in England. This is both illegal and incredibly dangerous, but he is resolute. Little does he dream that their perilous journey will involve him even further, and that it isn't the final chapter of the story.

Welcome to Sarajevo blends fact and fiction with a sense of urgency; at times it is painfully difficult to watch. Thankfully, screenwriter Frank Cottrell Boyce resists the temptation to preach. (Boyce's subsequent work includes *Hilary and Jackie,* and with director Winterbottom, *24 Hour Party People, Millions,* and *Tristram Shandy: A Cock and Bull Story.*) Scenes of Henderson drinking and debating with his colleagues—including an American correspondent played by Woody Harrelson—add flavor and, in some cases, welcome humor to the proceedings. They also serve to underscore the seriousness of the situation when a character who has been flippant is later knocked for a loop.

Director Winterbottom has proved, more than once, that he has a gift for creating a tangibly believable environment for his actors. With camera work that puts us in the midst of the action, pop music on the sound track, and a solid international cast, *Welcome to Sarajevo* makes us believe—and care.

144. WENT TO CONEY ISLAND ON A MISSION FROM GOD . . . BE BACK BY FIVE

(2000)

Directed by Richard Schenkman

Screenplay by Jon Cryer and Richard Schenkman

Actors:

JON CRYER

RICK STEAR

RAFAEL BÁEZ

IONE SKYE

FRANK WHALEY

DOMINIC CHIANESE

PETER GERETY

AKILI PRINCE

AESHA WAKS

For a long time, people knew Jon Cryer best as Ducky in the indelible teen movie *Pretty in Pink*. Nowadays he's the costar of the hit TV series *Two and a Half Men*. But a decade ago he cowrote and coproduced a low-budget film I like with a name that's hard to forget: *Went to Coney Island on a Mission from God . . . Be Back by Five.*

This is a story about friendship, with all its ups and downs. Daniel, played by Cryer, and Stan, played by Rick Stear, grew up together on the streets of Brooklyn. Even as young men, they still seem to be stuck in adolescence, working at dead-end jobs. But one wintry day they dump their jobs in order to follow a stream of rumors about a mutual friend who's vanished from their lives and is supposedly living among homeless people in Coney Island.

Their quest takes them on a circuitous route and they

have a series of encounters with people who may or may not have leads to the whereabouts of their pal Richie. Ione Skye plays Stan's long-suffering girlfriend, and you'll recognize some of the people they meet, including Frank Whaley as Skee-Ball Weasel, and Dominic Chianese, from the *Sopranos* cast, as Mickey the Photographer.

Went to Coney Island . . . is an alternately funny and moving meditation on the unpredictability of life and where it takes us. It also deals squarely with the meaning of friendship among guys. I like the look and feel of the film, especially the way it captures the now-melancholy landscape of Coney Island, which resonates strongly with New Yorkers like me who remember it in its heyday.

It's clear this movie was made as a labor of love for Cryer and director/cowriter Richard Schenkman, following their first collaboration, *The Pompatus of Love*. Something about the mood it creates and the relationship it portrays between two friends appeals to me, and it's long held a place on my list of films I recommend to *my* friends.

145. WHAT DOESN'T KILL YOU

(2008)

Directed by Brian Goodman

Screenplay by Brian Goodman, Paul T. Murray, and Donnie Wahlberg

Actors:

MARK RUFFALO

ETHAN HAWKE

AMANDA PEET

WILL LYMAN

BRIAN GOODMAN
DONNIE WAHLBERG
ANGELA FEATHERSTONE

F ilmmakers have made excellent use of Boston for region-
ally driven crime stories in recent years. *Mystic River* and
The Departed garnered the most attention; local boy Ben Af-
fleck captured a truer, grittier flavor in his directorial debut,
Gone Baby Gone. But in some respects another first-time director, Brian Goodman, trumped them all in his little-seen
drama *What Doesn't Kill You.* Not only is it a true story, it's
autobiographical.

Goodman grew up on the streets of South Boston, a
world all its own. He and his best pal (played by Mark Ruffalo and Ethan Hawke, respectively) started out as punk
kids, running errands for a local hood and learning not to
ask questions. A decade later, as young men, nothing has
changed, except that now, Ruffalo has a family. He's never
accepted responsibility for anything in life; he's just taken
things as they come, going from one small-time "job" to
another. Inevitably, he and Hawke wind up in prison where
they serve five years.

When Ruffalo is released he quickly discovers that ad-
justing to normal life is hard enough; trying to go straight
and stay away from booze makes it even tougher, and a
neighborhood police detective (played by Donnie Wahlberg, who cowrote the screenplay) is always on his case, refusing to give him the benefit of the doubt in any situation.

Told in outline form the story may sound familiar. What
sets this movie apart is its brutal honesty; there isn't a false
note in the picture.

In real life, Goodman faced all the challenges we see his character contend with on-screen. He started acting in the late 1990s and won small roles in several films shot in Boston (*Monument Ave.* and *Southie,* which starred Donnie Wahlberg); this was an especially lucky break because at that time he wasn't allowed to leave the state! In time he made his way to Hollywood. When he worked for Steven Spielberg, first in *Catch Me If You Can* and then in *Munich,* he spent every spare moment observing the director at work.

Eventually he started putting his story down on paper, and with the help of Wahlberg and Paul T. Murray, turned it into a screenplay. He then impressed a producer and a financier—and ultimately his actors—with his utter conviction to tell the story as honestly as possible. That included shooting the entire movie in Boston, often on the actual locations where incidents took place.

Mark Ruffalo and Ethan Hawke are superb. And Goodman fares well on camera playing Pat Kelly, the neighborhood racketeer.

What Doesn't Kill You opened in the midst of the busy December 2008 movie season in New York and Los Angeles just as its distributor, Yari Film Group, went out of business (more or less). Like *Nothing But the Truth* (written and directed by Rod Lurie, who also coproduced this movie) it never played elsewhere and made its DVD debut in the spring of 2009. If ever a film deserved a second chance, this one does.

146. THE WHOLE WIDE WORLD

(1996)

Directed by Dan Ireland

Screenplay by Michael Scott Myers

Based on the memoir *One Who Walked Alone*

by Novalyne Price Ellis

Actors:

VINCENT D'ONOFRIO

RENÉE ZELLWEGER

ANN WEDGEWORTH

HARVE PRESNELL

BENJAMIN MOUTON

MICHAEL CORBETT

HELEN CATES

At the same time moviegoers were discovering Renée Zellweger in the smash hit *Jerry Maguire,* a distributor was attempting to generate interest in a much smaller-scale film featuring the young actress—but without the name value of Tom Cruise to help it along.

The Whole Wide World is a compelling drama about a most unusual relationship between a prim, unworldly Texas schoolteacher and aspiring writer named Novalyne Price and an eccentric but fascinating young man named Robert E. Howard. He lives with his mother, talks out loud as he clatters away on his typewriter, and has few if any social skills, but unlike Novalyne he is making a living through his words—as the creator of the pulp magazine heroes Conan the Barbarian and Kull the Conqueror!

Howard is played by the gifted Vincent D'Onofrio, whose attention-grabbing performance in Stanley Kubrick's

Full Metal Jacket (1987) propelled him to the front ranks of young character actors. Subsequent films include *Mystic Pizza, JFK, Ed Wood* (in a memorable cameo as Orson Welles), and *Men in Black*. In recent years he's become a familiar face to television viewers on *Law & Order: Criminal Intent*.

Only an actor with the skill and range of D'Onofrio could pull off a role as peculiar as Robert E. Howard and help us understand what Novalyne Price saw in him. Michael Scott Myers based his expressive screenplay on her memoir *One Who Walked Alone*.

Zellweger is equally believable as the teacher who hasn't experienced much of life as yet but finds herself in the thrall of Howard's company—even though each time they get together, she doesn't know what to expect. They develop a deeply felt friendship even though it (apparently) never becomes a sexual partnership.

Incidentally—or not so incidentally—the film was made in Texas, where it takes place, and where Zellweger got her first film and television experience in locally made features like *Dazed and Confused*. Little did she dream that this modest film would finally reach theaters the same month as the Hollywood movie that would change her life. Yet the experience of making *The Whole Wide World* stayed with her: when she won her Best Supporting Actress Academy Award years later for *Cold Mountain* she thanked D'Onofrio for "teaching me how to work."

The Whole Wide World also changed the life and career of Dan Ireland. The cofounder of the Seattle International Film Festival, he was determined to parlay his lifelong love of film into a career behind the camera. He has shown great care in his choice of projects and while he's never had a box-office smash, he has made some excellent films. You'll find another one of them, *Mrs Palfrey at the Claremont,* elsewhere in this volume.

147. THE WIDE BLUE ROAD

(1957)

Directed by Gillo Pontecorvo

Screenplay by Ennio De Concini and Gillo Pontecorvo

Based on the novel *Squarciò* by Franco Solinas

Actors:

YVES MONTAND

ALIDA VALLI

FRANCISCO RABAL

UMBERTO SPADARO

PETER CARSTEN

FEDERICA RANCHI

MARIO GIROTTI (TERENCE HILL)

RONALDINO BONACCHI

GIANCARLO SOBLONE

During the 1950s Americans were introduced to great films from France, Italy, Sweden, and Japan. It was during this period (which extended into the 1960s) that many people got hooked on foreign films. Yet Gillo Pontecorvo's *La Grande Strada Azzurra,* or *The Wide Blue Road,* never received theatrical distribution in the United States. The director went on to make such notable films as *The Battle of Algiers* (1966) and *Burn!* (1969), but his early effort was virtually unknown on these shores until Dennis Doros and Amy Heller of Milestone Film and Video resurrected it (in a beautifully restored print) in 2001, with the support of Dustin Hoffman and filmmaker Jonathan Demme.

Yves Montand stars as a prideful, stubborn man named Squarciò who lives in an insular Italian fishing village off the Dalmatian coast. He refuses to obey the law and sets off dynamite charges in the water to guarantee a big haul every time he goes out to fish. This puts him in conflict with his family, his neighbors, and one determined Coast Guard lieutenant.

The Wide Blue Road is a moving and robust slice of life that's both original and completely unpredictable. Montand was never more handsome or charismatic. (Never mind that a Frenchman is playing an Italian fisherman.) Pontecorvo wrote the screenplay with Ennio De Concini and Franco Solinas, whose novel *Squarciò* was its source material.

The director has acknowledged that the classic Italian neorealist films of the 1940s and '50s were an inspiration, and while this film has well-known leading actors (Montand and Alida Valli) and is beautifully shot in color, it still pays homage to that style of filmmaking in its vivid depiction of everyday life in the village. And one could never find faces like the ones in this film at Central Casting.

148. WINTER SOLSTICE

(2005)

Directed by Josh Sternfeld

Screenplay by Josh Sternfeld

Actors:

ANTHONY LAPAGLIA

AARON STANFORD

MARK WEBBER

MICHELLE MONAGHAN

ALLISON JANNEY

BRENDAN SEXTON III

RON LIVINGSTON

EBON MOSS-BACHRACH

For some people, taking in a quiet, subtle film like *Winter Solstice* is akin to watching paint dry. On the other hand, I am attracted to films that make you do some of the work understanding the characters and sensing what's going on just beneath the surface.

This was Josh Sternfeld's first feature as writer-director, and I think it's an impressive piece of work. When he brought his film to my class at USC I asked him about his approach and he said, "I always feel like there's so much more going on with what people feel as opposed to what they say, so when I started writing I think that was a natural part of my process, to try to have levels of subtext operating in the script."

That's one reason such good actors as Anthony LaPaglia and Allison Janney were attracted to his screenplay. Ron Livingston agreed to play a small role as a schoolteacher, not

because it would help his career, but because he admired
Sternfeld's writing.

The setting is a quiet suburban town in New Jersey.
LaPaglia plays a widower who's trying to meet the challenge of raising two sons and running a business, but he gets
so caught up in his daily routine that he doesn't recognize
his boys' emotional needs.

Aaron Stanford and Mark Webber play the sons who miss
their mother. They love their father but see their lives in this
tranquil community as running into a dead end. The one spark
of life comes along when a woman (Janney) moves in down
the street who might be open to a relationship with LaPaglia.

In this movie looks, glances, body language, and silence tell
as much as the dialogue. You never doubt for a moment that
the three central characters care about each other, but you can
also feel the tension that's building with the older son—and
the open wound that the loss of his mother still represents to
all of them.

Josh Sternfeld told me that the highest compliment he received after screenings of his film was when people would say,
"It's just so real." That it is.

149. WORD WARS

(2004)

Directed by Eric Chaikin and Julian Petrillo

Spellbound movingly captures the suspense of America's
national spelling bee and the young contestants who
give their lives over to that competition. *Wordplay* celebrates

the world of crossword puzzle addicts and their hero, *New York Times* puzzle master Will Shortz. Overlooked in this select field of documentaries, *Word Wars* (full title: *Word Wars: Tiles and Tribulations on the Scrabble Circuit*) deserves to be better known, even though its protagonists are not nearly as endearing as those in the other two films.

Word Wars explores the world of full-time Scrabble players. That's right: there are people who spend every day of their lives playing Scrabble, mostly for money and what little glory they can muster. The four individuals profiled here don't make much of a living this way—from the evidence at hand, they exist at the margins of society—but they all share the same goal, to win the country's leading tournament, held every summer in San Diego, where the grand prize is $25,000.

In fly-on-the-wall fashion we meet these motley participants earlier in the calendar year and get an idea of their everyday lives leading up to that crucial trip west. These characters are oddballs with a capital O, and fascinating in their own bizarre way.

What struck me most about these people is that they're just like any other obsessives. I was reminded of people I know who are consumed by old movies or comic books. Only the object of their passion sets them apart. Yet filmmakers Eric Chaikin and Julian Petrillo don't judge them: they leave it to us to draw our own conclusions.

Another distinction of *Word Wars* is its stylish cinematic treatment, establishing a visual motif of Scrabble letters as anagrams—seemingly random lineups of letters that we quickly discover can be transformed into seven-letter words by an experienced eye. The action is further propelled by a snazzy music score by Thor Madsen. All of this takes what some might consider dry material and making it vibrant and fun . . . even if you're not a Scrabble connoisseur.

150. THE WORLD'S FASTEST INDIAN

(2005)

Directed by Roger Donaldson

Screenplay by Roger Donaldson

Actors:

ANTHONY HOPKINS

DIANE LADD

PAUL RODRIGUEZ

AARON MURPHY

ANNIE WHITTLE

CHRIS WILLIAMS

JESSICA CAUFFIEL

CHRISTOPHER LAWFORD

CHRIS BRUNO

BRUCE GREENWOOD

WILLIAM LUCKING

This disarming film was thirty-five years in the making. In 1971 a young New Zealand–based filmmaker named Roger Donaldson directed a half-hour television documentary about a genuine "character." *Burt Munro: Offerings to the God of Speed* focused on a colorful old codger whose devotion to his 1920s Indian motorcycle inspired his friends and neighbors to take up a collection so he could travel to the United States and race it on the Bonneville Salt Flats in Utah.

As Donaldson became a successful feature filmmaker, with such titles as *Sleeping Dogs, No Way Out, Cocktail,* and *Thirteen Days* to his credit, he repeatedly pitched the story of Munro, certain that it would make a compelling movie. He had several near misses and turned down concrete offers from producers and studios that wanted to subvert the true story. Finally the pieces fell together with Anthony Hopkins (who'd starred in Donaldson's *The Bounty*) committed to playing Burt.

The distributor hoped Hopkins's wonderful performance would earn him an Academy Award nomination, but that did not come to pass, and the film received a half-hearted U.S. release.

I went out of my way to screen *The World's Fastest Indian* for my class at USC because I wanted my students to see a movie that didn't contain an ounce of cynicism. That's rare nowadays, fueled by many producers' belief that young audiences won't accept a film that isn't "edgy." Here is a happy exception to that rule.

When single-minded, small-town New Zealander Burt Munro arrives in Los Angeles in 1967, he depends on the kindness of strangers to help him make his way to Utah . . . and because he is so guileless and straightforward, they do. Everyone from a Hollywood transvestite (Chris Williams) to a used-car salesman (Paul Rodriguez) falls under his spell.

Once he arrives at Bonneville, he again relies on people's good nature to help him out, even though he isn't registered and his MO is unconventional. But Burt believes in himself—and his ancient bike—and as a result, people respond. He, in turn, surprises them all when he revs up his vehicle.

Anthony Hopkins is absolutely perfect as Munro, a man who seems to exist in a world of his own. He awakens his neighbors every morning with the roaring of his engine as he putters in his workshop, and seems undeterred by any and every obstacle that gets in his way, at home and on the road. The movie wouldn't work if we didn't believe Hopkins, and we do.

My students loved the movie and gave it almost unanimous approval. Several of them complained that the previews made it seem like just another formulaic underdog story and didn't hint at the qualities that made it so appealing. That's just one more case of "expert" movie marketers selling their audience short.

151. ZATHURA: A SPACE ADVENTURE

(2005)

Directed by Jon Favreau
Screenplay by David Koepp and John Kamps
Based on the book by Chris Van Allsburg

Actors:

JONAH BOBO

JOSH HUTCHERSON

KRISTEN STEWART

TIM ROBBINS

DAX SHEPARD

FRANK OZ (VOICE)

DEREK MEARS

JOHN ALEXANDER

aving loathed *Jumanji,* I was not looking forward to another fantasy/adventure derived from a book by the same author, Chris Van Allsburg. Judging from the luke-warm reception that greeted *Zathura: A Space Adventure,* I may not have been alone, and that's a shame: it turns out to be a very entertaining, original movie.

Zathura won me over from the very start with an in-genious title sequence. Most popcorn movies nowadays eschew such niceties; they can't wait to explode in your face. But director Jon Favreau understood that he needed to set the stage for this unusual tale, and realized that a visual prologue was the perfect way to do it. *Zathura* is all about a magical, "retro" board game, the type I grew up playing— only much, much cooler. In the opening montage we see how this wonderfully designed game involves a wind-up mechanism that sets its tin-toy figures inching along a track. (This sequence, like so many great opening titles, was con-ceived and executed by Kyle Cooper.)

Having been properly introduced to the game, we are ready to meet the cast of characters, including a recently divorced dad (Tim Robbins), and his sons, ten-year-old Walter and six-year-old Danny. Like most kids they want their dad's nonstop attention, but he has to go off one af-ternoon and leaves them in their roomy, Craftsman-style house with their big sister (Kristen Stewart) to babysit.

The brothers fight, annoy each other, and get along in roughly equal measure; their sister wants as little to do with them as possible, and vice versa. While she is upstairs preen-ing in the bathroom, they try out the ancient board game Danny has found in the basement. Very soon they discover that this is no ordinary game: whatever is written on the fortune card dispensed after every turn actually comes to pass. Before long, their house is propelled into outer space, their sister is frozen, and they are visited by a U.S. astronaut (Dax Shepard), whose experience comes in handy as they try to fend off an attack from hostile aliens called Zorgons!

The boys never know what's going to happen next, and neither do we: that's what's so much fun, especially in a film where nothing is impossible. (What's more, Favreau didn't want to rely completely on computer-generated effects, so he built a full-size house set on a soundstage that could be hoisted in midair, tilted, and shaken. He sought to make the experience as tangible for us in the audience as it must have been for his young actors.)

Only a parent can determine whether this anything-goes adventure yarn is too intense for his or her children. But if you're a big kid, like me, I think you'll have a good time.

ABOUT THE AUTHOR

Leonard Maltin is a respected film critic and historian, perhaps best known for his annual paperback reference *Leonard Maltin's Movie Guide*, which was first published in 1969. It was joined by *Leonard Maltin's Classic Movie Guide* in 2005. Since 1982 he has appeared on television's *Entertainment Tonight;* he also hosts *Secret's Out* on ReelzChannel and introduces movies on DirecTV Cinema. For three years he cohosted the movie-review show *Hot Ticket.* He teaches at the University of Southern California School of Cinematic Arts and was a member of the faculty at the New School for Social Research in New York City.

His other books include *Leonard Maltin's Movie Encyclopedia, The Great American Broadcast, The Great Movie Comedians, The Disney Films, Of Mice and Magic: A History of American Animated Cartoons, The Art of the Cinematographer, The Great Movie Shorts (Selected Short Subjects),* and (as coauthor) *The Little Rascals: The Life and Times of Our Gang.* His articles have appeared in the *New York Times, Los Angeles Times,* the

Times of London, *Premiere, Smithsonian, TV Guide, Esquire,* and the *Village Voice.* For six years he was film critic for *Playboy* magazine. He has served as guest curator at the Museum of Modern Art and was president of the Los Angeles Film Critics Association in 1995 and 1996. In 1997 he was named to the National Film Preservation Board, and in 2006 he was selected by the Library of Congress to sit on the board of directors for the National Film Preservation Foundation. He also hosts and coproduces the *Walt Disney Treasures* DVD series. Perhaps the pinnacle of his career was his appearance in a now-classic episode of *South Park.* (Or was it Carmela consulting his *Movie Guide* on an episode of *The Sopranos?*)

He lives with his wife and daughter in Los Angeles. He publishes a newsletter for old-movie buffs, *Leonard Maltin's Movie Crazy,* and holds court at www.leonardmaltin.com.